W9-BPJ-210

FAMILY OF FREEDOM

ALSO BY KENNETH T. WALSH

Feeding the Beast: The White House versus the Press

Ronald Reagan: Biography

Air Force One: A History of the Presidents and Their Planes

From Mount Vernon to Crawford: A History of the Presidents and Their Retreats

FAMILY OF FREEDOM

PRESIDENTS AND AFRICAN AMERICANS IN THE WHITE HOUSE

BY

KENNETH T. WALSH

Paradigm Publishers
Boulder • London

Copyright © 2011 Paradigm Publishers

Published in the United States by Paradigm Publishers, 2845 Wilderness Place, Boulder, CO 80301 USA.

Paradigm Publishers is the trade name of Birkenkamp & Company, LLC, Dean Birkenkamp, President and Publisher.

Library of Congress Cataloging-in-Publication Data

Walsh, Kenneth T.
  Family of freedom : presidents and African Americans in the White House / Kenneth T. Walsh.
     p. cm.
  Includes bibliographical references and index.
  ISBN 978-1-59451-833-1 (hardcover : alk. paper) — ISBN 978-1-59451-834-8 (pbk. : alk. paper)
  1. Presidents—Relations with African Americans. 2. Presidents—United States—Attitudes. 3. Presidents—United States—Biography. 4. African Americans—Government relations. 5. African Americans—Politics and government.
6. Racism—Political aspects—United States—History. 7. Presidents—United States—Staff—History. I. Title.
  E176.472.A34W35 2011
  305.800973—dc22
                                                                    2010033695

Printed and bound in the United States of America on acid-free paper that meets the standards of the American National Standard for Permanence of Paper for Printed Library Materials.

Designed and Typeset by Straight Creek Bookmakers.

15 14 13 12 11   1 2 3 4 5

For Barclay

CONTENTS

PREFACE

This book has two goals—to examine the racial attitudes and policies of America's presidents and to explain how those attitudes and policies intertwined with the presidents' day-to-day relationships with African Americans. In the process, I hope to illuminate not only the tortured history of how our leaders dealt with race but also the little-understood role that blacks have played in running the White House and, in many cases, helping the presidents to govern.

The narrative is rich with fascinating characters, such as Barack Obama, the first African American president, and other iconic chief executives such as George Washington, Thomas Jefferson, Abraham Lincoln, Franklin Roosevelt, and Ronald Reagan, and many African Americans who served or advised them, including Ona Judge, Sally Hemings, Frederick Douglass, Elizabeth Keckley, William Slade, Mary McLeod Bethune, Colin Powell, and Condoleezza Rice.

In assessing the history of the presidents and blacks in the White House, we can learn much about ourselves as Americans. Through that prism, we can trace our capacity for tolerance, our ability to deal with moral issues such as America's original sin of slavery, and our 200-year-old struggle to heed what Lincoln so memorably called "the better angels of our nature."

ACKNOWLEDGMENTS

First and foremost, my heartfelt thanks go to my wife, Barclay Walsh. I wouldn't have written this book without her encouragement, and I couldn't have written it without her participation. She was my researcher and all-around sounding board, and her role was invaluable, as was her constant support. I dedicate this book to her.

I also want to thank President Barack Obama for his time, interest, and insight. My interview with him was an important part of this project.

And I'd like to express my appreciation to former Presidents George W. Bush and George H. W. Bush, each of whom took the time to respond to my written questions via e-mail and provide thoughtful answers.

Former General Colin Powell was extremely helpful in talking to me about his experiences at the highest reaches of government.

Also providing invaluable help were David Axelrod, Ross Baker, Cornell Belcher, Doug Brinkley, Bob Dallek, Frank Donatelli, Matt Dowd, Ken Duberstein, Marlin Fitzwater, Al From, Bill Galston, Geoff Garin, Robert Gibbs, Ed Gillespie, Ed Goeas, Stan Greenberg, Valerie Jarrett, Frank Luntz, Kevin Madden, Thurgood Marshall Jr., Will Marshall, Mike McCurry, Bill McInturff, Mark Penn, Dan Pfeiffer, Roman Popadiuk, Michael Steele, Sean Walsh, Brad Woodhouse, Julian Zelizer, and the staffs at various presidential libraries. In addition, I found some sources particularly helpful, including many articles in the African American press over the years and the books of former White House staff members Lillian Rogers Parks, Elizabeth Keckley, and Preston Bruce.

Jillian Manus, my agent, was a believer in this project from the beginning.

And thanks to the creative team at Paradigm Publishers, especially Jennifer Knerr, Laura Esterman, Sharon Daugherty, and Jessica Priest.

I hope this book illuminates a key part of American history that has been neglected for too long, the close relationships between our presidents and the African Americans who have been an integral part of the White House from the beginning.

Kenneth T. Walsh
Bethesda, Maryland

Letter from Abraham Lincoln to Michael Hahn

Executive Mansion
Washington, March 13, 1864

Hon. Michael Hahn:

My Dear Sir: I congratulate you on having fixed your name in history as the first free-State Governor of Louisiana. Now you are about to have a convention, which, among other things, will probably define the elective franchise. I barely suggest, for your private consideration, whether some of the colored people may not be let in, as, for instance, the very intelligent, and especially those who have fought gallantly in our ranks. They would probably help, in some trying time to come, to keep the jewel of liberty in the family of freedom. But this is only a suggestion, not to the public, but to you alone.

Truly yours,
Lincoln

Chapter One
The Family of Freedom and the Arc of Racial History

On election night, November 4, 2008, a quarter of a million Americans gathered in Chicago's Grant Park under a crescent moon and a crystal-clear sky to celebrate a turning point in history. For several hours that evening, expectations in the racially and ethnically diverse crowd had been rising as one state after another went for Barack Obama in the presidential race, including normally Republican strongholds such as Virginia, North Carolina, and Indiana. As the polls closed for each time zone and the vote count rolled from east to west, it became increasingly likely that the impossibly young-looking rookie senator from Illinois would be America's next president.

A few moments after 10 p.m., a cheer went up, growing in volume and emotion until it became a roar. That's when the television networks confirmed that Obama was assured of victory. His ascent to the pinnacle of American leadership was all the more startling because he was a member of a group, African Americans, that had started at the very bottom of society, classified by law as property with no rights as human beings, and because 143 years earlier Obama himself could have been owned as a slave.

Watching on huge TV monitors, many revelers raised their fists and, updating Obama's campaign slogan of "Yes, We Can!" began shouting, "Yes, We Did! Yes, We Did!" Others chanted, "O-ba-ma! O-ba-ma!"

1

Strangers hugged, and many wept with joy. "It's not about his skin; it's about his heart," said Jane Fulton Alt, fifty-six, a white woman from Evanston, Illinois. "He gave me back my country." Added Page Cooper, a commodities broker from Chicago's West Side: "My father had to ride on the back of the bus. Now look at where we are." Paul Reinhardt, a white man from Detroit, sat with his four adopted children, who are black, and said, "One day, they will look back and say they were here in Grant Park when the first African American became president of the United States. To me, that means anything is possible."[1]

Obama had won 52.8 percent of the popular vote and 365 electoral votes to 45.6 percent and 173 electoral votes for Republican candidate John McCain, and along the way motivated millions of new voters, young people, women, Hispanics, and a vast majority of black voters to create a new coalition for change in Washington.

"If there is anyone out there who still doubts that America is a place where all things are possible, who still wonders if the dream of our founders is alive in our time, who still questions the power of our democracy, tonight is your answer," Obama told the vast rally shortly after 11 p.m. "... It's been a long time coming, but tonight, because of what we did on this date in this election at this defining moment, change has come to America."

*   *   *

FAST FORWARD to two years later, and things didn't look nearly so bright. Change had come to America in the form of a new president, but the country's problems were still festering. And Obama's once-stratospheric approval ratings had tumbled by 20 points to below 50 percent. Americans were still trying to figure out exactly what their new president was all about, how ideological he was, how much he would fight for his beliefs, how competent he was, and whether he really understood their values and their lives.

Something else had happened that surprised his supporters and confounded his critics. Once he took office, Obama did not focus on racial issues as a main priority at all. In fact, he attempted to lead a racially neutral administration, endeavoring to move beyond the black and white divisions of the past and enter a new "post-racial" era. Ironically, this is the same pattern that most of his white predecessors had adopted for more than 200 years—ignoring racial issues because they were so difficult to deal with and avoiding dramatic action to help blacks because doing so would bring too much of a backlash from whites.

Instead of adopting any kind of "black agenda," Obama immediately moved to address a series of broad crises that confronted him and the country from day one. These included the near collapse of the financial industry, a painful recession, rising unemployment, acts of terrorism, two wars, a serious decline in America's optimism, and, starting in April 2010, a horrendous oil leak from a failed drilling rig in the Gulf of Mexico.

It was clear that Obama's larger goal was to move America into an era in which race was no longer a massive divide in the nation's life. And he felt that, as a black president, he was better equipped to reach that goal than any of his predecessors. He had the trust of African Americans when he counseled patience, and he had enough confidence among whites so they would give him a chance to succeed. "I actually believe that right now the same things that would help most African Americans are the same things that would help the society at large," Obama told me in an Oval Office interview for this book. He cited his initiative on health-care reform and the need to reduce the soaring unemployment rate and added: "We don't have to get into a bunch of questions about whether some are getting helped more than others. The principles of equality are upheld."[2]

His advisers buttressed the point. "There was an enormous amount of historical significance to this country being able to elect a person who was African American as president," said Valerie Jarrett, a senior Obama adviser and an African American. "I think that there are probably people who still see him as an African American president favorably and unfavorably, but the vast majority of people, I think, see him as *their* president. I think that because he inherited such a crisis on all fronts—two wars, an economic meltdown, a fiscal meltdown, the largest deficit in our nation's history, and a health crisis, energy crisis, education crisis, confidence crisis around the world—because of this extraordinary moment in history when he stepped in, I don't think there has been a lot of time to focus on his race. People just want to know, are you going to be able to improve the quality of my life?" Jarrett added that in the final analysis, "You rise and fall based on your accomplishments, not your race."[3] She was echoing the philosophy of Reverend Martin Luther King Jr., the iconic civil rights leader of the 1960s who said he hoped that one day people would be judged by the content of their character. That remains to be seen as the Obama presidency unfolds.

But in a broader sense, the rise of America's first black president was only the latest update in a much larger story—the history of the presidents and African Americans in the White House. As this book will show, there is a fascinating and important relationship between blacks and the presidency that traces the wider arc of America's race relations and the overall history of the country for more than two centuries.

First and foremost, blacks played an indispensable role in running the White House and in helping the presidents fulfill their duties from the beginning of the Republic. Black slaves, servants, advisers, confidants, and friends of the presidents have always played a strong role that was rarely discussed in public and that has never before been described and analyzed comprehensively and in detail. These African Americans persevered in remarkable ways, starting with the years of bondage and Jim Crow, proceeding through the civil rights movement, and moving on to today, when a black man is the master of the White House.

Through it all, the presidents have generally had a disappointing and sometimes appalling record on racial matters. Most of them believed in white supremacy.[4] According to the *Journal of Blacks in Higher Education,* eight of the first twelve presidents—Southerners who held the office before Lincoln's election in 1860—owned slaves and brought men and women in bondage to work in the president's house.[5] The second baby born in the White House, in fact, was the offspring of a female slave owned by that icon of freedom Thomas Jefferson.[6] Those who held slaves while in office were George Washington, Jefferson, James Madison, James Monroe, Andrew Jackson, John Tyler, James Polk, and, finally, Zachary Taylor, the twelfth president, who died in office in 1850.[7]

The sad fact is that even the presidents who favored racial equality stepped back from embracing it fully because they didn't want to alienate conservatives in the South and racist members of Congress. There was always a powerful faction, sometimes a politically dominant one, that sought to keep blacks down or that believed the federal government had no right to intervene in matters at the state and local level.

Over the years, many opportunities to advance the cause of racial justice were squandered. George Washington might have made great strides toward limiting or abolishing slavery if he had placed his enormous influence behind abolition. Instead, he decided that taking on the slavery issue would be too divisive and he left it alone. The same was true for Jefferson, who also had enormous influence but refused to use his moral and legal authority to narrow the racial divide.[8]

Abraham Lincoln did the opposite—moving to end slavery once and for all. But even Lincoln thought the races should be kept apart after emancipation, partly because he believed that blacks had been treated so badly that they could never truly trust whites. He felt that attempting to integrate blacks fully into white society would inevitably lead to violence and upheaval. Lincoln advocated black "colonization"—sending freed slaves outside the borders of the United States where they could create their own communities.[9]

Andrew Johnson, Lincoln's successor, sided with states' rights advocates and backed away from not only black suffrage but also equal rights for freed slaves, and he set back the cause of African Americans by many years. On the other hand, in the 1960s Lyndon Johnson brought about the biggest breakthrough on civil rights since the Civil War.

Only recently did presidents begin to name appreciable numbers of blacks to their administrations as they sought to demonstrate racial outreach at a time when blacks were pressing for their rights and becoming a key voting bloc in many states. Under John F. Kennedy and Lyndon Johnson, 2 percent of political appointees were African American. Under Richard Nixon and Gerald Ford, the number was 4 percent. Under Jimmy Carter, it jumped to 12 percent. Under Ronald Reagan, it dropped to 5 percent, and under George H. W. Bush it was 6 percent. Bill Clinton named African Americans to 13 percent of his political appointments, and George W. Bush, 10 percent.[10] Under Obama, the number is 15 percent in a country where an estimated 12.4 percent of the population is black.[11]

*   *   *

THE OTHER PART of the racial history of the White House comes from the perspective of African Americans themselves. Blacks were assigned by the presidents to help run the White House as slaves and, after emancipation, as trusted members of the household staff such as valets, butlers, carpenters, chefs, doormen, electricians, gardeners, groundskeepers, housekeepers, painters, and plumbers. The bonds between the black household staff and many of the presidents have been intimate and strong. The staff members have been witnesses to revealing private moments and historic decisions, the arguments between spouses, the stresses and strains, the pressures that every commander in chief must face in dealing with the inevitable crises of office. And most of the presidents and first ladies appreciated their loyalty, discretion, and commitment to service.[12] Later, blacks such as Colin Powell and Condoleezza Rice, each of whom served as secretary of state under President George W. Bush, were among the nation's most powerful government officials. And of course with President Obama today, a black man is in charge of the entire government.

Alonzo Fields, an African American who worked for twenty-one years on the household staff starting in 1931 under Herbert Hoover, once said, "I didn't feel like a servant to a man, I felt I was a servant to my government, to my country."[13] This was a common view.

Fields said the household staff has always prided itself on keeping the first family's affairs private. "Hear nothing, know nothing, see nothing, and keep everything to yourself! That's the best quality of a good butler," he said.[14] Fortunately for the purposes of this book and the historical record, however, some members of the close-in staff have left memoirs, diaries, and interviews behind.

In nearly every case, the blacks who have served our presidents have been models of traditional values like the work ethic, loyalty, and discretion—upstanding citizens who believed in the ideals of America, such as justice and fair play, even when those ideals were not applied specifically to them. And they were devoted to the institution of the presidency. "They all just feel that it's the office that is an honor to serve, and that transcends party affiliation," says Valerie Jarrett, the Obama adviser, in an interview with the author. "It transcends race. It would transcend gender."[15]

"Some have developed relationships with the first family that have been just incredible," says Gary Walters, retired chief usher at the White House.[16]

In an e-mail interview for this book, former President George H. W. Bush reflected a common view of the presidents when he told me, "Barbara [the first lady] and I were very close to the household staff. We got to know them and their families and knew everything going on with them. We stay in touch with them and some of their kids. Of course it was a great joy for us when we saw them occasionally when George and Laura (his son the 43rd president and his wife) lived there. We had cried when we said good-bye in 1993, and then we cried when we said hello again. It was like a family reunion. A whole group of them came down [to Texas] when my presidential library opened in 1997, and then they came again when the USS *George H. W. Bush* was commissioned in 2008. They meant a great deal to me."[17]

*   *   *

BLACKS PLAYED a key role in the construction of the White House itself. Planners in Washington, DC, originally thought they would import workers from other cities and even from overseas to work on the building, but they quickly realized that slaves would be cheaper and would do the job just as well. In 1791, chief planner Pierre L'Enfant hired slaves from their masters to help dig the foundation of the White House. They were hired by the month but over time the slaves were "rented" from their masters by the year. The arrangement was for the city commission to provide food and the master to provide clothing and a blanket for each man.[18]

While these slaves were digging the foundation, other slaves in Virginia were quarrying stone for the walls. Historian William Seale says that in 1792 the city commission hired what it called twenty-five "able bodied negroe [sic] men slaves" for the quarries and they used pickaxes, wedges, and other basic tools for the arduous tax of chopping the stone out of the ground in large slabs. It was then hauled forty miles north to the work site in Washington. Other slaves were hired from their masters to dig up clay for bricks, lay the bricks, saw lumber, and do basic manual labor such as loading supplies.[19]

The slaves, along with free men, worked six days a week, twelve hours a day, from dawn to dusk, with a one-hour midday break for a meal, usually of salt pork or mutton, hoe cakes, and grease sandwiches. The slaves were not chained, but they were closely supervised. There is no record of escapes from the district's labor camps, probably because there were few places where slaves could go and find freedom.[20]

During the early years of the Republic, slaves were vital to the operation of the president's house. The presidents needed about a dozen people to run their household operations, and that staff often consisted of slaves, free blacks, and whites. (The number of people on the household staff has increased to about 100 today.) Some of the slaves were from the presidents' own plantations and some were hired from other masters in and around the capital city.

Under President Lincoln, a few free blacks were given positions in government. Then Andrew Johnson, Lincoln's successor, promoted William Slade, an African American who had been invaluable to Lincoln as a valet and confidant, to be the official Steward of the White House, with responsibility for supervising the property and grounds. Winston Sinclair, also an African American, became steward under Grover Cleveland in the late nineteenth century. And for most of the late nineteenth and early twentieth centuries, blacks and whites worked together on the White House domestic staff.[21]

In 1909, President William Taft segregated the household staff, even to the point of forcing the workers to eat separately. He continued the tradition of not inviting blacks to social functions. Segregation continued for years.

Separating the races was deeply offensive to the black staff members. One of their leaders, Alonzo Fields, said, "They had separate dining rooms—black and white. We all worked together, but we couldn't eat together.... Here in the White House! I'm working for the president. This is the home of the democracy of the world and I'm good enough to handle the president's food—to handle the president's food and do everything—but I cannot eat with the help. Well, I was a little miffed over that because I'd come from New England where in the service we would all sit down at the same table together. And I thought, 'Well, in the White House of all places, this is where it should start.'"[22]

In reaction to this discrimination, in 1910 African American employees on the household staff, including the butlers and doormen, formed the Chandelier Club, named after a huge chandelier in the East Wing. They held an annual ball of their own outside the building; this ball continued for many years, featured music by the Marine Band, and was the social high point of the year for the staff. It was frequently attended by some white workers from the White House as well.[23]

As noted in the *Journal of Blacks in Higher Education,* "A domestic position at the White House was the most prestigious post for an African American in the pre–World War II era. Often, several generations of one black family served on the White House staff."[24]

These jobs were highly coveted and often helped middle-class black families move up the economic and social ladder. For example, James Edward Ellington, the father of iconic composer and musician Duke Ellington, worked part-time on the White House household staff while Duke was young.[25]

* * *

FROM THE START, blacks had a remarkable degree of contact with and access to the presidents, allowing them to observe the nation's leaders at private moments when their strengths and weaknesses were exposed. They often talked to the presidents about issues large and small and got to know their spouses and children and their wider circle of friends and advisers.[26]

President Warren Harding trusted his black valet, Major Arthur Brooks, so completely that he made Brooks the custodian of love letters between himself and Nan Britton, his mistress. Britton said she addressed her letters to the care of Brooks, and he was always discreet and reliable in delivering them and passing along Harding's letters to her. Britton said Brooks once inadvertently walked in on one of their romantic moments in what she called a secret passage under a pergola at the White House. "I asked Mr. Harding who he was and he told me," Britton wrote later. "In my brief glance backward I saw that his valet was a good-looking light colored man. This was the one and only time I ever saw the trustworthy servant in whose care I addressed so many letters to my sweetheart." Brooks also maintained Harding's impressive wardrobe.[27]

The household staff was aware of a persistent rumor about Harding's background—that he had "African blood," allegedly because a distant relative in the past had married a black woman with several children who carried the "Harding" name. The president's advisers always denied the story and tried to squelch it because they felt the rumors would badly damage his image.[28]

Preston Bruce, a doorman and longtime household staff member, wrote in his memoirs that, "My job gave me greater access to the presidents than anyone else in the White House except for the valets. I saw them first thing in the morning, and at night just before they went to bed. It was a very rich experience to be that close to them; I saw they weren't perfect, yet my respect and affection carried through from one day to the next. As doorman I was the first to greet a newly inaugurated president and the last to say goodbye when he left. Like so many of my colleagues, I became extremely protective of every president. My own convenience no longer mattered to me as it had before I came to work at the White House. Working overtime without pay when the first family needed me seemed natural; I didn't care about the time.... The sacrifices I made seemed small, compared to the cares of a president."[29]

* * *

ONE OF THE most important ways for blacks to gain job security and importance was through work in the kitchen, which was central to family life. George Washington, in recognition of the cooking talents of his slave Hercules, made him head chef at the family estate of Mount Vernon, Virginia, and later at the president's residence in the temporary capital of Philadelphia.[30]

Later, Dolly Johnson cooked for President Benjamin Harrison and his wife after serving as their cook in their pre–White House years.[31] She replaced a French chef, Madame Madeleine Pelouard, at the White House in 1889. Mary Campbell cooked for Franklin and Eleanor Roosevelt. Vietta Garr prepared meals for Harry and Bess Truman. Zephyr Wright cooked for Lyndon and Lady Bird Johnson. Mrs. Johnson had hired Wright when Wright was a home economics student at Wiley College in Texas; Wright ended up cooking for the Johnsons for twenty-seven years in both Texas and Washington, DC.

Beyond those with culinary skills, some African Americans found different routes to establishing close relationships with the presidents they served. In the 1860s, Elizabeth Keckley had similar experiences to those of Preston Bruce as a confidant. An African American dressmaker and sounding board to both the president and First Lady Mary Todd Lincoln, Keckley was privy to the Lincolns' candid assessments of the president's advisers (Mrs. Lincoln suspected some of them of disloyalty).

Lizabeth, also known as Lizzy, was relied upon to provide solace to both husband and wife when their son Willie died and, later, to comfort Mrs. Lincoln when the president was assassinated.

In the mid-twentieth century, Lillian Rogers Parks, a White House maid, got to know four presidents—Herbert Hoover, Franklin Roosevelt, Harry Truman, and Dwight Eisenhower—and their families, and became a keen observer of White House life during her career there from 1929 to 1960. (Her mother had worked at the White House as a maid for thirty years, starting in 1909.) She wrote in her memoirs about many of the foibles of the presidents and first ladies for whom she worked. The book contained so many juicy details when it came out in 1961 that the first lady at the time, Jacqueline Kennedy, insisted that her household staff sign pledges not to write books about their White House experiences.

In her gentle and polite style, Parks managed to skewer a number of presidents and first ladies. Parks said President William Taft, who served from 1909 to 1913, would doze at inopportune moments such as during dinner parties and staff meetings and once at a funeral. "Guests would be embarrassed when he would fall asleep in the middle of their stories," Parks wrote, "and poor Mrs. Taft would have to cover for him. Sometimes, when they were alone, she would scold him for this bad habit.... About the only time he wouldn't fall asleep was when he was talking to a pretty girl, and those were the times when Mrs. Taft wished he would. Backstairs, the help joked about the way the President loved to talk to pretty women. He would bore them to death with his long legal explanations, and they would try to look bright and interested. Whenever the President singled out the most beautiful woman at any party, Mrs. Taft, always the perfect lady on the surface, did not fool the staff, who knew she was boiling inside."[32]

Parks also wrote that Taft's obesity—he weighed more than 300 pounds—was a frequent source of chagrin for his wife, who was a stickler for maintaining a favorable public image. His weight caused many problems behind the scenes. A huge bathtub was installed in the residence because President Taft would get stuck in a normal-sized tub "and it would take two men to pull him out," Parks wrote.[33] Mrs. Taft tried to control her husband's weight by imposing dietary restrictions, but he would regularly escape from her control and she eventually learned that he was gorging himself at every opportunity, such as when he was traveling.[34]

Parks also told how Edith Galt Wilson, the second wife of widower Woodrow Wilson, helped to run the government after her husband suffered several strokes, which resulted in his partial paralysis, in late 1919. "In the kitchens and back halls of the White House, the regulars were shaking their heads," Parks recalled.[35] "They were glad that the president had weathered the storm and was improving, but most of them thought he should resign and allow a competent man to take over the reins of Government." Wilson stayed in his weakened condition for the rest of his term and retired in Washington after the inauguration of his successor.

*　*　*

PRESTON BRUCE, THE LONGTIME doorman, described President John F. Kennedy and First Lady Jacqueline Kennedy as "night owls" who would sometimes romp between each other's bedrooms.

Zephyr Wright, Lyndon B. Johnson's cook, told many stories about Johnson behind the scenes. "The first night that I met President Johnson, he was late as usual," she said. "He was always late for meals.... Now there have been times that he'd get on the phone himself and call me and ask me how long it would take to get something ready for the whole Cabinet, and sometimes he'd walk in with them and you didn't even know he's coming. And I've seen a time that I've fixed a meal in 10 minutes for 25 or 30 people."[36]

Some of Johnson's advisers believed that his awareness of the bigotry that Wright endured in the segregated South—not being served in restaurants, being refused rooms at whites-only hotels when she traveled—made him more sympathetic to the civil rights movement and prodded him to push aggressively for corrective legislation.

Roland Harley, a doorman, got so comfortable with President George H. W. Bush and his wife Barbara that in 1990 he escorted a *Baltimore Sun* outdoor writer named Bill Burton to the family quarters in the East Wing for an appointment with the president one morning. They walked into the president's bedroom where Bush and Barbara were in bed. Bush, ever the gentleman, was surprised but wasn't upset. He asked Harley and Burton to please step outside the bedroom so he could get dressed for the interview. "If that happened with Reagan or Clinton we'd all be executed," remarked a household staffer later.

But behind the scenes, there were problems. By tradition, for many years (until recently) there were no blacks in the usher's office, only whites, according to several longtime staff members. At the same time, for many years the butlers, doormen, housemen, maids, executive housekeepers, and elevator operators were almost always blacks. "Some feel the White House is the last plantation," says Chris Emery, former assistant chief usher. "It's been that way for 200 years."[37]

When Colin Powell served as national security advisor under Reagan, the general got to know the household staff that worked in the White House kitchens and dining rooms. Nearly all of them were blacks. Powell said it struck him as a "leftover from ante-bellum days." The general recalled, "I started to agitate" and sought more racial diversity. But the black workers pushed back. These were very good jobs that they didn't want to lose because comparable positions were so hard to come by on the outside. "They told me to mind my own business," Powell said in an interview for this book. He let the matter drop.[38] Actually, jobs on the White House domestic staff had been prized in the local black community for many years because they were among the best positions that African Americans could find in Washington.

*   *   *

THERE WAS A tradition at the White House that household staff should be as invisible as possible in dealing with the first couple. Lillian Rogers Parks related how "People are always asking me what we do when the servants meet the president or first lady in the halls. Do we ignore them? Or call out a cheery 'Hello, sir' or 'Ma'am.' Or what? Strange as it may seem, we make ourselves as scarce as possible. We try not to run into the president and first lady if we can possibly help it, in order to give them a feeling of privacy."[39]

"Every President has faced the servant problem in a different way and with different reactions," added Parks, who at four-foot-ten was known as "Little Lillian." "The Hoovers were fierce about servants being neither seen, nor heard, and heaven help you if you were caught in the hall when the President was coming. It was sort of a scandal around the White House, the way we would dodge into a particular closet so the President wouldn't see us. It was a closet near the elevator on the second floor that was used mostly for brooms and mops. But it was definitely for the help in an emergency, and butlers with trays would pop in and fall into a closetful of maids and housemen waiting for the coast to be clear."[40]

The tradition was for a bell to be rung three times when the president was leaving his second-floor quarters, and twice for the first lady. "Like jack-in-the-boxes, we would jump in and out of hiding places, because maids and housemen would be severely scolded—on sight," Parks recalled.[41]

When Franklin Roosevelt took office, he told the staff to stop hiding and just go about their work. Harry Truman felt the same way, but the old habits died hard and the staff still tried to stay out of sight. Once, Truman noticed gardeners crouching behind some rose bushes as he approached the Oval Office. This prompted him to ask, "Why are these people peeping at me?" After that, the gardeners and yard workers simply continued their jobs when the president walked by.[42] When Dwight Eisenhower arrived, the staff resumed trying to remain unobtrusive, and they succeeded so well that Ike asked, "Why don't I ever see anyone working?" After he was told of the stealthy tradition for the household staff, Eisenhower said, "Let these people do their work, and stop this foolishness about keeping out of sight." That ended the matter.[43]

*   *   *

AS RECENTLY AS the 1980s and 1990s, under the administrations of Ronald Reagan and George H. W. Bush, the race of White House staffers was rarely discussed because the white officials who ran those administrations didn't want to be misunderstood as bigots. Beneath the surface, however, racial difficulties persisted.

Kristin Clark Taylor, the first African American to serve as director of White House media relations and a key communications adviser to Bush going back to his vice presidential days, has written that she felt slighted sometimes despite her rank.[44] As with other African Americans in other administrations, she considered herself constantly under scrutiny and felt a duty to succeed as a way of vindicating her race. Yet she also shared the feeling, common among black staff members at the White House, that it was not appropriate to talk about race. Bill Clinton remarked on this during his White House years, telling a friend that "black members of the White House staff were circumspect about overt racial awareness, let alone advocacy, considering it unprofessional."[45]

After the death of her mother in 1988, Taylor was anxious to return to the White House so no one would think she was a quitter. "In my eyes," Taylor wrote in a memoir, "maintaining my professionalism was almost a test; I knew I would be judged and graded. I felt a commitment to stand tall, not only for myself but for all women, and for all African-Americans.... It was also imperative that 'the black woman' on Bush's vice presidential staff, whom these blue-blooded, fairly high-brow white men saw every day, remain strong, proud, and sure of herself—no matter what. I represented a race, a culture, an entire world which these white males would never know intimately or personally; I was fully aware that perceptions of black folks could subtly, in some indecipherable way, be influenced by their interaction with me. In many cases, I was their primary connection to all things ethnic, or at least all things black. I owed it to my black female sisters everywhere—be they Republican, Democrat, Independent, or, hell, even unregistered—to convey a positive image."[46]

* * *

THE SENSE OF being a good example has been common among African Americans in the White House. Colin Powell, who served as not only President Reagan's national security advisor, but also chairman of the Joint Chiefs of Staff under President George H. W. Bush and briefly in the same job for President Bill Clinton, as well as secretary of state under President George W. Bush, says, "My career should serve as a model to fellow blacks, in or out of the military, in demonstrating the possibilities of American life. Equally important, I hoped then and now that my rise might cause prejudiced whites to question their prejudices and help purge the poison of racism from their systems, so that the next qualified African American who came along would be judged on merit alone."[47]

On one of his last nights at the White House as Reagan's national security advisor, Powell was attending a reception in the ceremonial East Room when a black usher came up to him and said, "Sir, I was a private in the Army in World War II, the old segregated Army. I never thought I would see the day when a black general would be in this house. I just want you to know how proud we all are." Powell replied, "I appreciate that, but you don't have it quite right. I'm the one who's proud of what all of you did to pave the way for the rest of us."[48]

This theme has persisted throughout the history of the American Republic. One generation builds on progress that can, in turn, be built upon by the next generation. It is a cycle that applies to both individual citizens and the presidents who strive to lead them.

*   *   *

OVERALL, IT HAS been a remarkable journey, as America moved from the days of Hercules, Elizabeth Keckley, and Zephyr Wright to the era of Barack Obama.

It is an arc of progress in which all Americans can take enormous pride.

Chapter Two
The Slave-Owning Presidents

All of America's earliest presidents, except for John Adams, the second chief executive, were slave owners. This, of course, contradicted the ideals of freedom and human rights that supposedly shaped the new nation. It was also a massive hypocrisy for the founders to proclaim their right to rebel from England while at the same time denying independence to their slaves.

These contradictions especially applied to three iconic leaders whose decisions and policies guided the United States in its infancy and set many precedents for the future—George Washington, the father of his country; Thomas Jefferson, author of the Declaration of Independence, and James Madison, father of the Constitution. Each became president of the United States within a few years after the founding, and each was a slave owner who profited personally from the institution and, even when moral doubts set in, did nothing during his own lifetime to end the practice either on his own plantation or in the nation as a whole.[1]

* * *

GEORGE WASHINGTON'S FAMILY had owned slaves for many years, and he apparently did little serious second-guessing about the morality of the institution until late in life. "His forbears had long since justified slavery as necessary to the preservation of the social order, and surrounded the system with the fullest protection of the law and the sanction of the church," writes author Walter H. Mazyck.[2] In sum, Washington was a typical Virginia planter in his views about race. Martha, his wife, also accepted slavery and was, like her husband, most concerned not with the welfare of the African Americans in bondage but their efficiency as workers.[3]

Mrs. Washington was blunt in expressing her low regard for the slaves. "Black children are liable to so many accidents and complaints that one is heartily sore of keeping them," she wrote a friend in discussing a freedman servant. "I hope you will not find in him much sass. The blacks are so bad in their nature that they have not the least gratitude for the kindness that may be showed them.... [T]he women that wash, they always idle half their time away about their own business and wash so bad that the clothes are not fit to use."[4]

Throughout his adult life, including his eight years as president, George Washington closely supervised the treatment of his slaves, just as he carefully managed the rest of his property in Mount Vernon. His goal was to get the most out of his huge plantation and avoid the kind of debt that plagued many of his fellow planters (including Thomas Jefferson).

He was a strict disciplinarian who insisted on hard work from his human chattel and approved of flogging slaves to keep them in line. He clothed and housed them as cheaply as he could, consistent with maintaining their health and efficiency. He endorsed the custom of raffling off and dividing enslaved families, including children, owned by bankrupt slaveholders who owed him money.[5] He sold unruly slaves, especially those who ran away from the plantation, to buyers in the faraway West Indies where they couldn't cause him any more trouble.[6]

He also tried to devise the best diet for his slaves to maximize their output, as he might do for a mule or an ox. After discussing with Washington the pros and cons of raising corn, Benjamin Henry Latrobe, a family friend, wrote, "As food for the Negroes it was his opinion that it was infinitely preferable to wheat bread in point of nourishment. He had made the experiment upon his own lands and had found that though the Negroes, while the novelty lasted, seemed to prefer wheat bread as being the food of their masters, they soon grew tired of it. He conceived that should the Negroes be fed upon wheat or rye bread, they would, in order to be fit for the same labor, be obliged to have a considerable addition to their allowance of meat."[7]

* * *

AFTER BEING ELECTED president in 1789, Washington made his way to New York, the first capital, and received a tumultuous welcome.

Martha stayed behind at Mount Vernon to prepare the household for the move north. Nine slaves were chosen to serve the first family in New York: William Lee, the president's valet, who accompanied Washington to his new post; Ona Judge, the sixteen-year-old personal attendant for the first lady; Ona's brother Austin, a waiter; and slaves named Christopher, Giles, Hercules, Joe, Moll, and Paris.[8] The Washingtons had no qualms about bringing slaves into the capital of the supposedly freedom-loving nation; in fact, it seemed perfectly natural as part of their entitlement as white American aristocrats.[9]

Washington could have made a good start toward abolishing slavery had he desired to do so. "Washington's unequaled influence afforded him the opportunity to be the hub with respect to fighting for wondrous changes and unpopular causes," writes historian John Ferling. "During his first year in office, he was in a position to employ his matchless standing to conceivably bring on a profound transformation in one area that would have given all of American history a different, and more salubrious, contour."[10] That was the issue of slavery.

In fact, at the start of the revolution, slavery had been legal in every colony, and 500,000 blacks, or one-fifth of the population of the United States, were enslaved in 1776.[11] The new Constitution provided that in 1808 Congress would be empowered to abolish the foreign slave trade if it wished, but otherwise the Constitution preserved the institution of slavery.

Nine months after Washington's inauguration, anti-slavery Quakers forced the issue by presenting petitions to Congress calling for the immediate end of the slave trade and the gradual end of slavery in the new nation. The revered Benjamin Franklin gave the petitions credence when he endorsed them, prompting a debate on the issue among the legislators.

At this point, Washington could have sided with Franklin and at least moved the debate in what we would today consider a more enlightened direction. But he took no action rather than risk dividing the new national legislature between those who opposed slavery and those who supported it.[12]

In personal terms, Washington was far from a profile in courage. The man who in legend promised never to tell a lie resorted to deception to hold onto his slaves and avoid alienating Northerners who might have objected to his commitment to preserving the institution. In the spring of 1791, after the capital had moved from New York to Philadelphia, he became keenly aware that Pennsylvania had passed a law under which slaves brought into the state became free after six months of residency. Not wanting to lose the handful of slaves he had brought with him, President Washington evaded the law by shuttling slaves back and forth from Philadelphia to Virginia within the six-month time limit to avoid any legal problems. He also hoped that the slaves would not learn of the Pennsylvania emancipation law and then seek freedom by escaping from his control in that state. Washington wrote his assistant, Tobias Lear, that "the idea of freedom might be too great a temptation for them to resist."

In sending them back to Virginia to circumvent the law, Washington wrote, "I wish to have it accomplished under pretext that may deceive both them [the slaves] and the public; and none, I think would so effectually do this as—Mrs. Washington coming to Virginia next month, toward the middle or latter end of it, as she seemed to have a wish to do—if she can accomplish it by any convenient and agreeable means, with the assistance of the stage horses, etc. This would naturally bring her maid and Austin; and Hercules, under the idea of coming home to cook whilst we remained there, might be sent on in the state.... I request that these sentiments and this advice may be known to none but *yourself* and *Mrs. Washington* [emphasis in original]."[13] One visitor to Mount Vernon in 1800, a Polish writer named Julian Niemcewicz, was shocked at the slaves' living conditions. Niemcewicz found that their quarters were worse than those of poor peasants in his homeland of Poland. And Niemcewicz thought that their back-breaking work routine was excessive and the rules that were imposed on them made little sense, such as the fact that they were allowed to raise hens but could not own geese, ducks, or pigs.[14]

But some historians say Washington didn't treat his slaves badly, at least when assessed according to the standards of his day. "The regime in the presidential mansion represented slavery at its most benign," writes Henry Wiencek. "Washington occasionally barked in rage at his slaves, but he barked at his white servants as well, and even the highest government officials shrank from him when they sensed his temper rising. There is no record of it, but it is inconceivable that anyone was ever whipped at the Philadelphia Executive Mansion, a practice that was still going on at Mount Vernon at that time. The slaves were well treated, well fed, well clothed— and Ona, Austin, and Hercules went by themselves to the theater!"[15]

Still, all this was relative. These people remained slaves and many of them chafed at their subjugation; some plotted their escapes. Meanwhile,

George and Martha probably mistook obedience for loyalty, as did many other slave owners. But there is a clear record of tension and occasional defiance.

Paris, a teenager, was disobedient repeatedly, and Washington sent him back to Mount Vernon. Hercules's son, Richmond, was also sent back after being caught stealing money, and Washington speculated that Hercules, a cook much respected by the president for his culinary skills, and Richmond were trying to accumulate cash for a joint escape. Hercules supervised the president's kitchen at both Mount Vernon and the president's house in the capital. At one point, a slave named John Cline left the president's house in Philadelphia, the temporary capital, and Washington did not try to find him, probably realizing that Pennsylvania had many free blacks and many whites who would harbor a slave or send such a fugitive out of the area if that seemed a safer alternative.[16] At another point, Christopher, who knew how to read and write, sent a note to his wife about his own planned escape attempt and the note was found, foiling the attempt.[17]

In February 1793, President Washington signed the Fugitive Slave Act, which established the precise procedure for masters to reclaim their escaped slaves. And eventually the issue hit close to home.

In 1796, he tried to use the law in the pursuit of Ona (also called "Oney") Judge, one of his slaves and Martha's attendant, who escaped from his household in Philadelphia and fled to New Hampshire, where slavery was legal but frowned upon. When the capital was moved from New York to Philadelphia in November 1790, Ona had started working with Martha at the president's residence as the first lady's maid. Ona was young, gave a good appearance, and was light-skinned—all traits that the Washingtons liked. So she became one of the first couple's most popular workers, slave or free. The president and Mrs. Washington also valued Ona's skills as a seamstress and as an attendant who styled Martha's hair and took care of her clothes, but it was the first lady who became incensed at what she considered her slave's display of disloyalty and ingratitude by running away.[18]

After careful planning and making contacts among freed slaves in Philadelphia, Ona, then twenty-three, disappeared in May 1796, the last year of Washington's presidency. What apparently pushed her over the edge was being told that she would be given to one of the Washingtons's great-grandchildren as a wedding gift, which she interpreted to mean that "I should never get my liberty."[19] She slipped away one night while the Washingtons were at dinner in their Philadelphia mansion. At some point later that spring, she left her Philadelphia sanctuary, where she was apparently hidden by local blacks, and boarded the *Nancy*, a ship bound for Portsmouth, New Hampshire, where she took up residence and eventually married a free man and had a child.[20]

Learning that Ona was in Portsmouth, Washington told Treasury Secretary Oliver Wolcott to have the federal customs officer in that city capture her and send her to Mount Vernon aboard another ship. "The ingratitude of the girl, who was brought up and treated more like a child than a servant ought not to escape with impunity if it can be avoided," Washington wrote to Wolcott. This was illegal. Federal law required that a slaveholder or his representative appear in person before a magistrate to prove that he owned the slave in question before that person could be sent across state lines.[21]

The customs officer wrote the president that Ona was willing to negotiate for her freedom, but Washington was offended. He replied that "for however well disposed I might be to a gradual abolition, or even to an entire emancipation of that description of people (if the latter was in itself practicable at this moment), it would neither be politic or just to reward unfaithfulness with a premature preference; and thereby discontent beforehand the minds of all her fellow-servants who by their steady attachments are far more deserving than herself of favor."[22]

Washington kept up the pressure to return Ona to servitude at Mount Vernon, by force if necessary. Yet Ona managed to elude capture, moving at least once at the last minute as Washington's agents prepared to take her away, and eventually the Washingtons gave up their pursuit. Some of Washington's defenders say he did all this to please his wife, and he would have left Ona alone if it were not for the prodding of Martha. In any case, it was not a flattering insight into Washington's dealing with slavery, that he would treat Ona like his prey while he was supposedly an apostle of new thinking about human rights. And the episode showed the persistence and cleverness of the president's slaves in seeking their freedom. Ona died in a small New Hampshire town in 1848, living as a free woman. But she had endured under a cloud of fear that she might someday be captured and returned to bondage.

Ona Judge was not the only slave to escape permanently or, in the idiom of the time, "elope" from Washington's control and elude capture. In March 1797, on the morning that the first couple was leaving Philadelphia for their home in Virginia at the end of Washington's presidency, they noticed that Hercules, their chef, was gone, according to various accounts. He was never heard from again and apparently slipped away to take advantage of the Pennsylvania law requiring that slaves living in the state would be free if they stayed more than six months. An alternative theory is that Hercules actually escaped in February after being sent back to Mount Vernon.[23] But regardless of the circumstances, President Washington was upset, thinking that this was an act of ingratitude. And even though Washington sent out search parties, Hercules was never found. One of Hercules's daughters at Mount Vernon was asked by a visitor how she felt about her father escaping. "I miss my father," she replied, "but I know that he is free and so I am happy for him."

As was true for so many of America's presidents and white leaders in general, Washington did not appear to understand how deeply African Americans yearned for their freedom and how many risks they would take to gain it.

The escape was especially unsettling for the president because Washington had given Hercules enormous leeway, including permission to sell leftovers and other food from the kitchen and make enough money to buy fine clothes.[24]

Hercules had become invaluable to the first family, and he was immensely proud of his professionalism, a tradition that has been passed along from generation to generation of the presidents' household staff. An indication of this proud tradition can be found in a portrait said to be of Hercules that depicts the chef as a confident-looking man wearing a toque, a white kerchief around his neck, and a white chef's jacket. George Washington Parke Custis, Martha Washington's grandson, said Hercules was as "highly accomplished and proficient in the culinary arts as could be found in the United States." He was able to cook everything from a roast chicken to soufflé and almond pudding.[25]

Hercules was a sharp dresser, and he became a recognizable figure as he walked through the streets of Philadelphia, the temporary U.S. capital, wearing a velvet waistcoat and carrying a gold-handled cane. In one description at the time, Hercules was wearing "white linen, black silk breeches and waistcoat, highly polished shoes with large buckles, a blue cloth coat with velvet collar and bright metal buttons, a watch fob and chain, cocked hat, and gold-headed cane."[26]

*   *   *

HISTORIANS DEBATE WHETHER Washington ever took advantage of enslaved women and had affairs with them, as so many other slave owners did at the time. One theory is that he had sex with a slave named Venus at Mount Vernon and fathered a child named West Ford. I tend to agree with presidential scholar Wiencek and other historians who argue that Washington was so committed to personal discipline and self-control and so protective of his image as a man of rectitude that it is difficult to believe he would have allowed himself such a lapse. Washington wrote his philosophy in 1788: "I have studiously avoided, as much as was in my power, to give any cause for ill-natured or impertinent comments on my conduct: and I should be very unhappy to have anything done … which should give occasion for one officious tongue to use my name with indelicacy."[27]

*   *   *

OVER THE YEARS, Washington developed deep qualms about slavery. He wished to end the practice but felt it was up to the state legislatures. He told friends that to have the federal government push for abolition would pose a mortal threat to the Union because Southern states would never stand for such a move. Of course, this is exactly what happened in 1861 when the Civil War began. And in his own case, he felt that freeing his slaves would make it impossible to run his plantation at Mount Vernon and would consign him to financial ruin. But as his presidency proceeded, he grew increasingly distressed about being a slave owner. In 1794, he wrote to Tobias Lear, a friend, about why he wanted to dispose of some of his lands—and explained that it wasn't just for financial reasons. "I have another motive," Washington said, "which makes me earnestly wish for these things—it is indeed more powerful than all the rest—namely to liberate a certain species of property—which I possess very repugnantly to my own feelings; but which imperious necessity compels, and until I can substitute some other expedient, by which expenses, not in my power to avoid {however well I may be disposed to do it} can be defrayed."[28]

Also in 1794, he wrote to another friend, Alexander Spotswood: "With respect to the other species of property concerning which you ask my opinion, I shall frankly declare to you that I do not like even to think, much less talk of it. However, as you have put the question, I shall, in a few words, give my ideas about it. Were it not then, that I am principled against selling Negroes, as you would cattle at a market, I would not in twelve months from this date, be possessed of one as a slave. I shall be happily mistaken, if they are not found to be a very troublesome species of property ere many years pass over our heads."[29]

Historians James MacGregor Burns and Susan Dunn add: "Nothing could have more bluntly challenged Washington's view of happiness than slavery. To move from his public world of civility and decorum, statesmanship and diplomacy, revolutionary leadership and constitution making to his private world at Mount Vernon is to descend into a southern plantation of several thousand acres, two hundred slaves managed by hard driving overseers, directed from near or afar by entrepreneurs busy computing profit and loss, sales and expenses, the buying and selling of slaves as chattel property. Washington was the unchallenged master of these slaves, yet utterly dependent on them, in a hierarchical community."[30]

By the end of his life, Washington had turned firmly against slavery, considering it corrupting for everyone associated with it, both master and slave. But he declined to do anything immediately. Instead, in his will, Washington ordered that all his slaves—more than 300 by that time—be freed upon the death of his wife, Martha, and he added that the children of his slaves should be educated and trained so they could prosper as free adults. He was the only founder to order that his slaves be set free. But he came to this decision after a lifetime in which slave labor was the cornerstone of his wealth and central to his life at Mount Vernon. This was a basic contradiction of the principles espoused publicly by Washington and the founders in the Declaration of Independence and in their other writings.[31]

*   *   *

THE FIRST LADIES sometimes were important influences on their husbands regarding racial matters. As noted, Martha Washington reinforced her husband's prejudices. And in a sad denouement, she ended her life at Mount Vernon wrapped in paranoia about her slaves. According to Abigail Adams, a friend to Martha and wife of the second president, Martha was worried because her late husband had decreed in his will that the family's 300 slaves were to be freed upon Mrs. Washington's death. "She did not feel as tho' her life was safe in their hands," Abigail wrote, "many of whom would be told that it was in their interest to get rid of her. . . . If any person wishes to see the baneful effects of slavery as it creates a torper [sic] and an indolence and a spirit of domination—let them come and take a view of the cultivation of this part of the United States."[32]

Of course, Abigail Adams was a longtime opponent of slavery, as were her husband, President John Adams, and son, the future President John Quincy Adams. All of them were from Massachusetts, far from the plantation culture of the South. Abigail was particularly offended by the contradiction between slavery and the ideals expressed in the Declaration of Independence and said so, arguing that while Americans were fighting the "slavery" imposed by the British, white Americans owned slaves of their own. "I wish most sincerely," she wrote her husband, "there was not a slave in the province. It always appeared a most iniquitous scheme to me—fight ourselves for what we are daily robbing and plundering from those who have as good a right to freedom as we have." She expressed doubt about the patriotism of Southerners because "the passion for liberty cannot be equally strong in the breast of those who have been accustomed to deprive their fellow creatures of theirs." As first lady, Mrs. Adams refused to employ slaves hired out by their masters either in their home in Massachusetts or in the newly constructed White House (then called the President's House, where the Adamses moved in 1800). At one point, she sent a young African American servant, James, to a white public school in Massachusetts to get the best education possible. When the parents of white students objected, Abigail held firm.[33] Abigail's commitment to racial progress foreshadowed other presidential spouses who played a similar role (and will be discussed in later chapters).

* * *

THOMAS JEFFERSON WAS a man of the Enlightenment who delighted in learning about history, literature, science, architecture, inventions, and many other topics. But he was, unfortunately, a man of his time when it came to slavery and race relations. He kept slaves at Monticello, his beloved plantation near Charlottesville, Virginia, and considered them essential to running the property and keeping himself financially solvent. As America's third president (following Washington and John Adams), and serving from 1801 to 1809, he owned more than 100 slaves at the start of his presidency and brought about a dozen of them to the White House as household staff in 1801, a year after the building opened. He told friends that he considered the institution of slavery morally wrong but said it was indispensable at that time to the economy of the South— and his own livelihood.

Jefferson's hypocrisy strikes home very powerfully when one considers that he authored the most famous statement of American values—the Declaration of Independence—which proclaims, "We hold these truths to be self-evident: that all men are created equal; that they are endowed by their creator with certain inalienable rights; that among these are life, liberty, and the pursuit of happiness."

But Jefferson had what we consider today a huge and shocking blind spot. His personal attitudes about equality were primitive. In an 1807 letter, Jefferson said blacks were "as inferior to the rest of mankind as the mule is to the horse, and as made to carry burthens." In his *Notes on the State of Virginia*, which he wrote in 1781 and 1782, and arranged to be published in Paris in 1785, he condemned slavery as "a hideous evil" but said blacks were inherently inferior to whites in reasoning powers and imagination though superior to whites in music and equal in courage and the "moral sense." Jefferson also wrote in *Notes* that black men lusted after white women because they seemed more attractive than black women, just as an orangutan in the wild lusted for "the black women over those of his own species."[34]

Another Jefferson conclusion was that people of African descent were meant to be subordinate to whites while those of European descent were meant to be dominant. "It is not their condition then, but nature, which has produced this distinction," he wrote.[35] Under Jefferson's theories, blacks were not included in the definition of "men" when he wrote the Declaration of Independence.

He used his slaves in well-defined, hierarchical roles—body servants, house servants, cooks, artisans and, at the bottom of the ladder, field hands. "There also was a special inner family of slaves," writes historian Donald Jackson, "a matriarchy headed by mulatto Betty Hemings, which would eventually include twelve children. Betty had come to Monticello as part of Martha Jefferson's dowry, and apparently six of her offspring were sired by her former owner John Wayles, the father of Jefferson's late wife."[36]

Sally Hemings, one of Betty's daughters, who was described at the time as biracial, light-skinned, and beautiful, apparently had an affair with Jefferson and gave birth to at least one of his children. She spent much of her adolescence serving Jefferson and his two daughters while he was U.S. envoy to France, and then as a house servant and seamstress at Monticello, where she cleaned Jefferson's bedchamber, prepared his clothes, and gained much authority to run the main house.

The fourteen-year-old Sally accompanied nine-year-old Mary Jefferson, the future president's daughter, later called Maria, to Paris in 1787 when Jefferson was U.S. minister there. Some historians and Jefferson biographers believe he began an affair with her in 1788, when Jefferson began to pay Sally and her brother James, who was being trained as a chef, monthly wages (about half of what French servants were paid).[37]

*   *   *

JEFFERSON WAS RELATIVELY kind to his slaves, according to the standards of his day. He would not let them be overworked and would only rarely allow them to be whipped. He permitted some of his slaves to read but not to write, because he feared that slaves might forge papers to give themselves freedom.[38]

An insight into Jefferson's treatment of his slaves came in a diary dictated after the president's death by a slave named Isaac. Isaac called Jefferson "a mighty good master."[39] Jefferson sometimes learned that a slave had escaped by walking off his plantation, but he was not draconian in hunting the fugitive down or keeping watch on his slaves' day-to-day activities. He rarely sold slaves, preferring to keep them on his plantation with their families and friends.[40]

But there were serious lapses. Isaac tells how Jefferson allowed Colonel Archibald Cary, Jefferson's friend who periodically visited Monticello, to have a free hand in dealing with slaves. "He [Cary] has given Isaac more whippings than he has fingers and toes," according to Isaac. Anticipating a visit by Cary, Jefferson would instruct Isaac to keep three gates on the property open for the friend's arrival. "Whenever Isaac missed opening them gates in time the colonel soon as he git to the house look about for him and whip him with his horsewhip. . . . Colonel Cary made freer at Monticello than he did at home; whip anybody," Isaac said.[41]

Jefferson bargained with at least one of his slaves to keep him at Monticello—a testament to Jefferson's leniency and also the slave's savvy. When he was secretary of state in the temporary capital of Philadelphia, he brought with him James Hemings (a relative of Sally's), who had lived with Jefferson in Paris when Jefferson was a U.S. envoy there and was trained at considerable expense to cook French food. Jefferson realized that Pennsylvania had enacted a law emancipating blacks (the same law that Washington had evaded earlier). Jefferson and other Virginia slave owners understood that any slaves they brought with them could easily escape and gain freedom in Pennsylvania, where many free blacks already lived.[42]

The two struck a deal. In 1793, Jefferson agreed to free James but only if the slave returned to Monticello and taught other slaves how "to be a good cook." Three years later, having taught his brother, Peter Hemings, his culinary techniques, James Hemings was freed. After Jefferson was elected president, he asked James to join him in the White House as the chef, but James declined.[43]

Jefferson freed other slaves after his death, according to his will, but he allowed many to remain in bondage. He didn't think they were ready for freedom during his lifetime and didn't want to jeopardize the future of his debt-ridden plantation through a blanket emancipation, as Washington had done.

There is scant information about the slaves' routine at the White House when Jefferson was in office. One bit of insight, however, came from Edmund Bacon, who was overseer at Monticello from 1806 to 1822. On a sixteen-day visit to the White House as Jefferson neared the end of his second term, Bacon said Jefferson "had eleven servants with him from Monticello. He had a French cook in Washington named Julien and he took Eda and Fanny there to learn French cookery. He always preferred French cookery. Eda and Fanny were afterwards [two of] his cooks at Monticello."[44] Jefferson also had non-slaves in his employ, including a French steward named Lemaire and an Irish carriage driver named Daugherty.[45]

Overall, Jefferson's racial prejudice was his worst failure, notably his belief that blacks and whites "cannot live in the same government." Historian E. M. Halliday writes, "This was a besmirchment of his own great testimony to freedom and human rights, the Declaration of Independence, with which it cannot be reconciled.... It also is an amazing disregard, for a man as perceptive as Thomas Jefferson, of what may be called the crossover factor. At the very least, as he well knew, some blacks were intellectually far superior to some whites, so that categorical discrimination on the basis of color was intrinsically unjust. That he paid no attention to this factor is an indication of how predominantly emotional his racial prejudice was."[46]

* * *

JAMES MADISON followed the same pattern as Washington and Jefferson. He was a slave owner who had moral reservations about slavery but did little or nothing to combat the practice because of practical reasons, both personal and political. As his two predecessors had concluded, Madison believed that his own prosperity depended on his retaining the 100 slaves he owned at any given time, and, on a larger scale, he felt that maintaining the Union depended on keeping the institution of slavery intact or the Southern states would secede. This was probably an accurate political assessment, but it was never tested by the early presidents. Further, the political calculus doesn't absolve Madison of his personal obligation to live up to the moral standards of the new nation in terms of idealizing freedom and the sanctity of the individual.

Known as the "father of the Constitution" for his role in drafting that document, he was elected to two terms as America's fourth president in 1808 and 1812. Madison, after Washington and Jefferson and prior to James Monroe, was part of what was known as the "Virginia dynasty" of planters who dominated the presidency in the first few elections after independence. (Four of the first five presidents were from Virginia; John Adams, the second chief executive, was from Massachusetts.)

Madison is perhaps best known for being commander in chief during the War of 1812. In addition, he kept the institution of slavery on the back burner.[47]

On the issue of how Madison and his wife, Dolley, treated their slaves, perhaps the best evidence came from Paul Jennings, Madison's personal slave who stayed with him for many years until Madison died in 1836. Born in bondage at Montpelier, the Madison estate, in 1799, and believed to be the son of a white English trader and one of Madison's slaves, Jennings moved to the White House as a footman at the age of ten when Madison became the fourth president in 1809. He did not mince words about his new surroundings, reporting in a memoir that "the East Room was not finished, and Pennsylvania Avenue was not paved, but was always in an awful condition from either mud or dust. The city was a dreary place." Jennings remained there for Madison's two terms, until he was eighteen.

He was described as articulate and, in his own memoir, told of how he could play the violin. A photo of him kept today at Montpelier, Madison's estate in Virginia, shows a dignified, scowling light-skinned man with long sideburns and goatee, and dressed in what appears to be a fashionable coat and scarf.

Jennings described First Lady Dolley Madison as "a remarkably fine woman. She was beloved by everybody in Washington, white and colored. Whenever soldiers marched by, during the war, she always sent out and invited them in to take wine and refreshments, giving them liberally of the best in the house."[48]

Of the president, Jennings wrote, "Mr. Madison, I think, was one of the best men that ever lived. I never saw him in a passion, and never knew him to strike a slave, although he had over one hundred; neither would he allow an overseer to do it. Whenever any slaves were reported to him as stealing or 'cutting up' badly, he would send for them and admonish them privately, and never mortify them by doing it before others. They generally served him very faithfully."

In his memoir, *A Colored Man's Reminiscences of James Madison,* Jennings showed that blacks were eager to prove themselves in a variety of ways, and they regularly did so. On August 24, 1814, during the War of 1812 between the United States and Great Britain, as the British approached the weakly defended capital, an emergency force of Americans under a "Com. Barney" was put together and sent to meet the enemy at Bladensburg, Maryland. Jennings records that "They fought splendidly. A large part of his men were tall, strapping Negroes, mixed with white sailors and marines. Mr. Madison and a handful of his aides rode on horseback to review them just before the fight, and asked Com. Barney if his 'Negroes would not run on the approach of the British?' 'No sir,' said Barney, 'they don't know how to run; they will die by their guns first.'" Jennings goes on to say, "They fought till a large part of them were killed or wounded."[49]

After it became clear that the British had won the engagement, Madison dispatched James Smith, a free African American, to Washington with a warning to the first lady that the British were coming.[50] Meanwhile, back at the White House, having been assured by the military that there was no danger, Mrs. Madison ordered that dinner be ready at 3 p.m. as usual. Guests were invited, and Jennings set the table with a sumptuous meal, including ale, cider, and wine in coolers. Suddenly, Smith rode his horse at a gallop up to the house, waved his hat frantically, and shouted, "Clear out, clear out!"—the Americans were retreating. Jennings describes what happened next as "confusion.... People were running in every direction," with Mrs. Madison rushing through the dining room, stuffing silver into her handbag, then jumping into her carriage with a servant named Sukey and being driven to nearby Georgetown Heights.

"John Freeman (the colored butler) drove off in the coachee with his wife, child, and servant; also a feather bed lashed on behind the coachee, which was all the furniture saved, except part of the silver and the portrait of Washington.... I will here mention that although the British were expected every minute, they did not arrive for some hours; in the mean time, a rabble, taking advantage of the confusion, ran all over the White House, and stole lots of silver and whatever they could lay their hands on."[51]

Jennings adds that it wasn't Dolley Madison who in White House lore saved the now-famous portrait of George Washington by Gilbert Stuart Landsdowne (which hangs today in the East Room of the White House). According to Jennings, "John Suse (a Frenchmen, then door-keeper, and still living) and Magraw, the president's gardener, took it down and sent it off on a wagon, with some large silver urns and such other valuables as could be hastily got hold of. When the British did arrive, they ate up the very dinner, and drank the wines, etc., that I had prepared for the president's party."[52] They also set fire to the White House, the Capitol, and much of Washington.

* * *

DOLLEY MADISON HAD been raised a Quaker who believed that slavery was a sin. Her parents had freed their slaves when they converted to Quakerism. She joined the American Colonization Society, which favored resettling freed African Americans in Liberia, placing her at odds with abolitionists, who felt that sending the former slaves abroad was wrong because they had every right to live in the United States. She said she regarded "human chattels as human beings" and felt that "the black-hued had emotions like unto those of the more fortunately hued."[53]

When Madison left the presidency in 1817, Jennings became his personal servant, taking care of his clothes and his personal requirements, at his Virginia plantation of Montpelier. More than 100 black slaves and only a handful of white people lived on the estate at any given time, and Madison regarded Jennings as an essential part of the operation.

After the president died, almost bankrupt, Dolley desperately needed money and she sold Jennings in September 1846 to Pollard Webb, an insurance agent in Washington, for $200. Six months later, Senator Daniel Webster of Massachusetts bought Jennings for $120 and promised to free him after he worked off the money spent to make the purchase, at the cost of $8 per month.

Before he did that, however, Jennings decided to help the poverty-stricken Mrs. Madison with "small sums from my own pocket."[54] This delayed his freedom but he eventually got enough money together to buy it and he became a free man, working in the U.S. Pension Office in Washington, DC. He became a prominent citizen and leader of the black community of the capital and an abolitionist who helped organize a failed attempt to free slaves from the capital area by boat.[55]

Jennings's three sons, John, Franklin, and William, fought with the Union Army in the Civil War. Jennings died peacefully at his Washington home at age seventy-five.

*   *   *

AFTER MADISON, the racial pattern at the White House remained the same as the one established by the first three Virginia presidents. None of their immediate successors broke out of the mold of treating African Americans as chattel, both in terms of policy and in terms of the presidents' daily lives.[56]

Andrew Jackson, for example, owned slaves and had no qualms about the institution itself or extending it to new territories. The Census of 1830 recorded fourteen slaves living in the White House while Jackson was president, six males and eight females.[57] "The bravery that African American soldiers, both slave and free, and other nonwhite combatants had shown under his command during the Battle of New Orleans did not persuade him—as it had Washington, and would Lincoln, Grant, and Theodore Roosevelt—that such soldiers, having proven themselves as worthy in battle as others, might merit the right to enjoy the same liberties as other civilians afterwards," writes political scientist Alvin Felzenberg. "Jackson's nonchalant acceptance of slavery, his advocacy of a strong union, and his expansionist yearnings invite the conclusion that he would have been open to a continental union with slavery permitted in much, if not most, newly acquired territories."[58]

Zachary Taylor, who took office in 1849 and died in 1850, was the last president to actually have slaves in the White House. Like Washington and Jefferson, he said he was personally opposed to the institution of slavery on principle, but didn't free his own slaves because it would have undermined his financial well-being. According to biographer John S. D.

Eisenhower, "He would not disrupt the Union by trying to abolish slavery in states where it already existed, but he would not allow its expansion into the new territories."[59]

It was all part of America's sad and complex racial history. Even the presidents who did not own slaves did little or nothing to end the institution because they feared shattering the Union. It took the election of Abraham Lincoln in 1860, which triggered the Civil War, to set the nation on the path of emancipation and eventual abolition.

Chapter Three

The Emancipator

For much of his life, Abraham Lincoln was a racist. He thought blacks were inferior and, even if slavery were ended, he doubted that, except for some unusual individual cases, there could ever be full equality. In fact, for many years he supported the "separation of the white and black races" and the voluntary deportation of blacks to colonies outside the United States, in Haiti, Liberia, or elsewhere.[1] Lincoln sometimes used racist terms both privately and in his public remarks. In April 1862, for example, he commented on the offer of President Fabre Nicholas Geffard of Haiti to send a white man as his ambassador to the United States by saying, "You can tell the president of Haiti that I shan't tear my shirt if he does send a nigger here."[2]

When he assumed the presidency, Lincoln shared many of the same political concerns as his predecessors about ending slavery. He was not a slave master and believed owning human beings was wrong, but he was born in the slave state of Kentucky and had married into a slave-owning family, the Todds of Lexington, Kentucky, so he understood firsthand how deeply the institution pervaded the South and the border states. He also felt that abolition was up to each state because the Constitution didn't give the federal government the power to end slavery. He extended this logic to conclude that a law allowing slave owners to reclaim fugitive slaves was acceptable. In 1860, the year he was elected president, slavery existed in fifteen of the thirty-three states,[3] and four million men and women were held in bondage.[4]

In his political calculations, Lincoln particularly wanted to avoid alienating border states that could be lost to the Union if pressed too hard on the slavery question.[5] He believed total abolition would make it more difficult to hold the Union together, and after the Southern states did secede, he felt that while millions of people in the North were willing to fight and die to restore the Union, they would not do so to abolish slavery. Many Northerners feared that freed slaves would move en masse to the Northern states and take their jobs. And Lincoln believed, at the start of his presidency, that he might still persuade the Confederate states to rejoin the Union by promising to maintain slavery in the states where it was already legal and part of the social fabric.

On August 25, 1862, the *New York Tribune* published a revealing letter from Lincoln in response to editor Horace Greeley's call for complete emancipation and his criticism of Lincoln for failing to embrace that policy in full. Lincoln's letter confirmed the fears of strict abolitionists, including the former slave Frederick Douglass. "My paramount object in this struggle *is* to save the Union," Lincoln wrote, "and is not either to save or to destroy slavery. If I could save the Union without freeing *any* slave I would do it and if I could save it by freeing *all* the slaves I would do it; and if I could save it by freeing some and leaving others alone I would also do that. What I do about slavery, and the colored race, I do because I believe it helps to save the Union; and what I forbear, I forbear because I do *not* believe it would help to save the Union."[6]

But Lincoln's views on abolition gradually changed. His reasons for wanting to end slavery were, in the end, both moral—he thought it was wrong—and practical—he thought abolition would increase support for the North in Europe, where slavery was prohibited by law. And he felt that freeing the slaves in the South would deprive the Confederacy of needed manpower.

It's likely that his attitudes were shaped at least in part by his personal experiences with blacks, especially around the Soldiers' Home, a center for several hundred recuperating Union soldiers about three miles from the White House and where Lincoln and his family lived for about one-quarter of his presidency. He found the Soldiers' Home was less hectic and more restful than the White House, and cooler in the summer months, so he became a commuter. En route to and from the retreat, Lincoln would frequently stop at camps for "contrabands" or former slaves. "Aunt Mary"

Dines, an escaped slave from Maryland, was the Lincoln family's cook at the summer retreat, and she lived at such a camp.

These visits by Lincoln, who was becoming a figure of biblical importance to blacks, were much anticipated and treated with great pomp and ceremony. First, a sergeant would sound a bugle signaling the president's imminent arrival with his entourage of family members, friends, and aides. According to Dines's account of one such appearance, several hundred contrabands had lined up in a field wearing their best clothes, awaiting Lincoln's arrival. Many of the men had on blue and gray tunics gathered from battlefields where Union and rebel soldiers had died or had left their garments behind. Soldiers on horseback suddenly thundered onto the field, followed by the president and his wife in a carriage. They sat on a platform decorated with flags and a former slave opened the meeting with a prayer. Then everyone stood and sang "My Country, 'Tis of Thee."

When the congregation sang "Every Time I Feel the Spirit," Lincoln wiped tears from his eyes with his bare hands. The group sang for nearly an hour, including "I Thank God That I'm Free at Last," which was accompanied by shouts of joy. Lincoln bowed his head in silence. The last song was "John Brown's Body," and the president sang the chorus "as loud as anyone there" in a sweet, sad voice, Dines recalled.[7]

Some historians believe that it was at these emotional quasi-religious meetings that Lincoln deepened his convictions about the injustices of slavery and the need to care for the newly freed African Americans. His views also "were strengthened by his observation of the colored people who served him," writes African American author John E. Washington in *They Knew Lincoln*. "He soon learned that these people were easily affected by environment, and with a little help would rapidly learn how to provide for themselves. They furnished an example of what freedom would accomplish and that, given the proper assistance, freedmen would become progressive, independent and self-supporting."[8]

*   *   *

LINCOLN REVEALED HIMSELF at the Soldiers' Home as a human being with the same kinds of frailties, failings, and vulnerabilities as anyone else. He padded around the house in heelless slippers, a loose-fitting shirt, and pants, and he carried a big palm-leaf fan when it was hot.[9] More than one guest described him as disheveled and exhausted as the war dragged on.

Just as important, the human scenes around him must have been heart-wrenching for the commander in chief and must have deepened his appreciation of the immense cost of the war and the need to justify it in the most profound moral way, which brought him inevitably to the slavery question. There was a national military cemetery on the grounds, which was rapidly filling up with the remains of Union soldiers; eventually, 5,000 were buried there. Disabled veterans made their way along the paths and clustered in the buildings. Many of them had legitimate complaints about their treatment at the home, which was run in an authoritarian way and with few amenities. Many of them also had severe drinking problems, and there were frequent runaways.

Still, Lincoln gradually got to know the soldiers around him, both his bodyguards and, to a lesser extent, the disabled veterans. He valued their company, especially during the many weeks when his own family was away and he got lonely.[10] The soldiers gave him a sense of camaraderie, as did the presence of advisers and friends, including Secretary of War Edwin Stanton, who had a cottage at the Soldiers' Home.

*   *   *

IN JULY 1862, Lincoln read to his startled cabinet a draft of the Emancipation Proclamation, which local lore held that he had drafted while sitting under a tree a few yards from his cottage at the Soldiers' Home.[11] The proclamation would have freed all slaves in states that were in rebellion, but not in the border states. Lincoln thought this would keep hundreds of thousands of slaves from being forced to help the Confederacy because it would encourage them to flee to Union territory. Secretary of State William Seward feared that issuing the proclamation when the North was absorbing terrible defeats on the battlefield would seem like a desperate act not born of real conviction. So Seward asked Lincoln to postpone the proclamation until the Union won a major military victory somewhere. Lincoln agreed. After the federal success at Antietam on September 17, he issued the proclamation, which took effect on January 1, 1863.

The proclamation disappointed the abolitionists, who felt that Lincoln should have freed the slaves everywhere, not just in rebel territory that the Union did not control. But Lincoln was never a zealot about the issue. As he said time and again, his goal was to restore the Union, and if changing the status of slavery would help him restore the United States, he would change it.

Lincoln held onto the idea of shipping blacks outside the United States as a long-term answer to the nation's entire racial dilemma. In fact, Lincoln's support for the "colonization" of blacks was an important part of his theorizing about long-term solutions to the racial dilemma. Lincoln wrote to James S. Wadsworth in January 1864: "How to better the condition of the colored race has long been a study which has attracted my serious and careful attention."[12]

On August 14, 1862, Lincoln hosted five black leaders at the White House to discuss his plan to encourage freed slaves to set up colonies in South America.[13] The group was headed by Edward M. Thomas, who supported colonization. The meeting took place about a month before Lincoln issued the Emancipation Proclamation, and one of his reasons was to signal that, even if he freed the slaves, he didn't intend for all or even most of them to remain in the United States. This was designed to assuage concerns about the freedmen inundating job markets and disrupting social patterns in the North and the South.

Lincoln wanted Thomas and the other four black men to take the lead in setting up this colonization scheme and creating a new black nation. He specifically asked them "to head a voluntary colonization movement, which would take the soon-to-be-freed Southern slaves to what is now the Isthmus of Panama," writes historian Henry Louis Gates Jr.[14]

Lincoln "reminded them that they were suffering injustice in America," historian Michael Beschloss writes.[15] "Negroes suffered from living with whites, while the whites 'suffer from your presence.' It was 'better for both' to separate. Lincoln said there would have been no Civil War 'but for your race among us.' The African American leader Frederick Douglass was not present, but when told of Lincoln's message, he demanded to know why the president would wallow in 'Negro hatred.' Didn't he understand that Douglass and his people were Americans too?" Douglass, however, later concluded that Lincoln made amends for these views when the president issued the Emancipation Proclamation the following month.

Actually, Lincoln had two colonization plans. The first, which he discussed with the black leaders at the White House in August 1862, was to create a settlement of freed blacks in what was then Colombia—now Panama. But there were objections from black abolitionists, including the influential Douglass, and from the neighboring countries of Honduras, Nicaragua, and Costa Rica, and Lincoln gave up on the idea as unworkable.

Lincoln hatched the second scheme in the spring of 1863, after he had signed the Emancipation Proclamation.[16] He envisaged a black colony on L'Ile a Vace, Cow Island, off the coast of Haiti, and this plan was actually set in motion. In mid-April 1963, 453 former slaves left Virginia for Cow Island on a boat called the *Ocean Ranger*. But the venture went badly. The would-be colonists were debilitated by the tropical climate, the insects, and disease, and the poor soil made agriculture very difficult. Many died from malaria and smallpox; the Haitian government turned against the plan, and the experiment was abandoned. In March 1864, almost a year later, a ship carrying the surviving 368 blacks returned to Virginia; 85 had died. This soured Lincoln on the idea of colonization for the moment but some researchers say he never totally gave up on the concept.

*   *   *

IN ANOTHER SIGN of his increasing sensitivity to black pride and his innate pragmatism, Lincoln gradually moved a huge distance in his thinking about blacks in combat. At first, he refused to allow free blacks to serve in the front lines, considering them unreliable. In March 1863, however, he endorsed the recruitment of black troops. As the war proceeded with heavy casualties, Lincoln decided he could no longer leave the ever-growing pool of freed blacks untapped. Thousands of them were flooding Union encampments, and many were eager to fight.

They proved themselves almost immediately. Two regiments of the Corps d'Afrique, based in New Orleans, bravely participated in an assault on Port Hudson, Louisiana, on May 27, 1863. "They were unsuccessful," reports historian James McPherson, "but their courage and determination impressed many previously skeptical white soldiers."[17] That spring, Lincoln wrote General Ulysses Grant, whose army had just captured Vicksburg with the help of black troops, urging him to expand the recruitment of freed slaves. Lincoln said these potential soldiers were "a resource which, if vigorously applied now, will soon close the contest. It works doubly, weakening the enemy and strengthening us."

On July 18, African American soldiers proved themselves again when the Fifty-fourth Massachusetts, a black unit, attacked Fort Wagner, a Confederate fort at the entrance to Charleston Bay (an attack made famous in the film *Glory*). In a letter that was widely distributed in Northern newspapers that September, Lincoln said "some of the commanders of our armies in the field who have given us our most important successes, believe the emancipation policy and the use of colored troops constitute the heaviest blow yet dealt to the rebellion." Referring to the Fifty-fourth of Massachusetts at Fort Wagner, contrasted to the Northern whites who had recently rioted against the draft and said they "will not fight to free Negroes," Lincoln predicted that when the Union finally won the war, "there will be some black men who can remember that, with silent tongue, and clenched teeth, and steady eye, and well-poised bayonet, they have helped mankind on to this great consummation; while, I fear, there will be some white ones, unable to forget that, with malignant heart, and deceitful speech, they have to strove to hinder it."[18] In total, 180,000 black troops would serve in the Union army.[19]

*   *   *

ON A PERSONAL level, President and Mrs. Lincoln managed to develop a more enlightened view of black people than any of their predecessors. One of the reasons is that Lincoln had civil rights pioneer Douglass as one of his informal advisers, the first time a president had ever relied on a black man as a counselor at the highest level of policymaking. On at least one occasion, Lincoln sent his carriage to bring Douglass from a local boarding house to the White House.[20]

Douglass, an orator who had been born a slave, was an impressive individual, with his sweep of graying hair, fierce brown eyes, deep voice, and obvious intellectual gifts. Just spending time with him must have given the lie to the notion that blacks were inferior to whites and not capable of leadership. Likewise, Douglass was impressed with Lincoln's honesty and fairness. "Lincoln is the first white man I ever spent an hour with who did not remind me I was a Negro," Douglass said.[21]

During a meeting at the White House in August 1863, Douglass asked Lincoln to alleviate discrimination against black troops and he pointed out that their pay was lower than that of white soldiers. Lincoln replied that the legal authority for paying black soldiers was the Militia Act of 1862, which provided that any black recruits should receive $10 per month as "laborers" even if they served in combat. (Meanwhile, white privates received $13 per month and a clothing allowance.) Only Congress could change the pay allowance, and the legislators would not meet again until December, the president said.

Again showing his practical side, Lincoln told Douglass that "the employment of colored troops at all was a great gain to the colored people—that the measure could not have been successfully adopted at the beginning of war . . . that their enlistment was a serious offense to popular prejudice . . . that they were not to receive the same pay as white soldiers seemed a necessary concession to smooth the way to their employment at all as soldiers. . . . But I assure you, Mr. Douglass, that in the end they shall have the same pay as white soldiers."[22]

*   *   *

LATER, LINCOLN MET with abolitionist Sojourner Truth, the first African American woman to be formally received at the White House. Truth was living in an African American village at the current site of Arlington National Cemetery, and she met with Lincoln in the White House on October 29, 1864. The session was set up by Elizabeth Keckley, Mrs. Lincoln's black seamstress, and a white abolitionist named Lucy Colman.

As Truth recounted later in a letter,

> It was about 8 o'clock a.m., when I called on the president. Upon entering his reception room we found about a dozen persons in waiting, among them two colored women. I had quite a pleasant time waiting until he was disengaged, and enjoying his conversation with others; he showed as much kindness and consideration to the colored persons as to the whites—if there was any difference, more. One case was that of a colored woman who was sick and likely to be turned out of her house on account of her inability to pay her rent. The president listened to her with much attention, and spoke to her with kindness and tenderness. He said he had given so much he could give no more but told her where to go and get the money, and asked Mrs. Lincoln to assist her, which she did.
>
> I said to him, Mr. President, when you first took your seat I feared you would be torn to pieces, for I likened you unto Daniel, who was thrown into the lion's den; and if the lions did not tear you into pieces,

I knew that it would be that God had saved you; and I said, if he spared me I would see you before the four years expired, and he has done so, and now I am here to see you for myself.[23]

*   *   *

AT THE CENTER of White House operations was Elizabeth Keckley, who helped arrange Sojourner Truth's meeting with Lincoln. She was a former slave who had bought her freedom with proceeds from her work as a seamstress and been recommended as a dressmaker to Mrs. Lincoln in March 1861 by a friend.[24] Keckley became one of the first family's intimates, earning a remarkable amount of trust, as many black staff members at the White House were to do in subsequent years. She was "the most influential Negro at the White House during the Lincoln years," writes historian Benjamin Quarles. "In her late thirties, Mrs. Keckley was ... stately ... with a classic head—thin lips, aquiline nose, and high cheekbones—crowned by a mass of straight black hair parted in the middle with a neat bun in back. Mrs. Keckley carried herself like a woman of station, her bearing made more impressive by her clothes, which were of the best fabrics and fashioned in quiet style. Members of the congregation of the First Presbyterian Church, comprising the Negro elite of the city, hastened to Sunday morning services so as not to miss Mrs. Keckley as she made her entrance and moved down the aisle to her pew."[25]

Keckley, "tranquil, proud, patient, and intelligent, became the first lady's closest friend," writes historian Carl S. Anthony. "She embodied proof of the benefits of abolition. To Lincoln, who rarely complimented others, Keckley was a 'remarkable woman.'"[26]

From the start, Mary Todd Lincoln said she couldn't afford to pay large amounts for her wardrobe—the main point stressed by the first lady when she interviewed Keckley during the first days of her husband's administration. "I cannot afford to be extravagant," Mary Todd Lincoln said. "We are just from the West, and are poor. If you do not charge too much, I shall be able to give you all my work."

Keckley replied, "I do not think there will be any difficulty about charges, Mrs. Lincoln; my terms are reasonable."

It turned out, however, that Mrs. Lincoln was extravagant, and over the next four years amassed a huge debt from her purchases of clothes, furniture, and other personal items.

Keckley was hired, but her first assignment from Mrs. Lincoln didn't start off well. Given a few days to make a dress for one of the first lady's initial soirees at the White House, Keckley measured Mrs. Lincoln for "a bright rose-colored moiré-antique" and went home to make the adjustments. Then she was told that the "levee" had been postponed from a Friday night until the following Tuesday, giving her four extra days to complete her work. Mrs. Lincoln asked for further alterations, and Keckley made the adjustments. On Tuesday evening, Keckley folded the dress carefully and carried it to the White House.

"When I went upstairs," Keckley recalled, "I found the ladies in a terrible state of excitement. Mrs. Lincoln was protesting that she could not go down for the reason that she had nothing to wear."

At one point, Mrs. Lincoln said, "Mrs. Keckley, you have disappointed me—deceived me. Why do you bring my dress at this late hour?"

"Because I have just finished it," the seamstress replied, "and I thought I should be in time."

"But you are not in time, Mrs. Keckley; you have bitterly disappointed me," Mrs. Lincoln said. "I have no time now to dress, and, what is more, I will not dress, and go downstairs."

"I am sorry if I have disappointed you, Mrs. Lincoln, for I intended to be in time. Will you let me dress you? I can have you ready in a few minutes."

"No, I won't be dressed. I will stay in my room. Mr. Lincoln can go down with the other ladies."

Mrs. Lincoln's friends prevailed on her to proceed, and she finally allowed Keckley to help. She was pleased with the dress, and her mood quickly improved.

Suddenly, President Lincoln appeared, "threw himself on the sofa, laughed with [his sons] Willie and little Tad, and then commenced pulling on his gloves, quoting poetry all the while," Keckley recalled.

"You seem to be in a poetical mood tonight," his wife said.

"Yes, mother, these are poetical times. I declare, you look charming in that dress. Mrs. Keckley has met with great success." Lincoln also proceeded to compliment the other ladies, and then the first couple left for the party, with Mrs. Lincoln happily taking her husband's arm.[27]

* * *

ONE OF THE most poignant events ever to occur in the White House was the death on February 20, 1862, of twelve-year-old Willie Lincoln, the first couple's frail eldest son. He contracted either pneumonia or typhoid fever after he insisted on riding his new pony outdoors every day in the frigid depths of winter. He was confined for several days to a sick room at the White House, appeared to improve, but then suffered a relapse. During this period, Keckley was relied on by the parents to help watch over Willie and try to comfort him. As Keckley recalls in her memoirs:

> I was worn out with watching, and was not in the room when Willie died, but was immediately sent for. I assisted in washing him and dressing him, and then laid him on the bed, when Mr. Lincoln came in. I never saw a man so bowed down with grief. He came to the bed, lifted the cover from the face of his child, gazed at it long and earnestly, murmuring, "My poor boy, he was too good for this earth. God has called him home. I know that he is much better off in heaven, but then we loved him so. It is hard, hard to have him die!"

Keckley wrote that, "Great sobs choked his utterance. He buried his head in his hands, and his tall frame was convulsed with emotion. I stood at the foot of the bed, my eyes full of tears, looking at the man in silent, awe-stricken wonder. His grief unnerved him and made him a weak, passive child. I did not dream that his rugged nature could be so moved."[28]

Mrs. Lincoln was even more stricken. "The pale face of her dead boy threw her into convulsions," Keckley wrote. "... Mrs. Lincoln was so completely overwhelmed with sorrow that she did not attend the funeral."[29] At one point, the president had to caution his wife that if she did not pull herself out of her misery, she might end up in an asylum. But Keckley recorded that for many months, Mrs. Lincoln would break into tears at the thought of her beloved son and his untimely death.

It turned out that Keckley's only son had been killed on a Missouri battlefield in August 1861, and she understood what the first lady was going through. At one point, she recommended a medium to Mrs. Lincoln who might put her in touch with Willie. For months, a man named "Lord Colchester" visited the White House and held séances or circles, but Mrs. Lincoln never made the connection with her son.[30]

Calm and upbeat, Keckley over the next year became a confidant to Mrs. Lincoln in addition to serving as her personal maid and companion. Mrs. Lincoln even took Keckley with her on trips to Boston and New York. In a letter to her husband, dated November 2, 1862, from New York, Mrs. Lincoln spoke fondly of Lizzie's importance in easing her melancholy and reducing her anxieties. "A day or two since," Mary wrote, "I had one of my severe attacks; if it had not been for Lizzie Keckley, I do not know what I should have done."[31]

Under Keckley's influence, Mrs. Lincoln became a donor to Negro charities.[32] Keckley was the founder and first president of the Contraband Relief Association, made up of forty women from the growing and economically solid community of freed blacks who wished to help the former slaves who had come into the District of Columbia. Mrs. Lincoln gave the first donation to the association in 1862—$200, along with 15 boxes of clothing, 500 tin plates, 20 turkeys, and a supply of apples and cranberries.

*   *   *

KECKLEY'S MEMOIRS GAVE a rare insight into the difficult straits of escaped slaves trying to make new lives for themselves in Washington. "In the summer of 1862, freedmen began to flock into Washington from Maryland and Virginia," she wrote. "They came with a great hope in their hearts, and with all their worldly goods on their backs. Fresh from the bonds of slavery, fresh from the benighted regions of the plantation, they came to the Capital looking for liberty, and many of them not knowing it when they found it. Many good friends reached forth kind hands, but the North is not warm and impulsive. For one kind word spoken, two harsh ones were uttered; there was something repelling in the atmosphere, and the bright joyous dreams of freedom to the slave faded—were sadly altered, in the presence of that stern, practical mother, reality. . . . Poor dusky children of slavery, men and women of my own race—the transition from slavery to freedom was too sudden for you!" Too often, they could not find work or much assistance from charities or African Americans already living in Washington, and they became frustrated or despondent.

*   *   *

THE LINCOLNS TRUSTED Keckley—whom they affectionately called "Lizzie" or "Lizabeth" and, in the president's case, "Madame Keckley"—

enough to disclose many of their innermost thoughts in her presence, as many other presidents and first ladies did with the loyal black staff members in the White House over the years. Mrs. Lincoln revealed a deep dissatisfaction with some of her husband's advisers, and often warned him that he was too lenient and trusting.[33] She doubted the loyalty of Treasury Secretary Salmon P. Chase and was "especially severe" in criticizing Secretary of War William Seward for lack of scruples. She called Andrew Johnson, military governor of Tennessee and later Lincoln's vice president, "a demagogue."[34] She labeled General George McClellan "a humbug," and General Ulysses Grant was "a butcher."

The first couple sometimes debated their assessments of different members in front of Lizzie.[35] One morning, Mrs. Lincoln recoiled at the mention of Seward's name.

"Seward? I wish you had nothing to do with that man. He cannot be trusted."

"You say the same of Chase," the president replied. "If I listened to you, I should soon be without a Cabinet."

"Better to be without it than to confide in some of the men that you do. Seward is worse than Chase. He has no principle."

Lincoln said, "Mother, you are mistaken; your prejudices are so violent that you do not stop to reason. Seward is an able man, and the country as well as myself can trust him."

But Mrs. Lincoln would not relent. "Father, you are too honest for this world! You should have been born a saint."

Mrs. Lincoln even confided to Keckley her fear that her husband would be murdered.[36] "There is more at stake in this election than he dreams of," the first lady said on one occasion. Despite her qualms, she hoped he would win for the good of the country, even though the president thought that the North was so exhausted after three-and-a-half years of Civil War that the voters would turn him out of office and sue for peace with a new commander in chief.

Keckley was one of the few people at the White House who knew that Mrs. Lincoln had run up high bills for purchasing jewelry, dresses, and fur coats that she thought were fitting for a first lady. She told Keckley that Lincoln had "little idea" how much a wardrobe cost and he assumed she was paying for it with the small annual stipend he gave her of a few hundred dollars.

At one point, Keckley asked, "And Mr. Lincoln does not even suspect how much you owe?"

Mary sobbed and replied, "God, no! If he is reelected, I can keep him in ignorance of my affairs. But if he is defeated, then the bills will be sent in and he will know all!"[37] She even had dreams that the couple would go bankrupt and be humiliated.

Keckley was the only person except for Lincoln's remaining two sons that the first lady summoned to be with her on the night the president was shot.[38] The official messengers apparently had the wrong address, and Keckley wasn't located that night. But at 11 a.m. the following morning, a messenger arrived at Keckley's home by carriage and asked her to come to the White House immediately. "I was left alone with Mrs. Lincoln," Keckley recalled. After viewing the slain president's body in a nearby room, she returned to Mrs. Lincoln and "found her in a new paroxysm of grief.... I shall never forget the scene—the wails of a broken heart, the unearthly shrieks, the terrible convulsions, the wild, tempestuous outbursts of grief from the soul. I bathed Mrs. Lincoln's head with cold water, and soothed the terrible tornado as best I could."

* * *

WRITES HISTORIAN BENJAMIN QUARLES: "In his person-to-person relationships with Negroes, Lincoln was characteristically kind and considerate. He did favors for Negroes, favors that could bring him no political advantage or private gain. On one occasion a newspaper reporter visiting the White House found him counting greenbacks and putting them in an envelope. It turned out that the money belonged to a porter in the Treasury Department, who was hospitalized with the smallpox. Unable to sign for his pay, the stricken Negro had gotten word to Lincoln, who had gone to some trouble to get the money."[39]

"This, sir," Lincoln told the reporter, "is something out of my usual line, but a President of the United States has a multiplicity of duties not specified in the Constitution or acts of Congress. This is one of them. This money belongs to a poor colored man who is a porter in the Treasury Department, at present very bad with the smallpox. He is now in the hospital, and could not draw his pay because he could not sign his name. I have been at considerable trouble to overcome the difficulties, and get it for him, and have at length succeeded in cutting red tape, as you newspapermen say. I am now dividing the money and putting by a portion labeled, in an envelope, with my own hands according to his wish."[40]

This "poor colored man" was probably William Johnson, who in February 1861 had accompanied the President-elect on his nearly two-week train journey from Springfield, Illinois, to Washington, serving as his attendant and valet. His duties included carrying and dusting Lincoln's tall silk hats, Scotch-weave gray shawl, broadcloth overcoat and suits, satin vest, and winter boots. William won the approval of Henry Villard, who was making the trip as a newspaper reporter. William, "although not exactly the most prominent, is yet the most useful member of the party," wrote Villard in the *New York Herald* of February 20, 1861.[41] "The untiring vigilance with which he took care of the presidential party is entitled to high credit."

Extreme sensitivity to color was common even among African Americans themselves. "Lincoln had planned to use William at the White House as his attendant and private messenger, but the President reckoned without the incumbent domestics," Quarles reports.[42] "These old hands at the White House opposed William in part because he was a newcomer; this Lincoln could understand, being familiar with the seniority system. But he was astonished to learn that much of the opposition to William stemmed from his color. For a long time the White House had been staffed by light-skinned Negroes, to whom a richly pigmented person like William was simply beyond the pale. Bowing to the wishes of the White House colored, Lincoln gave up his plan to make William his valet."

Says Quarles: "Lincoln was bent on getting William placed somewhere. On March 7, 1861, he wrote a to-whom-it-may-concern letter, attesting to William's honesty, faithfulness, sobriety, and industry. A little more than a week later, he asked Secretary [of the Navy Gideon] Welles to give William a job, explaining that he had been forced to let him go because of 'the difference of color between him and the other servants.' When neither of these letters brought anything, Lincoln spoke to Secretary Chase. On November 29, 1861, Lincoln put his request to Chase in writing, and on the following day William was informed that he had been named for a laborer's job in the Treasury Department at $600 a year. Thereupon, William left the furnace room of the White House, where he had been working as a fireman while Lincoln had been looking around on his behalf."[43]

Lincoln approved a fund-raising festival organized by local black Catholics on the White House lawn in June 1964.[44] Gabriel Coakley, a freedman and leader in the black Catholic community, sought permission from the president by approaching him directly at the White House. The self-assured Coakley had a special advantage. His wife, Mary, was an expert seamstress known to the Lincoln family for the work she did for First Lady Mary Todd Lincoln, along with chief seamstress Elizabeth Keckley. Lincoln approved the project on the spot.

Lincoln also was kind to strangers, and seemed unable to resist a hard-luck story. A beggar on crutches stopped the president on the sidewalk on August 11, 1863, and asked for help as the president was returning to the White House from the War Department. Lincoln gave the man a check for five dollars, dated August 11, 1863, made payable to "Colored man, with one leg."[45]

*   *   *

MOST OF THE household staff in Lincoln's time were white and many were Irish Americans but there were several blacks, including butler-waiter Peter Brown, cook Cornelia Mitchell, cook and seamstress Rosetta Wheeler, and an usher named Edward.[45]

Lincoln found that nearly every black servant in the White House had slave ancestors. He talked openly with them, and they never betrayed his confidences. Robert Brown, Peter's son, came to visit often at the mansion and played with the children of white staff members on equal terms. Author John E. Washington writes that, "Bootblacks and other colored boys came and peeped through the fence, were invited in, and when they got too noisy Mr. and Mrs. Lincoln came out to see what they were up to."[46]

Before delivering his Gettysburg Address, Lincoln tested lines on William Slade, his black valet and personal assistant. Slade told his daughter Katherine that few people realized how close he was to the president, how many hours they spent alone together, and the fact that the president would often write a speech or other text "and try it out" on him. Lincoln considered Slade a man of common sense and intelligence, and he believed that if something sounded good to him, it would probably sound good and be understandable to others.

When Lincoln arrived at Gettysburg on November 18, 1863, to dedicate the battlefield, he stayed overnight with Slade at the Wills House and consulted with Slade on every major thought in the address. After writing a sentence or two, he would pause and read the words to Slade, who would pass judgment. "William, how does that sound?" Lincoln would ask. After this process, he sent Slade to bring his secretary and others to hear it.[47]

Slade and his entire family grew very close to the Lincolns. His daughter Katherine, also known as "Nibbie," recalled that she had "stayed many nights in the White House" with her parents when storms came up and they couldn't get home. She and her brothers played with Tad, the president's son, and he often came and played with them in their home on Massachusetts Avenue, between 4th and 5th Streets, NW. According to biographer John E. Washington, "Many times when Slade had had the opportunity of spending his nights at home with his family, he would put his three children—Katherine (Nibbie), Andrew, and Jessie—in his carriage (which he used in traveling back and forth to the White House and also for taking him from place to place with the messages of President Lincoln) and take them to the White House where they would spend the entire day playing with Tad in the basement, in the White House grounds, or in any other part of the house that the little son of the president wanted to use."[48]

Nibbie said her father told her that Lincoln, while reading or sitting alone, would tear off a piece of paper and write something on it and put it away in his desk, or in his vest or pants pocket, and continue reading. Slade would often discover these shreds of paper and save them for the president.

Slade was of medium height and olive complexion, with light eyes, straight chestnut-brown hair, and a goatee. He was described as cheerful, optimistic, and steady, and was able to raise Lincoln out of depression when the president was feeling down. He was full of wisecracks and funny stories. Slade had his own private room in the White House. He eventually was given responsibility for supervising all the black workers in the Executive Mansion, making arrangements for food and service at public and private functions, and playing a key role operating the Soldiers' Home.

Slade was so trusted by the Lincolns that it was he who arranged Lincoln's clothing after he was assassinated, choosing for his burial the suit he wore at his last inauguration. He washed and dressed Lincoln's body and supervised the final trim of the slain president's hair, clipping off a lock for himself and his family. Slade's wife Katherine was given the dress Mary Todd Lincoln wore to Ford's Theater the night Lincoln was shot.[49]

* * *

MARY TODD LINCOLN played a vital role in encouraging the president to take a more positive view of African Americans, just as Eleanor Roosevelt would play that role for her husband Franklin in the 1930s and 1940s. "She was from a Kentucky slaveholding family and had relatives serving in the Confederacy," writes historian Carl S. Anthony, "but as a child she had seen the slave trade from her bedroom window and loathed the concept. She was further indoctrinated against it by her maternal grandmother, who helped slaves gain their freedom through the Underground Railroad."[50] She became the first first lady to welcome African Americans, including an African American nurse, as White House guests, and Frederick Douglass was invited to take tea with the president.[51]

Jane Grey Swisshelm, a leading abolitionist, said Mrs. Lincoln was a "liberty-loving woman" who was "more radically opposed to slavery" than even the president, and that she had "urged him to emancipation as a matter of right long before he saw it as a matter of necessity."[52]

When her husband issued the Emancipation Proclamation, Mrs. Lincoln praised it as "emancipation from the great evil that has been so long allowed to curse this land. The decree, has gone forth, that 'all men are free,' and all the perfidious acts—cannot eradicate the seal, that has been placed on the 'Emancipation Proclamation.' It is a rich and precious legacy."[53]

CHAPTER FOUR
OPPORTUNITY LOST

Andrew Johnson, a white supremacist and former slave owner from Tennessee, succeeded to the presidency after Lincoln's assassination in 1865, and he wasn't up to the task of healing the country. Almost immediately, he got into a historic confrontation with Congress over executive power. One huge source of friction was his go-slow attitude regarding racial issues.

Emancipation and racial equality were never priorities for Johnson. Throughout his public life, he was preoccupied instead with limiting the power of the plantation aristocracy of the South and improving the lives of working white people.[1] Prior to the Civil War, he even said he would support a slave for every white family if that's what the American people wanted, as long as slavery was evenly extended beyond the rich planters. What he opposed was the use of slaves for the economic advantage of the rich estate owners in the South, whom he despised. He felt that slavery gave the planters too much power over common white people. But as the Civil War began, he reluctantly favored preserving slavery in order to save the Union, if that's what it took.

Johnson said in a Senate speech in July 1861, "It is upon the intelligent free white people of the country that all government should rest, and by them all government should be controlled."[2] He supported annexing Mexico and sending blacks there so they could form their own government and live by themselves.

After the war progressed, he changed his view, as did Lincoln, and became opposed to slavery and in favor of national emancipation through a constitutional amendment.[3] And as wartime governor of Tennessee, he freed the slaves in his home state by personal order. But all this wasn't really designed to help the blacks. Instead, it was aimed at undermining the Southern planter system and shattering its power.

Lincoln, in order to appeal to as many voters as possible, chose Johnson as his vice presidential running mate in 1864 because Johnson, as a U.S. senator from Tennessee and a member of the Democratic party, had been pro-Union.[4] To broaden their appeal even further, Lincoln and Johnson ran not as Republicans but as candidates of a new National Union party.

It remains unclear exactly what Lincoln would have done had he survived, but some historians argue that he would never have allowed the freedmen to be left unprotected by the federal government and subject to the abuses of their former owners.[5] Lincoln believed that freed blacks could do relatively well in the future if they were given education and opportunity.

Johnson took a more hands-off approach. He favored a lenient form of Reconstruction that turned over the state governments in the South to whites, with little or no federal safeguards for the rights of the estimated four million freed slaves. He also wanted to allow all but the top Confederate leaders to serve in government, while Republicans in Congress favored a "radical" Reconstruction that gave the vote to the former slaves and barred most former Confederates from government. Enfranchising the slaves and barring former Confederates would have strengthened the Republicans because the new voters would theoretically be freedmen and freedwomen who would vote for the party of Lincoln.

For a while as president, Johnson talked publicly about his becoming a "Moses" to blacks, leading them to a better life.[6] But this was only rhetoric designed to puff up his reputation as a historic figure akin to Lincoln. He quickly changed his tune and reverted to his racist past, arguing that America should be a white man's country.[7] In 1866, during a meeting with black leaders, Johnson said abolition of slavery had not been the aim of the war but simply "an incident in the suppression of a great rebellion."[8] He settled on advocating a merit system of race relations in which whites and blacks would start at the same point in competing for jobs, with no special legal help to the former slaves, even though they were starting from far behind.[9]

With his support fading among majority Republicans who controlled Congress, Johnson vetoed civil rights legislation and the Freedmen's

Bureau Act, putting him into direct confrontation with Congress, and when the legislators overrode his vetoes, he refused to abide by their decision and wouldn't carry out the law as required by the Constitution.[10]

Johnson's crucial decisions came between Lincoln's assassination in April 1865 and the reconvening of Congress in December, a time when the new president had near total control over Reconstruction policy. "In those critical eight months, Johnson delayed by a century the granting of full citizenship rights to blacks and prolonged the time it would take for the South to catch up to the North in economic development," writes political scientist Alvin Felzenberg.[11] "...When he took office, the defeated South—with Union forces omnipresent—was at its most vulnerable point. Johnson had it within his power to extend the full rights of citizenship to all within his native region. No less an authority than Robert E. Lee believed that Virginians would have looked upon extending the franchise to the freedmen as but a result of the war. Had Johnson done so, he would have spared the nation a century of continued sectional strife and African Americans a century of continued second-class citizenship, degradation, and worse. Had he acted to hasten the economic development of the region, Johnson might also have improved the lot of the poor Southern whites for whom he insisted he cared so deeply. Instead, Johnson provided erstwhile Confederates with reason to believe that political and social relations in the South—as they existed prior to the war—would resume, as before."

Basically, Johnson left it to each Southern state to decide how to treat the former slaves. It was a recipe for the abuses of the next hundred years. The states enacted "Black Codes" that deprived African Americans of basic rights such as suffrage and equality under the law.[12] For example, blacks were required in many places to show proof of employment when they were in public or they were subject to fines and imprisonment. Many blacks were reduced to accepting work at poverty-level wages or worse, and others were bound to the land in employment arrangements that amounted to a new form of servitude. And they had no legal recourse. Johnson engaged in a series of increasingly harsh and mean-spirited clashes with Congress over his insistence on states' rights.[13]

By April 1866, the radical Republicans had gained enough strength to pass a civil rights law over the president's veto, granting citizenship to the former slaves. Johnson thought this was unnecessary and wanted to leave such decisions to the states. The confrontation intensified as the majority

Republicans enacted in the spring of 1867 a series of tough laws penalizing the Confederate states and attempting to remake Southern society to at least partially accommodate the black population. Among the techniques was replacing the civil governments set up by Southern Democrats with military governments. In some cases, blacks and their white allies took control of state legislatures, outraging many Southern whites.[14]

Johnson was adamant. He said Congress's actions "would engender a feeling of opposition and hatred between the two races, which, becoming deep rooted and ineradicable, would prevent them from living together in a state of mutual friendliness."[15]

A constitutional crisis erupted when the radical Republicans passed, over the president's veto, the Tenure of Office Act in the spring of 1867. This law unconstitutionally prohibited the president from removing from office any federal official who had been appointed with the advice and consent of the Senate. In August 1867, Johnson removed from office Secretary of War Edwin Stanton, a radical Republican. He appointed General Ulysses Grant to that job, but in February 1868, Grant gave the office back to Stanton in defiance of Johnson. A furious Johnson again removed Stanton on February 21 and appointed Major General Lorenzo Thomas. Three days later, the House of Representatives voted to impeach Johnson for violating the Tenure of Office Act and other alleged transgressions. The Senate, however, declined to remove him from office, by one vote.[16]

* * *

IN PERSONAL TERMS, Johnson and his wife Eliza could show compassion to slaves. For example, when the black servant Slade (who had also worked for Lincoln) was dying, Eliza prayed for him and the first couple sent food to his family to tide them over, as a good neighbor might do anywhere in the country.[17]

But President Johnson could never see beyond his racist past. "The injustice done black people was simply not the problem [for Johnson]," writes historian David Warren Bowen.[18] "They were not human beings in the normal meaning of the word and were certainly not 'the people' who should rule in society.... His [Johnson's] extreme democratic ideology made no distinction between natural and political rights. A man was either equal, and thereby a politically functioning member of society, or he was not. Because most people ... assumed that the Negro was inferior, society was not obligated to grant any 'rights' at all. In fact, to do so would be interfering with the natural development of society, giving unfair advantage to a group that did not deserve special treatment."

In 1842, Johnson had bought a black girl named Dolly, his first slave, for $500.[19] Soon after, he bought her half-brother Sam, who became Johnson's favorite slave. They were not an important part of the family's economic well-being, and were apparently purchased to do household chores and to keep up appearances. In short, Johnson, an East Tennessee former mechanic, tailor, and real estate salesman, wanted to show that he was a rising member of the "master class." He owned at least four slaves in 1850 and at least five in 1860.

Some in the family thought the future president was too lenient in dealing with those he kept in bondage. Sam was described as "a dignified old man dressed in his Sunday best every Sabbath in a high hat and a black silk coat."[20] Charles Johnson, Andrew's son, complained in a letter to his father in 1860: "I will just make one suggestion,—I think were I in your place I would sell *Sam*; it does not suit him to stay in this country;—a few days since Mother sent him word to cut wood at Pattersons,—he came up in the house and said, he would 'be damed' [*sic*] if he wanted to cut wood there; and if you wanted to sell him you could just do so, just as soon as you pleased, he did not care a dam.... I do not desire to own negroes, but if I did, they should know their place or I would not have them about me, do not understand me, as complaining at your course; not so; but it does seem the more attention, the more kindness you show a negrro [*sic*], the less account he is; they seem to misconstrue it;—but after all the negro to be of any value, must be subjugated; and they are the fewest number of men that are fit to have negroes; this is especially the case in E Tennessee the negro must have a Master; and those who use them severly [*sic*] seem to have the best slavs [*sic*]."[21]

Even if he treated them with "leniency," Johnson believed blacks were members of "an inferior race whose natural lot was one of dependency," according to historian Hans L. Trefousse.[22] "Like Lincoln," writes biographer David Warren Bowen,[23] "moderate and conservative Republicans might have been described as racists. They undoubtedly shared the generally held assumption that blacks were naturally inferior to whites. Still, the majority of Republican leaders also came from some kind of antislavery tradition, and with the exception of the most reactionary usually accepted blacks as members of the human race. This simple acceptance could result, and often did in the North, in the belief that Negroes, even if inferior, retained certain basic 'natural' rights within society as fellow human beings. Under a republican system, the government would invariably be called upon to protect such rights."

Johnson opposed the Freedman's Bureau bill passed by Congress in 1865, widening a serious rift with Republicans.[24] He vetoed it, arguing that the federal government lacked the constitutional power to protect the freedom and property of former slaves. He also vetoed a civil rights bill, again on constitutional grounds but also with a racist appeal. He said the legislation would unwisely attempt to establish the "perfect equality of the white and colored races" by federal law and might set a precedent for Congress to later repeal state laws forbidding marriage between the races.

*   *   *

ON FEBRUARY 7, 1866, Johnson hosted a small group of black men at the White House—a notable occasion in itself because prior to Lincoln's administration these men would not have been admitted because of their race.[25] Some of the attendees had, in fact, recently been slaves. Now, as free men, they were granted a meeting by the new president to discuss the status of African Americans in the post–Civil War period.

The delegation was part of an African American convention being held in Washington at which blacks from several states including New York, Pennsylvania, Florida, and Maryland had called for federal action to guarantee equal rights to blacks, including the right to vote. President Johnson was at that time considered at least potentially sympathetic. He was thrown into the presidency by the assassination of Lincoln, but he had, after all, been the Emancipator's running mate and vice president. Yet Johnson was a lifelong and partisan Democrat who had joined Lincoln's 1864 Republican ticket not because the two men particularly saw eye to eye but to appeal for unity, and his attitude toward blacks remained primitive.

This became clear almost as soon as the meeting started. Among those in the delegation was Frederick Douglass, the famous black abolitionist whose comments were pointed. "In the order of Divine Providence," Douglass said, "you are placed in a position where you have the power to save or destroy us, to bless or blast us—I mean our whole race. Your noble and humane predecessor placed in our hands the sword to assist in saving the nation, and we do hope that you, his able successor, will favorably regard the placing in our hands the ballot with which to save ourselves."[26]

Johnson seemed offended and he immediately turned hostile. He proceeded with a forty-five-minute lecture that he later described as prompted by "repressed anger." He billed himself a "friend of humanity, and especially the friend of the colored man." He added: "I have owned slaves and bought slaves, but I never sold one. I might say, however, that practically, so far as my connection with slaves has gone, I have been their slave instead of their being mine. Some have even followed me here, while others are occupying and enjoying my property with my consent. For the colored race my means, my time, my all has been perilled; and now at this late date, after giving evidence that is tangible, that is practical, I am free to say to you that I do not like to be arraigned by some who can get up handsomely-rounded periods and deal in rhetoric, and talk about the abstract ideas of liberty, who never perilled life, liberty, property. This kind of theoretical, hollow, unpractical friendship amounts to very little. While I say that I am a friend of the colored man, I do not want to adopt a policy that I believe will end in a contest between the races, which if persisted in will result in the extermination of one or the other. God forbid that I should be engaged in such work!"[27]

President Johnson went on to say he favored giving black men their freedom but not the right to vote.[28] He seemed to get angrier by the minute. He said he had opposed slavery because "it was a great monopoly, enabling the few to derive great profits and rule the many with an iron rod." He also opposed it "upon the abstract principle of slavery." When Douglass tried to interrupt in disagreement, the president cut him off and continued his diatribe, arguing that most white Southerners had not owned slaves, yet they had been placed by blacks and others in the same category as the slave-owning aristocrats. Each state legislature should determine for itself who votes and who doesn't, not the federal government, Johnson argued.

Douglass and other black leaders tried repeatedly to rebut the president but the tirade continued. At one point, Douglass said, "You enfranchise your enemies and disenfranchise your friends."

Johnson declared that it would be best if the freed blacks left the Southern states altogether and found somewhere else to live. After some snippets of cross-talk, the president ended the meeting.

The black leaders were deeply disappointed and unsettled. President Johnson was still fuming about the "darky delegation."[29] "Those damned sons of bitches thought they had me in a trap!" he told an aide. "I know that damned Douglass; he's just like any nigger, and he would sooner cut a white man's throat as not."

Yet at the end of his life, it was a black servant who came to Johnson's aid. This was William Andrew Johnson, who had been Andrew Johnson's slave prior to emancipation and who remained his personal assistant at the White House and thereafter. During the ex-president's final illness in 1875, it was William Andrew Johnson who slept in the same room with the former chief executive and for six days and six nights never left his side.[30]

Chapter Five
Jim Crow

Ulysses Grant

Ulysses S. Grant, who followed Johnson into the presidency after winning the election of 1868, had been the commander of all the Union armies in the Civil War. As president, he is generally regarded by historians as a failure because of corruption in his administration and because he allowed many abuses by greedy businessmen. But in recent years, Grant has been credited with a more enlightened view on racial issues than had been earlier realized.

Grant's father, Jesse, was strongly anti-slavery, and refused to attend his son's wedding to a woman from a slave-owning family, but this did not seem to shape the son's attitudes one way or the other.[1] Grant seemed ambivalent about slavery until the Civil War actually began, when he turned against it.

His wife, Julia Dent of St. Louis, Missouri, had as childhood playmates the daughters of slaves who tended her father's crops and worked in her family's house.[2] But she was not in the least troubled that her family owned human beings, and there is evidence that she believed blacks were an inferior race.

When he was working his farm in rural Missouri during 1858, Grant endured hard times and scraped by as best he could. He never succeeded at farming and named his self-built house Hardscrabble. Grant worked the farm with two slaves he hired from their owners and one, William Jones, whom he borrowed from his father-in-law.[3] Grant later bought Jones outright but freed him on March 29, 1859. Julia owned four slaves: Eliza, Julia, John, and Dan. When the family later moved to Galena in the free state of Illinois, all of their slaves became free, but the future first lady kept the former slave Julia as her personal maid.

Like so many others in the North, Grant held views similar to Lincoln's at the start of the Civil War: His main goal was saving the Union, with slavery or without it. He wrote in August 1863, "I never was an abolitionist, not even what could be called anti-slavery."[4] However, after the bloody battle of Shiloh in 1862, he concluded that the North had to crush the rebels totally, and that meant destroying slavery, a pillar of the Southern economy.

Grant also supported using blacks in combat, and after he saw them fight, was more convinced than ever that they would make good soldiers. His trips into the South during the war gave him important insights into the anti-black culture there.[5] This helped to persuade him that the federal government was needed to protect blacks in the South. One outcome was enactment of the Ku Klux Klan Act of 1871.

As president, he tried to enforce the civil rights laws vigorously and favored granting African Americans universal suffrage and equality under the law. Grant also appointed blacks to federal office for the first time. The abolitionist Frederick Douglass said Grant never showed "vulgar prejudices of any color."[6]

"For Grant," writes historian Sean Wilentz, "Reconstruction always remained of paramount importance, and he remained steadfast, even when members of his own party turned their backs on the former slaves. After white supremacists slaughtered blacks and Republicans in Louisiana in 1873 and attempted a coup the following year, Grant took swift and forceful action to restore order and legitimate government. With the political tide running heavily against him, Grant still managed to see through to enactment of the Civil Rights Act of 1875, which prohibited discrimination according to race in all public accommodations. [This law was declared unconstitutional by the Supreme Court in 1883.] . . . That he accomplished as much for freed slaves as he did within the constitutional limits of the presidency was remarkable. Without question, his was the most impressive record on civil rights and equality of any president from Lincoln to Lyndon B. Johnson."[7]

Grant won ratification of the Fifteenth Amendment to the Constitution, which guaranteed every citizen the right to vote. "He sent federal troops into the South to support state militias that policed elections," Felzenberg notes. "He took action against the Ku Klux Klan, formed in 1866, which tried to intimidate and bully blacks into not voting. His administration's anti-KKK efforts led to the prosecution and jailing of hundreds of violent racists in the South."[8] Grant felt that the resistance to suffrage and to any semblance of equal rights for blacks in the South was based on the worst of motives. He said bitterly that when white Southerners spoke of having their rights "respected," what they really wanted was "the right to kill Negroes and Republicans without fear of punishment and without loss of caste or reputation."[9]

As a way to provide blacks with a safe harbor, Grant favored annexation of the island republic of Santo Domingo in the Caribbean, partly as a naval base and partly to allow blacks to relocate there as a new part of the United States.[10] Grant believed that such an option would give blacks a way to persuade their employers to raise their wages and improve their living conditions in order to retain their labor. And while some key black leaders, including Frederick Douglass, endorsed the plan, Grant was unable to get much support for the idea in Congress.

Responding to critics who said they were tired of his brand of racial politics, Grant said, "Treat the Negro as a citizen and a voter, as he is and must remain, and soon parties will be divided not on the color line, but on principle. Then we shall have no complaint of sectional interference."[11]

Although Grant disavowed social equality between the races, he also began appointing blacks to important federal positions, including Ebenezer D. Bassett, principal of the Institute for Colored Youth in Philadelphia, as U.S. minister to Haiti, the first black man to hold such a diplomatic job, and Frederick Douglass as marshal of the District of Columbia and, later, minister to Haiti.[12] Yet in his personal life, he apparently had little contact with African Americans except for a few personal assistants such as Jeremiah Smith, a former slave who was one of Grant's valets, and a black cook. He also had an orderly, James Young, during the Civil War and he kept Young on as a valet in the White House and during his post-presidency until Grant died in 1885.[13]

At the end of his administration, Grant offered an apology to the country in his farewell message to Congress. "It was my fortune, or misfortune, to be called to the office of Chief Executive without any previous training,"

Grant said.[14] "Under such circumstances it is but reasonable to suppose that errors of judgment must have occurred." He admitted there were serious problems gaining support from Congress for his Reconstruction policies but explained that his goal was to decide "whether the control of the Government should be immediately thrown into the hands of those who had so recently and so persistently tried to destroy it or whether the victors should continue to have an equal voice with them in this control. Reconstruction, as finally agreed upon means this and only this, except that the late slave was enfranchised, giving an increase, as was supposed, to the Union-loving and Union supporting votes. If free in the full sense of the word, they would not disappoint this expectation."

Rutherford B. Hayes

After Grant, the trend was clear: The North backed away from attempts to force black equality on the South, and Southern states passed laws and imposed rules designed to keep blacks in an inferior status, suppress voting, and impose segregation in schools, businesses, and other public places. Meanwhile, the nation focused on other tasks, such as taming the frontier, constructing a vast industrial economy, and dealing with immigration.

During the 1876 campaign, Alfonso Taft, Grant's last attorney general, wrote Republican nominee Rutherford B. Hayes with a warning. "It is a fixed and desperate purpose of the Democratic Party in the south that the Negroes shall not vote, and murder is a common means of intimidation to prevent them," Taft observed.[15] Under Hayes, little was done to keep this from happening, even though Hayes during the campaign claimed to be a friend of the freed slaves.

At first Democrat Samuel J. Tilden, the governor of New York, seemed to have won the presidential election of 1876, after eight years of Republican rule under Grant. But the electoral votes of Florida, Louisiana, and South Carolina were in doubt. Without them, Tilden had only 184 electoral votes, one short of a majority. If Hayes carried those three states, he would have 185 electoral votes and would win the presidency.

Each of the states sent two sets of electoral voters to Washington to be counted, one set for Tilden and one for Hayes. Congress responded by creating a fifteen-member electoral commission with eight Republicans and seven Democrats, to figure out who won.[16] At this point, the Compromise of 1877 was struck: In return for congressional Democrats' acceptance of Hayes's election, the Republicans promised to remove occupying troops from the South. So on March 2, 1877, the electoral commission rejected the Democratic returns from the uncertain states and declared Hayes the winner by a margin of one electoral vote. This was accepted by the House of Representatives, and President Hayes then removed federal troops from the South, ending virtually all attempts to enforce the Fourteenth Amendment's guarantee of civil rights to every citizen, including former slaves. It also meant an end to efforts to enforce the Fifteenth Amendment, which since 1870 had affirmed the right of citizens to vote, regardless of race, color, or previous condition of servitude.

Hayes had the naïve view that Southerners would do the right thing in dealing with blacks.[17] But after he removed federal troops from the region, the Democrats in whom he entrusted the future of the freedmen did all they could to keep the blacks in second-class citizenship or worse. Democrat-controlled state legislatures, for example, enacted impossibly arcane literacy tests in order to restrict black voter registration—a technique that remained in use for many years. After Hayes left office, white supremacy was stronger in the South than before he became president.

After Hayes, there followed several decades when most presidents displayed little interest in the problems of race. White public opinion was indifferent or hostile to the African American quest for freedom, and American presidents, whatever their personal attitudes, were content to follow public opinion rather than lead it.[18]

Theodore Roosevelt

President Theodore Roosevelt did things differently. He redefined the presidency as an activist institution that aimed to take the side of everyday people against the financial barons and corporate giants. Unfortunately, except for some personal gestures toward blacks, the progress he presided over on racial issues was very limited.

Roosevelt developed his theories about white supremacy from studying history and science. He believed that whites from Europe had proven themselves as the dominant race on Earth through their successes in war, in science, and in the arts, from 1492 to the early 1900s. He wrote that "peoples of European blood [held] dominion over all America and Australia and the

Islands of the sea, over most of Africa and the major half of Asia."[19] And he attributed "substantially all of the world's achievements worth remembering [since 1492] ... to the people of European descent," especially the white, English-speaking people of the United States and Great Britain, although he did credit the Japanese for developing an advanced and successful civilization, too.[20] He thought that, over many generations, other races could improve themselves, but that it would not happen any time soon.

As a corollary, Roosevelt believed that it was the duty of the white race to propagate as much as possible, and he advocated that every white married couple have no fewer than four children.[21] To do otherwise would be to commit "race suicide," he argued.

And Roosevelt believed in the inferiority of blacks. "I entirely agree with you that as a race, and in the mass, the [blacks] are altogether inferior to the whites," he wrote to author Owen Wister in 1901.[22] He added: "I do not believe that the average Negro in the United States is as yet in any way fit to take care of himself and others as the average white man—for if he were, there would be no Negro race problem."[23] He wrote to another friend, Grenville Dodge: "I wish to emphasize that we are not fighting for social equality, and that we do not believe in miscegenation; but that we do believe in equality of opportunity, in equality before the law."[24]

Roosevelt had told black educator Booker T. Washington that he "would help not only the Negro, but the whole South, should he ever become president," writes historian Lewis L. Gould.[25] At the time the South was generally poor but African Americans were at the very bottom of the economic ladder. They were segregated and endured rampant poverty, illiteracy, and powerlessness. Life expectancy in 1901 for white men and women was almost 49.5 years. For non-whites it was 33.7 years. There were about 100 lynchings of blacks annually as a means of terrorizing them.

Throughout his public life, Roosevelt was troubled and puzzled by what to do about the divisions between blacks and whites. He never found the answer, but some historians believe that Roosevelt had more meetings and conferences at the White House on what he called "the question of the colored race" than any president until Lyndon Johnson in the heyday of the civil rights movement in the 1960s.[26] There is no reliable count of such meetings, but among those he met with were educators, politicians, religious leaders, journalists, social philosophers, and activists, both black and white. Among them was Booker T. Washington, whom Roosevelt respected for his prudence and restraint. Roosevelt said this black adviser "was not led away, as the educated Negro so often is led away, into the pursuit of fantastic visions."[27] Roosevelt also held meetings on race with Edward A. Alderman, president of the University of Virginia; Judge Thomas Jones of Alabama; Silas McBee, editor of the *Churchman*; Lyman Abbott, editor of the *Outlook*; and many others.

Roosevelt was distressed about the virulence of Southern opposition to equality for blacks and the South's determination to resist advances for the African American, and privately he castigated Southern country gentlemen as "grown-up and often vicious children" on the question of race.[28] Even though he opposed special government programs to assist blacks, Roosevelt said he judged every individual on his or her merits, and his rhetoric was uplifting. "A man who is good enough to shed his blood for the country is good enough to be given a 'square deal' afterward," he told black soldiers standing guard at Lincoln's tomb, in an apparently spontaneous moment early in his presidency.[29] "More than that no man was entitled to, and less than that, no man shall have."

In November 1901, having been president for less than a year, he said, "I have not been able to think out any solution of the terrible problem offered by the presence of the Negro in this continent, but of one thing I am sure, and that is that in as much as he is here and can neither be killed nor driven away, the only wise and honorable and Christian thing to do is to treat each black man and each white man strictly on his merits as a man.... Of course I know that we see through a glass dimly, and, after all, it may be that I am wrong; but if I am, then all my thoughts and beliefs are wrong, and my whole way of looking at life is wrong. At any rate, while I am in public life, however short a time it may be, I am in honor bound to act up to my beliefs and convictions."[30]

He condemned lynching as fundamentally immoral and corrupting. After Governor Winfield T. Durbin of Indiana supported the right of a black man accused of murder to a fair trial, Roosevelt sent Durbin a public letter on August 9, 1903: "My dear Governor Durbin, permit me to thank you as an American citizen for the admirable way in which you have vindicated the majesty of the law by your recent action in reference to lynching.... All thoughtful men must feel the gravest alarm over the growth of lynching in this country, and especially over the peculiarly hideous forms so often taken by mob violence when colored men are the victims—on which occasions the mob seems to lay most weight, not on the crime, but on the color of the criminal."[31] Roosevelt continued: "Whoever in any part of our country has ever taken part in lawlessly putting to death a criminal by the dreadful torture of fire must forever after have the awful spectacle of his own handiwork seared into his brain and soul. He can never again be the same man."

But Roosevelt quickly concluded that this condemnation was sufficient. He didn't want to risk his presidency in the election of 1904 by turning the South completely against him, and he pivoted away from the issue of lynching, on which he took no action, and race, and focused on other policy areas. During the 1904 presidential campaign, he wrote a friend, "I have nothing to gain and everything to lose by any agitation of the race question."[32] As with so many of his predecessors, Roosevelt showed little sustained moral courage on race because he feared a political backlash. And he wasn't proud of his decision. At another point in the 1904 campaign, he said, "If I am to be blamed by anyone for any failure in my duty, active or passive, toward the South, it must be for failure to take action as regards the nullification of the Fourteenth and Fifteenth Amendments in the South." He also felt constrained because he claimed that blacks had failed to demonstrate "both intelligence and moral vigor" in confronting the white power structure in the South.[33] Finally, there was little or no support in the North for reopening the old racial wounds of the past. Roosevelt complained in 1904 about "the indifference of the great masses of people [in the North] to whom the wrongdoing in the South is a matter afar off and of little immediate consequence, and who are impatient of any attempt to make things better in any way."

After his election victory that year, he told associates that he wanted to improve the racial climate but wasn't sure how to proceed. He felt that one huge obstacle was a "partially successful movement to bring back slavery."[34]

In the end, however, Roosevelt retreated from his racial goals and ideals. He simply decided that the issue of race was intractable, and he couldn't do much about it. He told friends that a president led best by avoiding unpopular social causes and seeking goals he could actually achieve. And racial justice was not one of them.

*　*　*

YET IN PERSONAL TERMS, Roosevelt apparently had no problem associating with blacks. He had a black valet, James E. Amos, who accompanied him on many trips around the United States. Amos remained as his personal assistant after he left the presidency and returned to the family estate at Sagamore Hill, New York.[35]

In particular, Roosevelt reached out to educator Booker T. Washington. Washington, who lived in Tuskegee, Alabama, was a leader of black Republicans in the South, a region that Roosevelt believed would be an important force at the Republican National Convention in 1904. And he reasoned that Southern delegates could be pivotal to ensuring him the presidential nomination. Some even thought that Washington was the dominant black political figure in the country. He was considered so important that Roosevelt, on the day he took office after William McKinley's death in 1901, asked Washington to visit the White House for a meeting "as soon as possible." His goal was to discuss and coordinate government appointments in the new administration. The two men met on October 4, 1901.

On October 16, 1901, Roosevelt went further by hosting Washington for dinner at the White House, the first time a president had brought in an African American leader to share a meal there on purely social terms. The president considered it quite routine, he said later. He told a friend that it seemed natural to "show some respect to a man whom I cordially esteem as a good citizen and a good American." During their discussion, Roosevelt focused on politics in the South and he treated his black guest with respect. In fact, Roosevelt considered the dignified, erudite Washington a proof of his theory that some blacks could achieve great success on an individual basis. He told friends that blacks were subject to "natural limitations" and that in nine cases out of ten, disenfranchisement was justified.[36] But he also said that a black man who managed to advance should be respected and rewarded by society. He believed that over many years, blacks could lift themselves up on the social ladder if they emulated whites, but it would take a long time.

Word of the dinner quickly spread in the newspapers, and it received favorable reaction in African American communities and in the North. But in the South, it was an entirely different story. This pleasant social encounter prompted condemnations of the most vile sort, including the comment by Senator Benjamin "Pitchfork" Tillman of South Carolina that, "The action of President Roosevelt in entertaining that nigger will necessitate our killing a thousand niggers in the South before they will learn their place again."[37]

Southern newspapers attacked Roosevelt for dining with "a darkey," said he was a "coon-flavored president," noted that "Roosevelt proposes to coddle the sons of Ham," and said he was promoting "mingling and mongrelization" of the white race.[38]

The *Memphis Scimitar* wrote:

> The most damnable outrage which has ever been perpetrated by any citizen of the United States was committed yesterday by the president, when he invited a nigger to dine with him at the White House. It would not be worth more than a passing notice if Theodore Roosevelt had sat down to dinner in his own home with a Pullman car porter, but Roosevelt the individual and Roosevelt the president are not to be viewed in the same light.
>
> It is only very recently that President Roosevelt boasted that his mother was a Southern woman, and that he is half Southern by reason of that fact. By inviting a nigger to his table he pays his mother small duty. . . . No Southern woman with a proper self-respect would now accept an invitation to the White House, nor would President Roosevelt be welcomed today in Southern homes. He has not inflamed the anger of the Southern people; he has excited their disgust.[39]

The outrage was so intense that Roosevelt and Washington agreed not to discuss their dinner in public, lest it generate more ill will, and Roosevelt never received African Americans in such a social setting again, only in business meetings. He continued to privately seek the advice of Washington on racial issues but the next time Washington visited the White House it was at 10 a.m., during official business hours.[40] No black person apparently received a social invitation to the White House for many years afterward, according to White House historian William Seale.[41]

Another blemish on Roosevelt's record was his handling of a violent racial incident at Brownsville, Texas. On August 13, 1906, about twenty to thirty black soldiers from the Twenty-fifth United States Infantry, a black unit commanded by white officers, left their garrison in Brownsville, walked into town, and began firing their rifles "directly into dwellings, offices, stores, and at police and citizens," the mayor reported in a telegram to President Roosevelt on August 16.[42] One citizen was killed in his yard, and a police lieutenant was shot through the right arm, which was amputated at the elbow, the telegram reported, adding: "After firing about 200 shots, the soldiers retired to their quarters. We find that threats have been made by them that they will repeat this outrage. We do not believe their officers can restrain them. . . . Our condition, Mr. President, is this: our women and children are terrorized and our men are practically under constant alarm and watchfulness. No community can stand this strain for more than a few days. We look to you for relief; we ask you to have the troops at once removed from Fort Brown and replaced by white soldiers."

It was an urgent appeal that no president could ignore, least of all the action-oriented Roosevelt. He ordered a full and immediate report from the War Department, and learned from the military and from initial accounts in the press that the black battalion had arrived in Brownsville about three weeks before, and racial tension with the white community had been growing ever since.[43] The black soldiers were banned from local bars, pushed off sidewalks, beaten, and threatened with murder. On the day before the incident, a white woman reported that a black man had made unwanted advances on her. The press reports said about fifteen of the men had violated a curfew imposed by their white commander, Major Charles W. Penrose, and went on a vengeful shooting spree.

There were contradictions in the accounts almost from the start, such as the fact that a head count during the incident found all the soldiers present and accounted for on the base.[44] But other evidence seemed to support the original accusations, including more than seventy casings from Army rifle ammunition and a soldier's cap found at the scene.

Roosevelt sprang into action on August 20, four days after receiving the telegram and after a follow-up request from a Brownsville citizens' committee that Fort Brown be temporarily abandoned.[45] Roosevelt ordered the battalion to redeploy to Fort Ringgold nearby until a full military investigation could be completed. After a preliminary report from the military arrived, Roosevelt moved the battalion away so as to avoid mob attacks from the local community. Roosevelt proceeded to send most of the battalion to Fort Reno, Oklahoma, while twelve suspects were held in the guardhouse at San Antonio. Military authorities eventually concluded that some black soldiers had indeed conducted the violent raid and that there was a conspiracy within the unit and among the prime suspects to obstruct justice because none of the black soldiers would identify the shooters.

Roosevelt clearly sided with the whites of Brownsville. He didn't want to alienate white Southern voters in that fall's mid-term congressional elections.[46] He said, "The colored man who fails to condemn crime in another colored man . . . is the worst enemy of his own people, as well as an enemy to all the people." The final military report recommended that if no soldier confessed or provided information on the perpetrators, all of the black enlisted men should be judged guilty and held responsible and all should be dishonorably discharged.[47] Booker T. Washington met with Roosevelt privately at the White House, at the president's request, and recommended that members of the Twenty-fifth Infantry receive their day in court. But Roosevelt was in no mood to compromise and he "discharged without honor"—and without trial—167 black soldiers. As a result, many of America's blacks turned against him.

Woodrow Wilson

Woodrow Wilson, former president of Princeton University and governor of New Jersey, was raised in the segregated South. He is widely known for his high-minded ideals about promoting peace around the world after World War I and his unsuccessful effort to have the Senate approve the creation of a League of Nations to promote peace. But on racial matters, Wilson was retrograde.

Wilson was a self-styled Virginia gentleman, steeped in the idea that educated, upper-class whites were the superior class and blacks were inferior and needed constant guidance and supervision. While president of Princeton University, Wilson had discouraged African Americans from seeking admission and none were admitted while he was in charge. He believed the violent and racist Ku Klux Klan in the 1860s through the 1870s properly preserved the right of Southern whites to run their states for their own benefit and keep blacks in subservient positions.[48]

His presidency was very damaging to racial progress. "Through a combination of his own racial attitudes, his willingness to act on them, and the influence southern Democrats exerted over his administration, Wilson set back the aspirations and hopes of African Americans by more than a generation," Felzenberg writes.[49]

Black leaders had high hopes for Wilson early on. As he campaigned for the presidency in 1912, Oswald Garrison Villard, editor of the *New York Evening Post* and grandson of abolitionist William Lloyd Garrison, talked to Wilson about ways to expand black support for him and the Democratic party. W. E. B. Du Bois, editor of *The Crisis,* the magazine of the National Association for the Advancement of Colored People (NAACP), endorsed Wilson in August and wrote: "He will not advance the cause of the oligarchy in the South, he will not seek further means of 'Jim Crow' insult, he will not dismiss black men from office, and he will remember that the Negro in the United States has a right to be heard."[50]

On October 21, as the election approached, Wilson sent a letter assuring African American leaders of "my earnest wish to see justice done them in every matter, and not mere grudging justice, but justice executed with liberality and cordial good feeling.... My sympathy with them is of long standing and I want to assure them through you that should I become President of the United States they may count upon me for absolute fair dealing and for everything by which I could assist in advancing the interest of their race in the United States."[51]

And he seemed to have an easygoing relationship with individual blacks. The black press reported that as governor of New Jersey in 1911, as he prepared to run for president the following year, Wilson met former slave Joseph Ford, a railroad employee at Union Station in Grand Rapids, Michigan. As Ford reached for Wilson's three suitcases, Wilson protested that they were too heavy for one person to carry.[52] But the porter, aware of Wilson's admiration for the author Rudyard Kipling, said, "Oh, no, governor, I am used to carrying the white man's burden." Wilson smiled broadly in appreciation of the literary reference. In 1917, when Wilson was president, he was again introduced to Ford, then active in political circles, and Wilson joked, "I remember him. He carries the white man's burden."

*   *   *

BUT DURING HIS first year in office, in 1913, Wilson's racial prejudices showed through.[53] He didn't object when in early April Postmaster General Albert S. Burleson of Texas, whose father had been a military officer in the Confederacy, sided with Southern whites who were angry that the races were mingling in federal offices and that black supervisors were overseeing white clerks. Burleson and Treasury Secretary William McAdoo went about systematically segregating blacks and whites at the offices, restrooms, and eating facilities of the government, starting with the Post Office, Treasury Department, and Bureau of Printing and Engraving.

This was a big setback. After the Civil War, Washington, DC, didn't have the Jim Crow laws legalizing segregation that existed in the Deep South. In fact, when the city of Washington had home rule after the Civil

War, laws gave blacks equal rights in public places. Over time, these laws were ignored and segregation became the rule in most public places, such as hotels and restaurants, which would not serve blacks at all or would keep them apart from whites. But it wasn't until the Wilson administration that segregation of federal offices, restrooms, and cafeterias became widespread.[54] In some post offices, partitions were installed to separate black workers from whites.

The NAACP quickly objected. Villard, a founder of the NAACP, wrote Wilson that, "I cannot exaggerate the effect this has had upon colored people at large." Villard said African Americans had assumed that Wilson's commitment to democracy, much ballyhooed during the campaign, "was not limited by race or color." Wilson was defensive when he wrote back. "It is as far as possible from being a movement *against* Negroes," the president said.[55] Wilson told his aides that he had made no promises to blacks during the campaign except to "do them justice," and while he didn't want them fired from their jobs, he felt that segregation reduced racial friction and he wanted the matter settled in the least contentious way possible.

In November 1913, Wilson met in the Oval Office with critics of his racial policies. Their spokesman, the fiery Boston editor William Monroe Trotter, an African American and a leader of the National Equal Rights League, delivered a lengthy indictment and challenged the president. "Not since Frederick Douglass came to Washington to lobby President Johnson for black suffrage in 1866 had such a bold and demanding black figure stood in the White House face-to-face with a president," writes historian Nicholas Patler.[56] "Now, almost fifty years later, Trotter wasted no time getting to the crux of the problem."

Trotter said segregation was an "indignity" and an "insult" that suggested that "African Americans are unclean, diseased, or indecent as to their persons, or inferior beings of a lower order."[57] He went on to say that denying equality was in "violation of the Constitution." Throughout the meeting, Wilson was polite and seemed sympathetic, although he claimed not to know all of the steps toward widespread segregation in the federal government that were being taken in his administration.

At one point, Wilson lamely responded, "I am not familiar with it all," and admitted, "Now, mistakes have probably been made, but those mistakes can be corrected."[58] The meeting ended with the African American representatives mildly hopeful that Wilson would look into the matter and do something to stop the abuses.

A year later, in November 1914, Wilson again met with Trotter and other anti-segregation leaders.[59] Little had improved, and Trotter was confrontational from the start, even more so than the first time. "Only two years ago," Trotter said, "you were heralded as perhaps the second Lincoln, and now the Afro-American leaders who supported you are hounded as false leaders and traitors to their race. What a change segregation has wrought!" Wilson didn't address the charges directly, noting that "it takes the world generations to outlive all its prejudices" and no one could be "cocksure about what should be done." But Trotter didn't back off. "We are not here as wards," he replied. "We are not here as dependents. We are here as full-fledged American citizens."

Trotter said the government's backing for segregation was based on prejudice and he reminded Wilson of the black support he had received in the 1912 election. But Wilson, in a rare lapse in his self-discipline, couldn't control his anger and fumed, "Please leave me out. Let me say this, if you will, that if this organization wishes to approach me again, it must choose another spokesman. . . . You are an American citizen, as fully an American citizen as I am, but you are the only American citizen that has ever come into this office who has talked to me with a tone with a background of passion that was evident." Trotter came back, "I am from a part of the people, Mr. President." And Wilson retorted, "You have spoiled the whole cause for which you came."

Wilson was ill disposed to accept their confrontational attitude, partly because he was dispirited and embittered by the recent death of his wife, Ellen. But an angry Trotter refused to back down and was defiant.[60]

"Mr. President," he said, "we are here to renew our protest against the segregation of the colored employees in the departments of our national government." He said segregation had been spreading through the government in the year since they last met, including the use of separate offices and "toilet rooms," and urged Wilson to reverse course and "abolish segregation of Afro-Americans in the executive department."[61]

Wilson responded hotly that the segregation was designed to minimize the friction that inevitably arises "when the two races are mixed." Besides, he said, he was assured by his staff that blacks were receiving separate but equal treatment, and that the arrangement really wasn't harmful or degrading to blacks. Trotter replied that this was false, and he went on to declare that black voters were very disappointed with Wilson, and his Democratic party would suffer for lack of black support in the future.

Wilson later told an adviser he regretted losing his temper and should have simply listened to Trotter's heated remarks and moved on.[62] But the incident was revealing because Wilson was much more upset over the perceived lack of respect for his office than the substance of what his visitor was saying about the poor state of race relations and the evils of segregation. Overall, the number of black-held positions in government was reduced during the Wilson administration.

The meeting, in the end, had no effect on policy. Segregation worsened, and civil rights activist Oswald Villard wrote in his memoirs that "the colored people were left much worse off than when Wilson took office, for the precedent had been set" of official sanction for segregation in federal facilities.[63]

The relationship between Wilson and black leaders deteriorated. At the start of 1915, the NAACP was protesting against showings of *Birth of a Nation,* a new film by D. W. Griffith that took a racist view of blacks and glorified the Ku Klux Klan in the post–Civil War period, even though it was considered a breakthrough in cinematography. Thomas Dixon, who wrote *The Clansman,* a novel on which the film was based, had been a student of Wilson's at Johnson Hopkins years earlier, so the president had a personal connection to the producers of the film. Wilson agreed to see the movie at the White House on February 18 with his family, aides, and their wives.

This incensed black leaders, and many African American voters took it as Wilson's endorsement of the movie.[64] The president explained to aides that he was unaware of the movie's content in advance and never expressed approval for it, and that his attendance was a courtesy for an old acquaintance. These feelings were conveyed by an adviser to political allies. But Wilson failed to condemn the racism conveyed in the film, and the damage to his reputation among blacks was irreparable.

As the migration of African Americans from the South to the North grew amid increased demand for workers in war-related industries, racial tensions grew in the North. In July 1917, a riot erupted in East St. Louis, Illinois; thirty-nine blacks and nine whites were killed and several black neighborhoods were badly burned.[65] Wilson asked Attorney General Thomas W. Gregory if the federal government could "check these disgraceful outrages" but Gregory replied that no federal action was warranted. Wilson made no public statement deploring the violence, but on August 14 he met with four black leaders and allowed them to say publicly that he condemned the violence and wanted to punish the offenders.

But on August 23, a confrontation occurred between black troops and a crowd of whites in Houston, Texas; fifteen whites and three blacks died before white troops and local police restored order.[66] The next day, an aide took shorthand of Wilson's reaction at a cabinet meeting: "Race prejudice. Fight in Houston, Texas. Negro in uniform wants the whole sidewalk." The Army quickly hanged thirteen black soldiers and sentenced forty-one to life in prison. Courts martial later resulted in sixteen more death sentences, and although Wilson commuted some of them, his partial leniency did little to strengthen African Americans' trust in him.

Lynchings were also a continuing problem. The NAACP reported that nearly 100 blacks were lynched in both 1917 and 1918, and black and white leaders pressured Wilson to speak out. On July 26, 1918, Wilson issued a statement "on a subject which so vitally affects the honor of the nation and the very character and integrity of our institutions."[67] He condemned the "mob spirit" of lynching and added: "I say plainly that every American who takes part in the action of a mob or gives it any sort of countenance is no true son of this great Democracy but its betrayer, and does more to discredit her by that single disloyalty to her standards of law and of rights than the words of her statesmen or the sacrifices of her heroic boys in the trenches can do to make suffering people believe her to be their savior." He urged governors and law-enforcement officers to end "this disgraceful evil."

But he did little at the federal level to back up his rhetoric. And Wilson showed no interest in an anti-lynching bill that made the practice a federal crime and that was pending before the Democrat-controlled Congress, where it died.

The irony is that while all these injustices were going on, Wilson committed the United States to what he called a war to "make the world safe for democracy." Just as disgraceful, America's armed forces—in which 350,000 African Americans served, as laborers and cooks, as well as in other jobs at the bottom of the social hierarchy—were racially segregated.[68]

*   *   *

MEANWHILE, THE BLACK household staff saw a private and troubling version of President Wilson and his second wife Edith that few others did, especially after Wilson suffered a series of strokes in 1919 and became partially paralyzed. "As the president hovered between life and death, no one dared tell him how grave his condition was, for fear he would lose his will to live," recounts African American maid Lillian Rogers Parks.[69] "Even as he lay at death's door, word came that the Senate had rejected the Versailles Peace Treaty, because the League participation was part of it. Mrs. Wilson was in continual consultation with the doctor over whether or not the President should resign."

"As the crisis passed," Parks adds, "the word got around the White House that the first lady could still not even suggest to the president that he resign, because if he could not work toward the eventual American acceptance of the League of Nations, he would quite possibly lose any hope or will to live. The League was his magnificent obsession, even in his sickbed ramblings. From then on, the White House saw Mrs. Wilson become more and more involved in the actual workings of the government. Documents were delivered directly to her. . . . In the kitchens and back halls of the White House, the regulars were shaking their heads. They were glad that the President had weathered the storm and was improving, but most of them thought he should resign and allow a competent man to take over the reins of government."[70]

The first lady was strongly criticized in the newspapers for amassing too much power and acting as the unofficial president. There were also reports that Wilson had gone insane. All this bothered Mrs. Wilson profoundly. She insisted that her husband was mentally sound, and she was just helping him and conveying his wishes to other staffers. "I just don't know how much more criticism I can take," she told Lillian Rogers Parks's mother, also a maid at the White House, as she pointed to a stack of newspapers.[71]

Herbert Hoover

Herbert Hoover and his wife, Lou, showed some signs of racial sensitivity, as they made clear in dealing with a controversy surrounding the treatment of newly elected Representative Oscar De Priest of Chicago and his wife in 1929. De Priest was the first African American elected to Congress in the twentieth century.

The trouble came in connection with the first lady's traditional White House tea for congressional wives. The question was what to do with Mrs. Jessie De Priest. To grant Mrs. De Priest her prerogative and avoid a boycott by the wives of Southern legislators, Mrs. Hoover divided the event into four separate receptions. Mrs. De Priest attended the smallest of the four sessions, whose participants said in advance that they didn't mind attending with a black woman.[72]

Despite Mrs. Hoover's attempt to find a compromise, the incident triggered vitriolic criticism throughout the South. The Texas Legislature passed a resolution censuring Mrs. Hoover.[73] *The Mobile Press* in Alabama said Hoover had "offered to the South and to the nation an arrogant insult.... Social admixture of the Negro and the white is sought by neither race." The Mississippi Legislature passed a resolution asking Hoover to give "careful and thoughtful consideration to the necessity of the preservation of the racial integrity of the white race."

In his memoirs, President Hoover recounts the incident tersely. He doesn't mention the De Priests by name and seems put off not only by the racist reactions but by De Priest's refusal to keep the incident as quiet as possible to avoid embarrassing anyone. "During my administration," Hoover writes awkwardly, "there was a Negro Congressman. He had a wife. In giving the usual teas for Congressmen's wives, Mrs. Hoover insisted upon inviting the Negro's wife equally with the others. She was warned by some of her Congressional lady friends not to do it. The Negro Congressman did not particularly help matters by announcing to the press that his wife had received such an invitation. In consequence, the southern press denounced this 'defiling' of the White House and the southern reporters lined up to watch the colored lady come and go, hoping to witness their prophecy that some Congressman's wife would drop out. Mrs. Hoover had more sense than to give any such occasion for affront to her guest or to the White House. Nor did she wish to offend ladies from the South. Therefore, she divided her Congressional tea into different days and placed the Negro lady on the first day with ladies who had been previously tested as to their feelings. The speeches of the southern Senators and Congressmen, the editorials in the southern press, and a denunciatory resolution by the Texas Legislature wounded her deeply. Her tears, however, did not melt her indomitable determination. I sought to divert the lightning by at once inviting Dr. Moton of Tuskegee to lunch with me. The White House was thus 'defiled' several times during my term."[74]

But overall, Hoover showed little interest in racial advancement and exhibited some strange personal traits regarding the household staff. "In the White House," wrote Lillian Rogers Parks,[75] "he seemed tense and utterly preoccupied with the nation's ills. Such were the security precautions that the order was given that none of the servants were to be in sight when the President came out into the halls. So whenever the help heard three bells—the signal that he was emerging from his quarters—they would jump in every direction in order not to be seen. They jumped into rooms, and they jumped into a particular hall closet.

"Mama was around the First Lady much more than I was, so she did much more jumping, but even I had to resort to the hall closet once in a while. That broom closet, near the President's elevator, was eliminated during the Truman period of White House reconstruction, but in the Hoover administration, it was a very popular place, and butlers would hold their trays high over their heads to make room for others as they tumbled in."

Mrs. Hoover, with her desire for uniformity, initially wanted all the butlers in the dining room to be the same size. But she hired 6-foot-4 Alonzo Fields, far taller than his colleagues, for the butler staff; she recognized his talents, and he quickly became chief butler.[76]

"Though Mrs. Hoover was a kind and considerate woman," Parks wrote, "she was so busy concentrating on making each party the finest that she didn't see the worried faces of the staff, who were losing their savings while the banks went under, and had to take care of their unemployed relatives on the small salaries of the White House."[77] Parks was making $48 per month, and her mother made $80.

"The servants couldn't get over the fact that the president, who had once been a great outdoor man, roughing it in the wilds, and a mining engineer, who was used to mixing with all classes of people, was completely aloof with the White House staff," Parks continued.[78] "He never spoke to them, and never paid the slightest bit of attention to anything they were doing. However, he was *respected* by everyone. They knew how busy he was. At Christmas, when the servants would have a big party in the East Room, the President would simply walk in, say, 'Merry Christmas,' and leave, and Mrs. Hoover would give us a little talk."

For years, Hoover refused to pose for photographs with black people.[79] He claimed it was because he was concerned that the photos would be misused for advertising purposes, his aides said, but that standard didn't apply to whites. The black press, including the *Baltimore Afro-American* and the *Norfolk Journal and Guide*, complained that Hoover's policy was an insult. But he refused to relent until he was up for reelection in 1932.

Late in the campaign, Hoover deigned to have his picture taken at the White House with several black leaders, including Howard University Secretary-Treasurer Emmett J. Scott.

In an editorial, the *Baltimore Afro-American* noted that the black press had complained repeatedly about the slights and pointed out how many other delegations Hoover had posed with. "The *AFRO* has carried word of the President's posings," the editorial said.[80] "These columns, week by week, have noted how the president was photographed with the Morris Plan Bankers (September 29) or the International Beauty and Barbers' Supply Association (September 28), the Boy Scouts, the Jobs, the Ninnies and the Boobs, all of them white, none of them colored. The Negro press took up the battle.... Hardly a week passed that some paper did not refer to anti-Negro President Hoover, who never posed with Negro delegations." Noting that Hoover had finally posed with blacks, the editorial said, "The Hoover in those photographs is the same who sent Gold Star Mothers to France in Jim Crow ships. He's the same Hoover who put the Tenth Cavalry to work doing chores and advised Liberia that what it needed was a white dictator. He hasn't reformed or repented, but he needs votes and like any ward politician in a pinch, he'll do almost anything to get them. The Hoover photograph is a gesture of despair. Let nobody make a mistake about that."

The *Baltimore Afro-American* also reported that President Hoover could be impatient, even rude, to visiting African Americans. When black educator Mary McLeod Bethune of Daytona, Florida (who would later become a close friend of first lady Eleanor Roosevelt), expressed the hope that the government might make an appropriation for a "National Negro Memorial," Hoover snapped, "That's a matter for Congress."[81] The paper suggested that, "The entire delegation must have felt rebuffed."

CHAPTER SIX
STIRRINGS OF CHANGE

Despite his efforts to protect everyday people from the Depression, Franklin D. Roosevelt was not a champion of Africans Americans.[1] Blacks took part in many of Roosevelt's programs, including the Civilian Conservation Corps (CCC) and other initiatives providing government-funded jobs to keep young people at work, but Roosevelt did nothing to end the Jim Crow system of legalized segregation. Roosevelt calculated that Southern Democrats would have rebelled even more violently against the New Deal had he attacked segregation, and this would have conceivably jeopardized his renomination by the Democratic party, since Southern states held a critical mass of votes.

It was First Lady Eleanor Roosevelt who pushed Franklin on behalf of blacks. She believed it was a matter of elemental fairness to guarantee African Americans equality and that segregation was a monumental injustice. And after the U.S. entry into World War II in December 1941, she argued that it was wrong to leave racism intact at home when the nation was fighting to end it abroad. Her activities raised public consciousness about the need for equality and gave blacks hope that someone in high places was looking out for them, even though most of the administration's actions were largely symbolic.

One such move was including a black Boy Scout with the honor guard on the White House lawn during FDR's inauguration ceremonies in 1933.[2] Eleanor also brought African American sharecroppers into the White House to meet with her and later visited them in their decrepit shacks.[3]

She joined a sit-in to desegregate a Washington restaurant. She attended meetings and visited dormitories at the historically black Howard University in Washington. When the King and Queen of England visited the White House, Eleanor included African American entertainers, such as Marian Anderson and the North Carolina Spiritual Singers, as performers. And at the urging of Irvin and Elizabeth McDuffie, a black couple on the household staff, Eleanor arranged for other African American singers, including Lillian Evanti and Etta Moten, to perform on various occasions. Jazz great Louis Armstrong performed at a White House birthday party for the president on January 30, 1942.[4] It was part of Eleanor's effort to bring black entertainers recognition from a wider audience.

The black press frequently noted the Roosevelts' efforts to break the "color line." On August 11, 1934, for example, the *Pittsburgh Courier* carried a page-one dispatch that "The chief executive of the United States entertained President Stenio Vincent, of Haiti, and then posed with him for a picture and the sound movies. He was no less [gracious] in the honor freely bestowed upon his classmates of Harvard University, among them some 14 distinguished colored citizens. They and their families found the sociability of the President and Mrs. Roosevelt as they chatted on the White House lawn most stimulating. The little 6-year-old colored boy during the Easter-egg rolling fete who was 'shot' in the picture with the three other youngsters got a great thrill out of holding the hand of the first lady of the land while she beamed the Roosevelt smile before the battery of cameramen for the edification of all and sundry everywhere, at home and abroad."[5]

Eleanor often invited civil rights leaders into the White House. And as her husband's presidency advanced, she became even more active and committed to racial justice. She attended civil rights conventions, wrote in her newspaper column and other articles about the need for racial justice, and allied herself with black leaders. She formed especially close friendships with Mary McLeod Bethune, educator and chief of the National Youth Administration's Division of Negro Affairs, and Walter White, the executive secretary of the NAACP.[6] Bethune became Roosevelt's primary contact on African American issues, while Walter White kept the first lady informed of specific cases of bigotry. Her inclusion of African Americans in the life of the White House "aroused the wrath of Washington, and of her mother-in-law [who was very traditional and ever-protective of her son], but raised the hopes of millions of Americans," writes former chief White House usher J. B. West.[7]

Dorothy Height, a leader of the National Council of Negro Women, said that African Americans "came to think that Eleanor Roosevelt could do anything."[8] The attitude she tried to convey to people of all races was that, as Height summarized, "No one can make you feel inferior unless you give them your consent."

Her friendship with African American educator Bethune, the daughter of slaves, was particularly close. "When Mrs. Bethune arrived," recalled former usher J. B. West,[9] "Mrs. Roosevelt always went running down the driveway to meet her, and they would walk arm in arm into the mansion. Few heads of state received such a welcome."

As African American maid Lillian Rogers Parks[10] recalled, "She was so black that she made many of us backstairs look ghostly white by comparison. Mary was famous for having founded the Bethune–Cookman College, but she was then stationed in Washington in charge of Negro activities of the National Youth Administration. Eleanor and Mary would sit by the hour talking about the needs of blacks all over the country, especially housing, health care, and jobs. She was always bringing Eleanor the name of some worthy and well-educated black person who deserved a higher-level job.... Once Eleanor told someone she was grateful to Mary for having freed her of the bondage of racial prejudice and she had proven it to herself by giving Mary a kiss. Another time the White House bouquet room was in an uproar because Eleanor had ordered that flowers be sent to her black friend on a regular basis, until she recovered from an illness."

In 1939, Eleanor and Mary Bethune went to Birmingham, Alabama, for a meeting of the Southern Conference on Human Welfare.[11] The blacks and whites were segregated on each side of the center aisle, and Eleanor decided to sit with her black friend. A policeman told the first lady that she was breaking Alabama law by sitting in the black area and, as a compromise, Eleanor moved her chair into the aisle between the blacks and the whites as a gentle gesture of defiance. During the war, she made a habit of making inspection visits to ensure that black soldiers had adequate places to go for recreation, another outgrowth of her relationship with Bethune. Sometimes she and her aides were the only white people in the areas she toured.

Yet since she was the first lady, not the president, there were severe limitations to the progress that she could achieve. A federal anti-lynching law was the prime example. Long sought by African American leaders but blocked by segregationist Southerners in Congress and further stymied by indifferent or timid presidents, such a law seemed the kind of change that her reform-minded husband might endorse, and Eleanor made a behind-the-scenes effort to persuade him. She scheduled a meeting between civil rights leader Walter White and her husband and she prepared White for the encounter by briefing him on the objections that Franklin had raised when she discussed the matter privately with him over dinner.[12] During the session with White, Roosevelt said he had been told that such a bill would be unconstitutional. But White presented evidence that it wasn't. After White seemed able to read Roosevelt's mind when the president raised other objections, Roosevelt got miffed. "Somebody's been priming you," the president said. "Was it my wife?" White remained silent, not wanting to get Eleanor in trouble. Roosevelt let that matter drop.

But Roosevelt's final argument to White was his most pointed—the necessities of politics, the same argument that so many presidents have used over the years to explain their inaction on racial issues. Roosevelt said an anti-lynching law might be the moral course, but it wasn't practical. "I did not choose the tools with which I must work," he told White, noting that senior Southerners in Congress controlled important committees.[13] "If I come out for the anti-lynching bill now, they will block every bill I ask Congress to pass," he said. "I just can't take the risk." And he didn't.

Later, Eleanor wrote White, "I'm sorry about the bill. Of course, all of us are going on fighting, and the only thing we can do is hope we have better luck next time."[14]

The whole incident left President Roosevelt annoyed. Eleanor, he felt, had encouraged White to press for a course of action that could have harmed the overall New Deal. When presidential press secretary Steve Early complained that White had been sending messages to the president that sometimes were "decidedly insulting," Eleanor admitted that White seemed to be obsessed with lynching, but she added, "If I were colored, I think I should have about the same obsession that he has."[15]

Then Eleanor had another idea in her campaign to promote civil rights. She invited African American contralto Marian Anderson to give a recital at the White House. The performance was brilliant. Howard University officials then got the idea of arranging a concert by Anderson at Constitution Hall, the biggest auditorium in Washington at the time. But it was controlled by the Daughters of the American Revolution (DAR), a conservative group that refused to allow Anderson, or any other black, to perform there.

Eleanor, a member of the DAR, resigned in protest.[16] And she took her objections to another level, encouraging Walter White and Sol Hurok, Anderson's manager, to arrange a concert on government property. Interior Secretary Harold Ickes thought it was a wonderful idea and got approval from the president. The concert was held on the afternoon of Easter Sunday 1939 at the Lincoln Memorial. Anderson sang "America," "Nobody Knows What Trouble I See, But Jesus," and other inspirational songs, while facing the vast National Mall with the Washington Monument in the distance and a racially mixed crowd of 75,000. Eleanor showed her own practical side by recognizing that her presence would provoke the racists and divert attention away from Anderson's performance. So the first lady did not attend.

Eleanor's advocacy of fairness toward African Americans angered the white establishment in Washington, DC, which was at the time a segregated town oriented toward the South. Even though her husband didn't follow her recommendations for comprehensive civil rights legislation, or to integrate the armed forces, she kept up the pressure and had limited success.[17]

"More than anyone else in the White House," writes historian Doris Kearns Goodwin,[18] "Eleanor was responsible, through her relentless pressure of War Department officials, for the issuance of the two directives that forbade the designation of recreational areas by race and made government-owned and -operated buses available to every soldier regardless of race. By the end of the war, only one major step was needed to insure true equality for Negro soldiers, and that step would come in 1948, when President Truman issued Executive Order 9981, ending segregation in the armed forces."

Eleanor also warned Franklin that the patience of blacks was wearing thin because of continued bias in employment. This was another area where Eleanor's private lobbying, in addition to the lobbying of African American leaders, paid off. On June 25, 1941, President Roosevelt issued an executive order banning racial discrimination in the burgeoning defense industries and in all government-related employment.[19] This order established the Fair Employment Practices Commission to investigate complaints of discrimination and accountable directly to the president. It was praised as the first executive order directly benefiting African Americans since the

Emancipation Proclamation, taking a stride toward ending the federal Jim Crow system that was established in the Woodrow Wilson years. Unfortunately, the commission was inadequately funded, and the order was widely ignored in the South.

But Roosevelt's response to the demand from black leaders for more jobs in the war industries came only after he was threatened with a massive march on Washington by several hundred thousand African American workers and their supporters.[20] Black leader A. Phillip Randolph called off the march after Roosevelt, on June 25, issued his executive order prohibiting employment discrimination against workers in industries that had government contracts.

Similarly, there was only halting progress in allowing blacks to benefit from Roosevelt's signature programs, such as the CCC, which was designed to provide temporary government jobs for unemployed young men. By July during its first summer, in 1933, 275,000 young men were put to work building roads, trails, camps, and picnic grounds and constructing erosion and flood control projects in the nation's forests and parks.[21] Most earned $30 per month and sent about $25 per month home, supporting an estimated one million people in countless families.

Blacks were allowed to participate in the CCC but not in the numbers corresponding to their proportion of the population. And they were usually placed in segregated camps where the supervisors were white. Roosevelt spokesmen said local whites felt more comfortable that way and there would be less friction.

Eleanor's warnings about rising black militancy were proven all too true when riots broke out in Detroit on Sunday, June 20, 1943.[22] Scuffles between blacks and whites intensified after initial confrontations that afternoon at Belle Isle, a public park, on a sweltering day. Rumors of violence spread across the city and emotions exploded. Groups of blacks and whites roamed the streets of Detroit, chasing and beating anyone of the other race. By midnight, several hours after the disturbances started, 10 people were dead and 400 injured. President Roosevelt finally sent in 3,800 federal troops Monday morning, after Governor Harry Kelly of Michigan requested help. By the time the troops restored order a few hours later, 25 blacks and 9 whites were dead, and nearly 1,000 people had been hurt.

In some areas of the country, Eleanor was blamed for this violence. Mrs. Roosevelt was "morally responsible" for the riot, declared the *Jackson*

Daily News on June 22.[23] "It is blood on your hands, Mrs. Roosevelt. You have been personally proclaiming and practicing social equality at the White House and wherever you go, Mrs. Roosevelt. What followed is now history."

Eleanor's reaction to such abuse was mild. "I suppose when one is being forced to realize that an unwelcome change is coming, one must blame it on someone or something," she wrote in a letter to a friend.[24] But she had been privately warning her husband about rising racial tensions, spawned by appalling living conditions for blacks throughout the country, for years. Shortly after the riots, she called for an interracial conference to defuse tensions and set forth an agenda for action, but it never came to pass.

For his part, a week after the Detroit riots the president considered making a statement on race but quickly abandoned the idea. Eleanor told a friend that Franklin believed "he must not irritate the southern leaders as he feels he needs their votes for essential war bills."[25]

It was the same explanation, the same excuse that presidents had been using from the start in dealing with racial issues. Again, fear of political retribution from the South and from other opponents of equality caused a president to defer bold and needed action.

*   *   *

NOT THAT ELEANOR was completely free of prejudice. Since the Wilson administration, both whites and blacks had worked on the household staff but they were segregated in two dining rooms for meals.[26] Mrs. Roosevelt felt that the racially mixed staff was a hotbed of tension and conflict, so she decided upon entering the White House in 1933 that having everyone of one race would solve the problem and that it was appropriate that all the servants should be black, except for the chief housekeeper, Henrietta Nesbitt, who was white.[27] Another reason may have been that Nesbitt was notoriously tight-fisted, and hiring only blacks allowed her to save money since the blacks were paid substantially less than whites.

Some other African Americans in the White House had a more harsh explanation. "There was a theory backstairs that one reason Eleanor Roosevelt decided to have only black servants was that she thought they would be less likely to spread tales of what they heard and less likely to understand it," according to maid Lillian Rogers Parks.[28] "If so, she was right on the first point, but certainly wrong on the latter. We understood, all right, but we only talked among ourselves. The help would often have a private chuckle about what we had heard, and how obvious it was that those speaking must have thought what they were saying went over our heads. Only the brightest survived at the White House. We had schoolteachers working as maids, for example. We learned to act dumb as part of the job."

This code of silence and supposed ignorance applied to the most intimate details of the first family's lives. Parks says few in the White House knew that the president had resumed a pre-presidential affair with a former White House social secretary named Lucy Mercer Rutherford, who was sometimes secretly brought to the White House to see Roosevelt when Eleanor was away.[29] But those who did know included three black household staffers—the McDuffies and Maggie Rogers, Lillian Parks's mother and a longtime White House maid—and they didn't talk about it publicly. The Roosevelts also had a black cook at Warm Springs, Daisy Bonner, who prepared Franklin's meals at his Georgia retreat for twenty years and who probably was aware of the liaisons.[30]

There were other examples of Eleanor's racial insensitivity and her tolerance for racial prejudice around her. At the Roosevelt family home in Hyde Park, New York, "whenever the colored help went there to serve the president, they were not permitted to eat in the dining room for the [white] help. They had to eat in the kitchen," African American butler Alonzo Fields recalled.[31] "Of course at the White House, with Virginia so nearby, the separate dining rooms could be attributed to the influence of that state's policy, but in New York you did not expect this."

And sometimes Eleanor had to be prodded to follow through on her benign instincts. Unhappy because the black staff's workload was increasing exponentially because of all the Roosevelts' entertaining (often, for example, Mrs. Roosevelt scheduled teas for 500 people, twice on the same afternoon), Fields and others, including doorman Arthur Jackson, asked Mrs. Roosevelt to institute an eight-hour day and compensation for overtime. Initially, she balked, responding that such an arrangement would limit her flexibility, complicate matters, and increase the White House budget too much.

"So Arthur and I came up with a solution," Fields recalled later.[32] "We started a rumor. He'd go to someone in the kitchen, someone who was very talkative, and say to him, 'Have you heard of organizing? Did anyone say anything to you about the White House?' And they'd say, 'No.' And that person would go to someone else and in no time it was back to the housekeeper. So the housekeeper calls me in. She says, 'What's this about John L. Lewis [a famous union leader at the time], the CIO's gonna organize the help in the White House?' I said, 'I don't know anything about it. You know they wouldn't come to me.' Then Mrs. Roosevelt and she talked it over. And Mrs. Roosevelt asked me to come up to talk to her. She says, 'Do you have any way of finding out?' I said, 'Well perhaps I could get the doorman, Arthur, to find out for us.' ... He came back and told us that they would organize us if 75 percent of the people would sign up. So I told her that news and she said, 'Well that mustn't happen. Tell me, what do they want?' I said, 'Well they'd like eight hours a day, and compensatory time off when they work overtime. They want pay for it.' So she said she and the president didn't think it should go up to the [Capitol] Hill [to Congress]. And so everybody then got eight hours a day." That was only a legal guide, however. Members of the household staff said they were still expected to work many additional hours per week to take care of the first family's needs.

Franklin and Eleanor also allowed segregation to continue at the president's recuperation center in Warm Springs, Georgia, which the president owned and where other polio patients were treated. For years, he traveled to Warm Springs to bathe in the mineral springs, which he considered therapeutic for his polio-paralyzed legs, and to relax from the pressures of Washington. But the blacks and whites were kept separate, with the black staff even having to sit in a small "colored" section when the white children watched movies in an auditorium at the rehabilitation center. On Roosevelt's trips to the facility, he would bring two black servants with him, including valet Irvin McDuffie.

But the president never integrated the staff. Blacks and whites were kept in separate dormitories, with the whites living in much superior conditions.[33] The blacks also were relegated to lower-level jobs at less pay. Black men were given $30 per month and black women $18 per month, while white men made a minimum of $90 per month. There were about 100 white patients at any given time, and black patients were extremely rare. When African Americans were admitted, they were kept in a basement room reserved for "the colored sick."

In 1941, Roosevelt endorsed a separate medical facility for black polio patients at Tuskegee Institute in Alabama, with an entirely black staff.[34] The Warm Springs center reversed policy and decided to routinely admit black patients in 1945, just after Roosevelt's death.[35]

Franklin's commitment to racial justice fell far short of his wife's ideals. Thurgood Marshall, who years later was to become the first African American appointed to the Supreme Court, saw Roosevelt's backward attitudes firsthand. Marshall, then a lawyer in private practice, met with Attorney General Francis Biddle to find some way to guarantee fair treatment for a black man accused of shooting a sheriff in Virginia. During the meeting, Biddle phoned the president and had Marshall pick up an extension so he could listen in. "I warned you not to call me again about any of Eleanor's niggers," Roosevelt threatened Biddle, unaware that Marshall was on another line. "Call me one more time and you are fired."[36]

One curious racial omission during the Roosevelt era was the refusal of the president or the first lady to meet with Jesse Owens, the black running star of the 1936 Olympics in Berlin. Owens achieved international fame for winning four gold medals for the United States, defeating a host of white athletes, and undermining German dictator Adolph Hitler's claims of Aryan superiority. But Owens said at the time, "Hitler didn't snub me—it was our president who snubbed me. The president didn't even send me a telegram."[37] With Roosevelt's reelection at stake that November, it appears that the president didn't want to stir up anti-black resentments by hosting the African American track star, which would have gotten enormous publicity in the South. Owens always felt slighted at never being invited to the White House until President Gerald Ford gave him the Presidential Medal of Freedom, the nation's highest civilian honor, in August 1976. "That's right, I never had been invited to the White House before, and it seems like even marbles champions are invited," Owens said after the ceremony in 1976.[38]

Both Roosevelts, however, were capable of beneficent personal gestures. When the son of Eleanor's personal maid, Mabel Haley Webster, died, the first lady went to the funeral, even though she was the only white person there. "It endeared her to us forever after," wrote Parks.[39] "In the [19]30s it was almost unheard of for a white woman to appear at an all-black gathering of any kind. And this was a first lady."

The president liked to host recitals for Lizzie McDuffie, a talented singer and the African American maid married to his valet Irvin McDuffie (both of whom came with the Roosevelts to the White House from the family home in Hyde Park, New York, in 1933).[40] Mrs. Roosevelt brought several of her black servants to Hyde Park to take care of the king and queen of England during a royal visit. This outraged Franklin's hidebound mother Sara, who allowed her own English butler to start his vacation just before the King and Queen arrived, as a protest.[41] However, the royal visit didn't go smoothly. With all the guests assembled in the Hyde Park library, a black butler tripped while carrying a tray of glasses, decanters, and ice bowls. He and everything on the tray clattered to the floor, causing much embarrassment and second-guessing by Franklin's mother that they should have used white help.[42] This was also the occasion when Eleanor caused a mini social scandal by serving the King and Queen hot dogs as part of a picnic buffet.[43] Mrs. Roosevelt said she wanted them to experience one of Americans' favorite foods, but the capital's socialite mavens weren't impressed.

Meanwhile, Lillian Rogers Parks, the African American maid and seamstress, was privy to all sorts of secrets and confidential moments. She had a special bond with the president because both of them were victims of polio. Roosevelt walked with crutches and used a wheelchair in private, and the four-foot-ten "Little Lillian," as she was known by the presidents she served, also had difficulty walking and used crutches.

"Few people knew that the President slept with a gun under his pillow," Parks wrote.[44] "Nor did they know that the Secret Service men had ordered Mrs. Roosevelt to carry a gun with her wherever she went. I used to see a storeroom helper, Mac, cleaning the first lady's gun in the supply room run by the husband of the housekeeper, Henrietta Nesbitt. Backstairs, we called the guns 'His' and 'Hers.'"

Parks added: "The President was human, and no one knew that better than the servants at the White House, who had to maintain a certain serenity in the midst of chaos. Yes, we knew that the father image, the hero, the 'perfect man' was besieged by his own set of problems. Now and then, he was torn between the two women in his life, his mother and his wife. Sometimes, he would revolt against his wheelchair, and the fates that had put him there; then he would complain and become irritable. At such times, there was only one thing to do—give him a rubdown to soothe his weary, wasted muscles and relax his mind."[45]

Roosevelt had a deep fear of getting caught in a fire and being unable to escape because his legs were paralyzed. The Secret Service installed special "chutes" to get him out of the second-floor window of his bedroom and down to the ground, and they held regular drills for moving the president to safety.[46] Irvin McDuffie helped Roosevelt with what the staff called "crawling exercises" to give the president practice in getting himself out of a room in case he had to escape a fire (or an enemy attack) on his own.[47] These exercises showed the extent of the president's disability and were very embarrassing to him, so he kept them secret from all but valet McDuffie and a few other trusted staff members. Not even his wife and children were allowed to see him in such a vulnerable condition. It was significant that Roosevelt trusted McDuffie with his secret, suggesting just how close the president was to his valet and his wife Lizzie.

McDuffie was a former barber in Atlanta who had injured his leg and couldn't remain standing for long periods of time, so he began looking for other employment. A well-connected associate for whom McDuffie served as a part-time valet arranged for him to "try out" with Roosevelt in 1927, two years before Roosevelt became governor of New York, as a personal assistant at the future president's retreat in Warm Springs, Georgia. Roosevelt quickly hired him, and McDuffie was assigned the jobs of cleaning and pressing Roosevelt's clothes, shining his shoes, cutting his hair, waking him each morning, and getting him to bed each night. He traveled with Roosevelt around the country and the world. McDuffie and his wife, Lizzie, who was hired as maid to Eleanor, followed the long-term pattern of presidents and first ladies entrusting black household staff with their secrets. "They were more than valet and president—they were confidants. McDuffie knew everything about [Roosevelt] and loved him more for it," recalled Parks. "Lizzie came to be trusted with all of [Roosevelt's] secrets as well, and she was warm and motherly with him. The McDuffies were among the few people who always knew the state of [Roosevelt's] romances with Lucy Mercer ... and they protected him from any prying eyes—especially Eleanor's."[48]

Lizzie, an accomplished speaker, also became a political surrogate for the president and the Democratic party in the black community during the 1936 campaign. On one tour that fall, she visited Illinois, Indiana, and Ohio and spoke to an estimated 50,000 people. The couple lived in a room on the second floor of the White House so they could always be close at hand.

In a rare newspaper interview, Irvin McDuffie said, "After eating his breakfast, the president reads the morning papers, including the leading Negro papers. He does lots of work before he gets up. He can work five men to death while he lies in bed."[49] McDuffie, whom Roosevelt called "Mac," added: "From my association and conversation with him, I can frankly say that the President does not think in terms of races, but in terms of Americans, and he believes the Negro is an American. I heard every speech he made during his campaign, and never did he single out the colored people. It was always 'Americans.'" McDuffie didn't get beyond the eighth grade, but said, "I have read all of the Harvard classics, several histories, the Bible, Balzac, Emerson, Tennyson, Byron, and Shakespeare."

The black staff also got some vivid private impressions of Eleanor. One was that while she put up a good front in dealing with jokes and criticism in the newspapers about her social activism and her frequent fact-finding missions for her husband to determine how his policies were working, privately she was bothered by the criticism.[50] To better determine what everyday people were saying, when she gave speeches or appeared somewhere she assigned one of her secretaries to take down the "critical" things she heard people saying in crowds.

And serving the Roosevelts took its toll. The couple required near-constant attention, and the pressure drove many household staffers to exhaustion. One of them was Irvin McDuffie. "We could see that the strain of taking care of [Roosevelt] and being on twenty-four-hour call was taking a terrible toll on McDuffie," wrote Parks. "He started to drink to calm his nerves. One night, though, relaxed from a few too many drinks, McDuffie didn't hear [Roosevelt's] bell. [Roosevelt] happened to be all alone for a little while, and by the time he was rescued, he was terribly upset. Someone went to McDuffie's room and found him zonked out and asleep. The next day he was terribly sorry. [Roosevelt] forgave him, but Eleanor heard of it and had a conference with some of her sons and decided McDuffie was no longer reliable enough—and worst of all, could not be counted on—in an emergency." After a decade serving Roosevelt almost around the clock, he was forced from his White House job in 1939.[51]

Yet all in all, the black household staff loved and respected the Roosevelts. Lillian Rogers Parks apparently spoke for most of them when she wrote, "I believe the Roosevelt White House was the catalyst for the whole civil rights movement that would eventually open all front doors."[52]

CHAPTER SEVEN
A FEW SHINING MOMENTS

Harry Truman

During his nearly eight years in office, Harry Truman dealt with many grave problems, including the aggressive behavior of the Soviet Union and China, the threat of communism in Greece and Turkey, the rebuilding of Europe after World War II, the establishment of a Jewish state in Israel, and a host of domestic challenges, including a troubled economy. He also was confronted with rising pressure to provide justice and fair treatment to African Americans.

In some ways, Truman couldn't escape his background. He grew up in segregated Missouri; his grandfather had owned slaves, and an uncle had served in the Confederate Army.[1] At the same time, Truman depended on black voters during his political career in Missouri, including as a U.S. senator, and he always tried not to stir up racist animosities.[2]

As president, Truman's basic sense of fairness was offended by the injustices he saw. "My forbears were Confederates," he wrote to political associates who wanted him to soften his views on civil rights in 1948. "I come from a part of the country where Jim Crowism is as prevalent as it is in New York or Washington. Every factor and influence in my background—and in my wife's for that matter—would foster the personal belief that you are right. But my very stomach turned over when I learned that Negro soldiers, just back from overseas, were being dumped out of army trucks in Mississippi and beaten. Whatever my inclinations as a native of Missouri might have been, as president I know this is bad. I shall fight to end evils like this."[3]

In the months after World War II ended, the Ku Klux Klan stepped up its brutality against African Americans, targeting black veterans of the war with assaults and lynchings. Walter White, chief secretary of the NAACP, complained directly to Truman, who asked Attorney General Tom Clark to investigate. White found that all-white juries often failed to convict other whites for crimes against blacks. Truman issued an executive order naming a commission to look into civil rights violations and recommend solutions. He was deeply troubled by the violence.[4]

Writes political scientist Alvin Felzenberg: "Truman pursued all these actions even though he shared some of the prejudices against blacks, Jews, Catholics, and other minorities that many of his contemporaries held and voiced. Truman was known to use the 'N-word' in casual conversation, wrote disparagingly of Jews after visits to New York City, and maintained that the Vatican would dictate policy should a Catholic be elected president. Truman, however, believed that his responsibility under the Constitution trumped his personal biases. Just to be on the safe side with his neighbors (and with some of his relatives), he cautioned his listeners not to mistake his embrace of equality before the law as an endorsement of social equality."[5]

Privately, his bias was sometimes crude. In a letter to his wife, Bess, in June 1946, Truman referred to black heavyweight boxing icon Joe Louis's rematch later that day with Billy Conn and said, "I don't like that yellow nig, and I wouldn't like to see him knock out a fool white Irishman."[6] (Presumably to Truman's displeasure, Louis proceeded to knock out Conn in the eighth round.)

Only 7 percent of Americans supported his civil rights agenda, according to the Gallup Poll, and little of that agenda passed Congress while Truman was in office.[7] But at the level of political pragmatism, Truman believed that backing civil rights for blacks would increase his popularity among African Americans in the 1948 election, when he also was warding off the third-party candidacy of liberal Henry Wallace. So there was a savvy political calculation in his moves to help black citizens.

In addition, historian Robert Dallek points out: "The long history of discrimination and segregation, particularly in the South, was at best an embarrassing blight on an America advertising itself to the world as the defender of freedom and democracy—and at worst a gross violation of constitutional commitments to equal treatment under the law. Lynchings, systematic exclusion from the ballot box, and job discrimination had become a source of national tension that jeopardized the country's domestic tranquility."[8]

When Southerners blocked comprehensive civil rights legislation in Congress, Truman resorted to unilateral action. In December 1946, he created a Committee on Civil Rights to study and recommend ways to eliminate or lessen racial discrimination.[9]

On June 30, 1947, he spoke at a rally by the NAACP at the Lincoln Memorial, the first president to address the NAACP since its founding in 1911, and promised that the committee would find ways to reduce racial prejudice. "The extension of civil rights today means not protection of the people against the government, but protection of the people by the government," Truman declared. Privately, he promised NAACP leader Walter White that he would follow up these remarks with action, and he did.

In October 1947, the Truman committee called for the equal treatment of blacks under the law in a report, "To Secure these Rights." Among its proposals were a federal anti-lynching law, federal action to ban poll taxes and other restrictions on black voting, integration of the armed forces, and a stop to segregation in public interstate transportation.[10] When the civil rights commission formally issued its report on October 29, 1947, Truman asked Congress to enact its recommendations.[11]

On February 2, 1948, Truman made good on at least one of his pledges to African Americans by asking Congress to enact sweeping civil rights legislation, a daring request considering that it was sure to endanger Truman's support among whites in the South in his bid for reelection that November. He supported an anti-lynching statute, and endorsed greater protections for the right of blacks to vote, such as elimination of poll taxes, making permanent the Fair Employment Practices Commission, created as a temporary panel by Franklin Roosevelt, and an end to racial discrimination at interstate transportation facilities.[12]

His June 29, 1948, address on equal rights was remarkable for its bluntness. "Every man," he said, "should have the right to a decent home, the right to an education, the right to adequate medical care, the right to a worthwhile job, the right to an equal share in making public decisions through the ballot, and the right to a fair trial in a fair court.

We must insure that these rights—on equal terms—are enjoyed by every citizen."[13]

Truman added: "The support of desperate populations of battle-ravaged countries must be won for the free way of life. We must have them as allies in our continuing struggle for the peaceful solution to the world's problems. They may surrender to the false security offered so temptingly by totalitarian regimes unless we can prove the superiority of democracy. Our case for democracy should be as strong as we can make it. It should rest on practical evidence that we have been able to put our own house in order."[14]

Truman believed it was a matter of elementary fairness to end segregation in the military, because the abuses were so serious and the requirement for fairness seemed so clear. Even though nearly 11 percent of enlisted men in the Army were African American, the highest-ranking black person in the Army was a solitary black colonel. The same level of discrimination existed in the Navy and the Air Force. The Navy was particularly outrageous in limiting black advancement. African Americans were cooks, dishwashers, and waiters, and did manual labor such as swabbing decks and cleaning rooms, but had virtually no other job opportunities.[15]

In July 1948, faced with a balky Congress, Truman also unilaterally ended segregation in the federal civil service and the armed forces and continued Franklin Roosevelt's ban on racial discrimination in companies contracting with the federal government. His Executive Order 9981, issued on July 26, 1948, is still considered a landmark in civil rights. It "declared to be the policy of the president that there shall be equality of treatment and opportunity for all persons in the armed services without regard to race, color, religion, or national origin" and that promotions would be made "solely on merit and fitness."

The executive order is particularly impressive because it came two weeks before the Democratic National Convention would choose its presidential nominee. It was certain to rile up Southern delegates, and it did. A number of them walked out rather than nominate Truman, but he won the nomination anyway. He also had to cope with the candidacy of South Carolina Governor Strom Thurmond, running as an independent on a states' rights platform. Truman's calculation, shaped in part by an unpublicized White House meeting with black leaders including Roy Wilkins, A. Philip Randolph, and Ralph Bunche, was that his success in that fall's election would be determined by blacks and other voters in the big cities. He was right, and he went on to win a stunning upset victory that November.[16]

*   *   *

IN DEALING WITH the household staff, Truman was decent and considerate. Maitre d' Eugene Allen told this story about an incident involving Truman and houseman George Thomas: "President Truman used to come over for lunch and he used to go into the Oval Room on the second floor and do some work at a desk in there. So when he'd leave and go back to the office, we had a houseman named George Thomas, and he would go in and look around and make sure the place was tidied up. So George looked around—of course, President Truman was neat and everything was in order. So George decided that he would sit down. So he got in the president's chair—he had one of these big leather chairs, you know—and sat down. And who comes in the door but President Truman. He looked at George—he had forgot something, you know—he looked at him and said, 'George, I'll tell you one thing, you're in a mighty hot seat!' He picked up his papers and went back to the office. That was the end of that."[17]

Lillian Rogers Parks, the maid and seamstress at the White House, became an intimate of the Trumans, as she had been with the Roosevelts. She recalled being in Blair House on November 1, 1950, when Puerto Rican nationalists tried to assassinate the president, who was napping inside. (The White House, across the street, was being renovated at the time.) The would-be assassins were shot before they entered the building and Truman wasn't hurt. "I remember exactly where I was, of course, when the bullets that killed my favorite White House guard, Leslie Coffelt, started flying," Parks wrote. "I was one of the maids you read about who were looking out the third-floor window."[18]

Parks was sitting alone in the front room of the third floor making curtains when the shots rang out. She and another maid, Rose Booker, looked out the window and quickly ducked back in when they realized a shootout was under way. "I was shaking like a leaf as I stood back and watched it all, and later, when Mrs. Truman went down and saw the blood and heard the story, she came back upstairs and cried. Then she pulled herself together and calmly phoned Margaret [the Trumans' daughter], who had a concert that night, to tell her everything was 'all right,' and to go ahead with her singing."[19]

When it came to family matters, Truman would tolerate no criticism of his wife or daughter. His threat to do physical harm to a reviewer who panned one of his daughter's concerts is part of Truman lore. Less well-known is his tangle with black U.S. Representative Adam Clayton Powell, a New York Democrat and Harlem pastor, over what Truman saw as rudeness to Mrs. Truman.

The incident started when the DAR refused to allow black pianist Hazel Scott, who was Powell's wife, to perform at Constitution Hall, which the DAR owned and which was the same venue from which Marian Anderson had been excluded under Franklin Roosevelt. Powell was furious. So, when Mrs. Truman subsequently attended a DAR function, Powell publicly called her "the Last Lady of the Land." Now it was Harry's turn to be furious at what he considered an insult to Bess. He excluded the Harlem congressman from all subsequent social occasions at the Truman White House and referred to Powell at a staff meeting as "that damned nigger preacher."[20]

"He apparently felt that the insult to his wife was worse than the insult to Powell's wife and to American Negroes," recalled J. B. West, then the chief usher of the White House. "And yet this same Harry Truman was an early champion of civil rights and the first president to integrate the armed forces. He was a complex man, but when it came to his family he was very single-minded. They came first."[21]

Harry also tangled with the famed baritone and black political activist Paul Robeson. When Robeson and a delegation of other civil rights leaders visited Truman at the White House in September 1946, the entertainer demanded immediate federal action against lynching, and Truman felt that his tone was too strident. Robeson particularly angered the president when he compared American lynchings with atrocities committed by the Nazis and the Japanese in World War II. "The president took great exception to that and declared that we should stand by our country in foreign affairs regardless of the domestic situation," Robeson told reporters afterward.[22]

When Robeson said it was wrong for the United States to take a leading role in the Nuremburg war-crimes trials if it wouldn't protect blacks at home, Truman objected, declaring that the United States and Great Britain were the last strongholds of freedom and democracy. Truman also became upset when Robeson declared that Secretary of State James Byrnes couldn't be effective in arguing with the Russians about democracy because he was from a Southern state where blacks were treated badly. And Truman fumed when Robeson said that if the government didn't do something about lynching "the Negro will"—a reference to the possibility of race riots.

But Harry and Bess became popular with their African American staff. The Trumans were effusive in their compliments and considerate in many other ways. The president, unlike many of his more aloof predecessors, would introduce individual household workers to visiting guests and family members, such as Democratic presidential nominee Adlai Stevenson in 1952, as well as his brother Vivian Truman and his sister Mary Jane Truman. He would make sure the staffers got annual leave from their all-consuming jobs. The president impressed the black workers by including 2 African American master sergeants at a dinner for 126 guests honoring then-General Dwight Eisenhower after Europe was retaken by the allies during World War II. The Trumans showed up for meals on time (breakfast at 8 a.m. sharp; lunch at 1, and dinner at 7).[23] On a very personal level, Harry insisted that no one should have to wash another person's underwear or socks, and he did the chore himself.[24]

The Trumans invited black household staffers to social events, and seemed even-handed in other ways. Butler Alonzo Fields recalled one impressive moment during the Trumans' first Christmas in the White House in December 1945. A week before the holiday, the president looked up from the breakfast table, where he was dining alone, and said, "Fields, I should like to request a favor. I want you to find a needy colored family and see to it that they have a real happy Christmas dinner."[25] Truman had already asked another staffer to find a poor white family for the same treat. Truman paid for gifts to the families out of his own pocket but ordered that the episode be kept secret. Fields proceeded to have a huge dinner of turkey and all the trimmings prepared at the White House and delivered to the families in private cars. The secret tradition continued each Thanksgiving and Christmas for the rest of Truman's presidency.[26]

Alonzo Fields wrote, "So if the question is, 'Which one of the Presidents did I understand and which one did I think understood me as a person?' I must say that the answer is President Truman. I always felt that he understood me as a man, not as a servant to be tolerated, and that I understood that he expected me to be a man, sincere in my duties and trying to do what is right at all times. President Roosevelt was genial and warm but he left one feeling, as most aristocrats do, that they really do not understand one. As if to a less fortunate human being, they extend a charitable, human tolerance, but never permit the right to understand them."[27]

The staff noticed other specific contrasts to the Roosevelts. Mrs. Truman had breakfast with her husband nearly every morning; the Roosevelts rarely saw each other before dinnertime, if then. Meals with the Trumans were at regular times. The Roosevelts ate at different hours and let other family members and guests straggle in whenever they chose. The staff nicknamed the Trumans—Harry, Bess, and daughter Margaret—"The Three Musketeers" because they were such a close-knit family.[28]

"The Roosevelts had been kindly and good to the staff, and had even kidded with us, but there had always been a sort of barrier, as if you had to look up," wrote Parks. "The Trumans' attitude said that you were just as important as anyone else, and you were treated with the respect of an equal. And for that, the whole gang of us looked up to them even more."[29]

"We used to talk about the difference in attitude between the Roosevelts and the Trumans, and we recalled how once Lizzie McDuffie had asked Mrs. 'R' if the help could watch a certain entertainment—it wasn't a State occasion but just some little affair which all the White House secretaries and such could attend. Mrs. Roosevelt said, 'Yes, they can come if they stay in the back.' So we knew that even she had reservations, and we didn't bother about going. We had come to know the difference between a high-sounding speech and actual performance."[30]

"But Harry Truman had felt that an American is an American, no matter what his color or the number of fillings in his teeth. And that was that," Parks wrote, at least in terms of the law if not always in social customs and relationships.[31]

Dwight Eisenhower

In 1953, the Supreme Court ruled in the *Brown v. Board of Education* decision that segregation of public schools was unconstitutional, violating the equal protection clause of the Fourteenth Amendment. Even though President Dwight Eisenhower, who had taken office in January, was a states' rights advocate and opposed the decision, he said he would enforce the ruling as the law of the land. He used the *Brown* decision to work behind the scenes to argue for desegregation in a number of ways.

He called the three members of the commission that governed the District of Columbia and told them to begin desegregating the capital city's schools immediately, which was accomplished by the end of his first term in early 1957. He saw to it that discrimination in government employment and contracting was officially prohibited, and named E. Frederic Morrow as a presidential assistant for special projects in 1955, the first black to be officially appointed an aide in an executive capacity at the White House.[32] And he tried to exert pressure to end the remaining discrimination in the U.S. armed services, where he had spent his career.[33]

"Eisenhower's brand of leadership put a premium on forbearance and restraint," writes Felzenberg. "Hoping that others might follow their example, he singled out for praise individuals and school districts that had successfully and peacefully dismantled segregation. He urged opponents of school integration to voice their objections only through peaceful and legal means. Having spent time in southern states earlier in his life, Eisenhower feared that, unless and until attitudes changed, white parents would remove their children from public schools rather than allow them to attend integrated ones. Eisenhower would have preferred that the Supreme Court not begin its assault on segregation with something as emotional to parents as their children's education. Nevertheless, once the court had acted, Eisenhower was intent on supporting it."[34]

In 1957, Arkansas Governor Orval Faubus ordered the Arkansas National Guard to prevent nine black students from entering Central High School in Little Rock. Then he withdrew the guard, leaving the children unprotected from the angry crowds that blocked their way. Eisenhower sent 1,000 members of the 101st Airborne Division to escort the students into the school, arguing that he was taking action to stop an insurrection (rather than side openly with the integrationists). Critics argued that Eisenhower should have made a public case for the virtues of integration, but he did make sure that the students attended school and he did enforce the Supreme Court decision. Eisenhower thereby became the first president since Ulysses S. Grant to send federal troops to the South to enforce civil rights laws protecting African Americans. This episode made a deep impression on a certain elementary-school student at another school in Little Rock who was shocked at the anti-black prejudice in the community and never forgot the experience. This was Bill Clinton, who was to be elected president of the United States thirty-five years later, in November 1992.

Also in 1957, Eisenhower sent a civil rights bill to Congress. Although it was markedly weakened, the measure established a Civil Rights Commission and a Civil Rights Division in the Justice Department, which Truman had requested earlier to no avail. To Eisenhower, the bill's provisions to expand black suffrage were worth the compromises he had to make to win passage. "With his right to vote assured, the American Negro could use it to secure his other rights," Eisenhower theorized. In 1960, Eisenhower proposed and won passage for another civil rights bill authorizing the hiring of federal poll inspectors to guarantee blacks the right to vote.[35] But neither measure had much impact because implementation was halfhearted.

The sad state of black America was illustrated in October 1957 when K. A. Gbedemah, the black finance minister of Ghana, was prohibited from drinking a glass of orange juice at a whites-only Howard Johnsons roadside restaurant in Dover, Delaware. Gbedemah protested to the State Department, and as a result an embarrassed President Eisenhower and Vice President Richard Nixon had breakfast with the diplomat, clad in a multi-colored kente cloth toga and leather sandals, at the White House to make amends. The group also posed for pictures, and the State Department apologized to the Ghana government.[36]

* * *

EISENHOWER SHOWED LITTLE interest in the household staff, black or white. But Mamie, his wife, was so exacting—"fussy" is the word used by the staff—that the long-suffering maid and seamstress, Lillian Rogers Parks, considered quitting. Parks was under pressure from Mrs. Eisenhower to complete all manner of special projects, including redoing the curtains and much of the other decor in Mamie's favorite color, pink. Mrs. Eisenhower also decreed that no one could use slang or nicknames, including calling the president "Ike," as his campaign had done. "Taking away nicknames was taking away the spice and fun of backstairs life," Parks wrote. "The handsome chief usher, James West, was called 'Perry Como' because of a real resemblance. George Thompson, the likeable houseman, was 'Jockey' because of his size. Head Electrician Johnson, who had operated the first movie projector under Hoover, was happily called 'Short Circuit.'"[37] But Mamie's edict was respected, at least when she was within earshot. When the Eisenhowers were at their farm in Gettysburg, Pennsylvania, about eighty miles from the White House, Mamie insisted that White House linens be sent back and forth rather than use any of her own.[38]

But Parks stayed on because she needed her salary to pay for her ailing mother's nursing care.[39]

And Mamie showed racial sensitivity by continuing Eleanor Roosevelt's policy of desegregating the annual Easter Egg Roll on the White House lawn and ordering that full protocol rights be given to the visiting black president of Haiti, for whom she arranged a state dinner.[40] Mamie and Ike agreed to have Marian Anderson, the center of so much controversy when she was barred from Constitution Hall in the Roosevelt years, sing the national anthem at Eisenhower's inauguration in 1953, the first African American to participate in such an event. Mamie invited Alice Dunnigan of the Association of Negro Press to her one press conference, and held a special reception for 100 members of the National Council of Negro Women in November 1953.[41] Eisenhower also met in August 1956 with twenty-two African American beauty contestants who were competing for the title of "Miss Shrine Princess" at a Washington convention.[42]

The Eisenhowers created a long-lasting positive impression with the staff by inviting nearly all of them to a buffet supper on June 6, 1959, at the first couple's Gettysburg farm. This corrected what the Eisenhowers said was an oversight in June 1955 when only a smaller group from the White House staff was invited to a picnic at Gettysburg to celebrate the first couple's thirty-ninth wedding anniversary and the completion of their Gettysburg house, which had been renovated.[43]

There was one African American to whom Eisenhower felt close—John Moaney, his longtime valet. Moaney had been an Army sergeant who started working for Eisenhower as his personal attendant in 1942. Moaney and his wife, Dolores, a housekeeper, lived in the White House and were on what amounted to twenty-four-hour call. To show their appreciation, in June 1957 President and Mrs. Eisenhower played host to the Moaneys and forty of their friends from the African Methodist Episcopal Church on the Eastern Shore of Maryland. The group assembled in the Rose Garden with the first couple and then went on a special tour of the White House.[44]

But overall, the household staff considered Eisenhower very distant, not the outgoing, friendly fellow projected in his public image. Parks observed that, "Since everyone had parroted the slogan, 'I Like Ike,' I had thought that the president would have many friends, but he seemed to be clannish and to stick to just a few friends—all millionaires—whom he had known only since he had become an important general, and who were quickly nicknamed 'The White House Clan.' The leader was George Allen, who also owned a Gettysburg estate. Backstairs, we speculated that the man behind the 'I Like Ike' slogan was really sort of an introvert who liked to get away from people, and enjoyed painting because it was a solitary occupation. The real extrovert of the family was Mrs. Eisenhower, definitely."[45]

Yet Mrs. Eisenhower, despite her bubbly disposition, had serious health problems that slowed her down, including headaches, asthma, and uneven stamina, and she spent much time in bed, often not rising until lunchtime. Behind the scenes, the staff nicknamed her "Sleeping Beauty."[46]

Frederic Morrow, Eisenhower's lone black White House policy aide, had a mixed assessment of his boss on racial issues. He said the president was a strong leader in many ways, and he did take quiet but aggressive action to desegregate public areas of the District of Columbia. But Morrow, a former news employee at CBS, was also critical. "President Eisenhower's lukewarm stand on civil rights made me heartsick," Morrow wrote in a memoir. "I could trust this man never to do anything that would jeopardize the civil rights or the personal dignity of the American Negro, but it was obvious that he would never take any positive giant step to prove that he unequivocally stood for the right of every American to walk this land in dignity and peace, clothed with every privilege—as well as every responsibility—accorded a citizen of our Constitution. His failure to clearly and forthrightly respond to the Negro's plea for a strong position on civil rights was the greatest cross I had to bear in my eight years in Washington."[47]

And there were appalling obstacles to Morrow's living a normal life. Even though he was a member of the president's staff, Morrow had trouble finding adequate lodging because he was excluded from many rental apartments and houses because of his race. He couldn't play golf at some local courses because of his color, and he had difficulty recruiting secretaries because at first every member of the all-female, all-white White House secretarial pool declined. "None wants the onus of working for a colored boss," Morrow concluded at the time.[48] Eventually, a handful of secretaries relented, but the experience understandably left Morrow with a bitter feeling.

Morrow was occasionally criticized by Southern whites for moving too aggressively and by black leaders for moving too slowly on civil rights and for being Eisenhower's lackey.[49] He didn't want to be stereotyped as "Eisenhower's black man," so he tried to avoid discussions of civil rights in the White House, which kept the president and his aides from getting a firsthand African American perspective on racial issues from someone on the staff.[50] But Morrow never achieved the status of a true insider in the White House, and rarely had any direct contact with the president.

Chapter Eight
Camelot in Black and White

At first, President John F. Kennedy didn't make civil rights a priority. As with his three predecessors, he was much more focused on foreign affairs, especially America's ongoing confrontation with the Soviet Union in the cold war. White House adviser Theodore Sorensen said Kennedy didn't have any "background or association or activity in race relations," and he "simply did not give much thought to the subject" until he took office.[1]

Arthur Krock, a columnist for the *New York Times* who knew the Kennedy family well, said, "I never saw a Negro on level social terms with the Kennedys" and "never heard the subject [of race] mentioned." Kennedy had little contact with blacks throughout his life, including his time in the military during World War II. "There were no blacks on PT boats [where Kennedy served]; black sailors in the navy were usually cooks," writes historian Michael O'Brien.[2] "He didn't read about racial problems, discuss them with his friends, or develop empathy for the problems of African Americans." During his first campaign for the U.S. House of Representatives in 1946, he showed political savvy mixed with racial and religious bias when he joked to a friend that his World War II exploits as captain of PT-109 attracted more votes when he included "a Jew and a nigger in the story."[3]

Baseball star Jackie Robinson was one of many blacks who were troubled by Kennedy's racial attitudes, and his meeting with Kennedy prior to the 1960 election did not go well. "My very first reaction to the senator was one of doubt because he couldn't or wouldn't look me straight in the eye,"

Robinson recalled.[4] "... My mother had taught me to be wary of anyone who talked to you with head bowed or shifty eyes. My second reaction, much more substantial, was that this was a man who had served in the Senate and wanted to be president but who knew little or nothing about black problems or sensibilities. He himself admitted a lack of any depth of understanding about black people." Robinson was appalled.

The meeting reached its low point, Robinson wrote later, when Kennedy asked, "How much would it take" to get Robinson "on board the bandwagon?" Robinson replied, "Look, senator, I don't want any of your money. I'm just interested in helping the candidate who I think will be best for the black American because I am convinced that the black struggle and its solution are fundamental to the struggle to make America what it is supposed to be." The meeting ended in awkward embarrassment, and Robinson went on to endorse Republican Richard Nixon, the losing candidate that year.[5]

As president, most of Kennedy's initial concern about racial discrimination, like Truman's, stemmed from his sensitivity to possible international embarrassment. Kennedy felt that the Soviets could use America's shabby treatment of blacks to gain an edge in propaganda, especially in Africa and other regions where people of color dominated. For similar reasons, Kennedy also was upset when he received reports that diplomats from African nations were denied service or otherwise discriminated against in the United States. (Kennedy was not as upset when American citizens of color received the same treatment.) At his direction, the State Department worked with businesses and local governments in Washington and surrounding areas to help the black diplomats get access to decent housing and public facilities.[6] Containing communism was Kennedy's biggest priority, and he quickly grew frustrated when black and white leaders at home treated race relations, not fighting the cold war, as their biggest concern.[7]

Still, Kennedy had raised expectations among civil rights leaders when, during the 1960 campaign, he said racial discrimination in housing could be ended with the "stroke of a pen" by the president. Eventually, he issued Executive Order 11063 banning discrimination in federally assisted housing, but black leaders considered this measure far too limited.[8]

During the 1960 campaign, he also inflated the hopes of black activists when he phoned Coretta Scott King, Martin Luther King Jr.'s wife, to express his concern that her husband had been arrested in Atlanta on false charges. Word was leaked to civil rights leaders and the incident found its way into the African American press. King was released from jail and Kennedy's sensitivity impressed many black voters.

*   *   *

THE RACIAL DIVIDE hit Kennedy with special force on Inauguration Day in January 1961. As he looked out from the reviewing stand on the vast parade of 32,000 marchers, he couldn't help but notice that the participants were segregated. He was especially upset and angry that the honor guard from the U.S. Coast Guard did not include a single African American. After the parade, he complained about it to aide Richard Goodwin and said, "That's not acceptable. Something ought to be done about it."[9] It took a year, but in February 1962, a black cadet named Merle J. Smith became the first African American student in the eighty-six-year history of the Coast Guard Academy. The new president showed openness to change when he danced with black women at his inaugural balls, which had never happened before.[10]

But Kennedy disappointed African American leaders when he announced that he would not be introducing civil rights legislation during his first year as president. And while he named a record number of blacks to federal jobs and was the first president to openly host blacks at the White House for social events, he also appointed several segregationists to judgeships in areas where civil rights organizations were waging important court battles.[11] As political scientist Alvin Felzenberg points out, "Initially, Kennedy regarded demands for increased enforcement of civil rights provisions and new protection more as problems to be managed than as major priorities."[12]

On the positive side, Kennedy made sure that blacks were named to his Secret Service detail and his ceremonial honor guard. He urged that his appointees name more African Americans throughout the government, and he chose Andrew Hatcher as the first black press assistant at the White House. And First Lady Jacqueline Kennedy took a small step forward by organizing a private White House kindergarten to protect her daughter Caroline from media exposure if she attended such a school outside the White House grounds.[13] Mrs. Kennedy invited Hatcher's five-year-old son Avery to join, creating the first integrated White House nursery school.

Still, the Kennedy administration's moves were not significant compared with what would happen under some of his successors. "As had been the case for the previous fourteen years, the black aide Kennedy spent most time with was George Thomas," the president's valet, writes Kennedy biographer Nick Bryant. "His job each morning was to lay out the president's clothes."[14]

Thomas, in fact, was probably the black man that Kennedy knew best, bar none. Thomas, who was from a small town in Virginia, had been recommended to Kennedy, then a young U.S. representative from Massachusetts, by *New York Times* columnist Arthur Krock, who called Thomas "a fat, good-natured Negro of high competence as a domestic."[15]

Kennedy, the American aristocrat, had a few complaints about Thomas's sophistication, asking at one point, "Why can't he learn to tie a white tie?" But Thomas gave Kennedy his unstinting loyalty for many years. Thomas would slip into Kennedy's bedroom each morning and whisper, "Mr. President, it's close to 7:30," and sometimes shook a sleeping Kennedy's feet to awaken him without disturbing the first lady, if Mrs. Kennedy was with him at the time.[16] Thomas counted out the many pills that Kennedy took each day for his various ailments, ranging from chronic back pain to gastrointestinal trouble.[17] On a more mundane level, the vain new president liked to change his clothes four or more times each day, and Thomas dutifully pressed the president's shirts and suits. He would hang the fresh clothes and set aside clean socks and boxer shorts in a small bathroom off the Oval Office so the president could make a quick wardrobe shift.

Thomas would also draw the president a hot bath each morning and each afternoon.[18] It relaxed Kennedy and eased the pain in his back. After lunch, Thomas would close the drapes in the president's bedroom and Kennedy would take a nap at about 2:30 p.m. Jackie would often clear her schedule so she could join him. The first couple issued strict orders: The doors were to be closed, no phone calls were permitted, no paperwork sent in, no interruptions allowed. Thomas would gently knock on the door and tell the president when it was 3:30 and time to get back to work.

* * *

IN THE SPRING OF 1961, Kennedy's first year as president, black and white civil rights activists known as "freedom riders" challenged segregation on buses and in other public areas of Alabama. Attorney General Robert Kennedy, the president's brother, sent 600 federal marshals to stop a riot in Alabama after 1,000 freedom riders protested at bus terminal restaurants, restrooms, and waiting rooms.

Young whites and blacks were ever more aggressively but peacefully confronting authorities throughout the South and getting court orders to force compliance with a Supreme Court ruling that banned segregation on interstate buses. Administration officials put pressure on local authorities to protect demonstrators from violence.

In 1962, Kennedy enforced a court order aimed at requiring the University of Mississippi at Oxford to admit James Meredith, a black Air Force veteran, at the school, despite the opposition of Governor Ross Barnett. Kennedy sent in only 500 U.S. marshals, rather than the 1,000 troops dispatched by Eisenhower to Little Rock, and they had trouble managing the crowds of angry segregationists. About a third of the ill-equipped marshals suffered injuries from bricks and bottles thrown by mobs.[19] Two bystanders were killed, and numerous other civilians were injured. Kennedy got the crisis under control only after federalizing the Mississippi National Guard, which was already on the scene, and sending federal troops to support them. This removed the guardsmen from the control of local racist authorities.

"In response to the strife," writes Kennedy biographer Robert Dallek, "the Kennedys exercised greater executive leadership in behalf of civil rights than any administration in American history. They won judicial orders enjoining local police forces and anti-civil rights groups like the Ku Klux Klan from interfering with interstate travel. They persuaded the Interstate Commerce Commission to end segregation in interstate bus terminals. They filed forty-two lawsuits on behalf of black voting rights, and helped win congressional approval of the Twenty-fourth Amendment to the Constitution—anti-poll tax. They also appointed forty blacks to important administration posts, and put Thurgood Marshall, the winning counsel in the landmark 1954 school desegregation case, *Brown v. Board of Education,* on the federal Circuit Court of Appeals in New York."[20]

"Yet most civil rights advocates saw the Kennedy administration's response to the struggle for black equality as inadequate," Dallek continues. "Above all, Kennedy refused to take on the Congress, and particularly its southern power brokers, by asking for a major civil rights law. The Kennedys justified their inaction by pointing out that not even a 1962 literacy bill guaranteeing voter registration for anyone with a sixth-grade education could overcome a southern filibuster. The argument carried little weight with civil rights advocates, who pointed to [Kennedy's] timidity in issuing an executive order desegregating federally supported housing. When the president finally acted in November 1962, using the simple 'stroke of a pen' he had promised in the 1960 campaign, his order was limited to future housing. Moreover, his refusal to lobby the Senate for a change in Rule 22 from a two-thirds vote to a three-fifths vote to end filibusters confirmed the view that he would not risk any part of his legislative program for the sake of civil rights."

*   *   *

KENNEDY'S PERSONAL DEALINGS with black leaders slowly grew more intense as civil rights protests proliferated and Kennedy found it more important politically to court African American voters.

On February 12, 1963, Kennedy hosted 800 African Americans at the White House for a reception marking Lincoln's birthday and the 100-year anniversary of the Emancipation Proclamation.[21] It was the largest gathering of blacks at the White House up until that time and more blacks in one night than had visited the White House, in total, in all its previous history.

The event was a huge political success, impressing black voters and civil rights activists across the country, but it was marked by an incident that also showed Kennedy's lingering racial prejudices. The president was distressed when he saw black entertainer Sammy Davis Jr. and his blonde Swedish wife, Mai Britt, at the reception.[22] Kennedy worried that a photo of them could cause him major embarrassment because so many Americans opposed interracial marriage. "Get them out of here," Kennedy ordered an aide.

He had earlier banned Davis and his wife from his inauguration because he feared offending white Southerners, even though Davis had backed Kennedy in the 1960 campaign. However, the Davises weren't ejected from the Lincoln's birthday event. Instead, Kennedy and his wife left the reception after half an hour to have a private dinner with associates upstairs at the White House residence, partly so no photos could be taken of the Kennedys and the Davises.

Davis was deeply hurt, and his feelings were still raw two decades later when he gave a rare interview to *Ebony* Magazine. "You see, the Democrats have always hurt me," Davis said. "I supported John F. Kennedy, I did everything I could for him and then I was told not to come to the

White House because it would embarrass the president. So here I am being treated as an outcast by the Democrats."[23]

Davis was later swathed in controversy when he hugged President Richard Nixon in public, sparking widespread criticism of Davis by other African Americans who disliked the GOP leader.[24] Davis said he warmed to Nixon after the candidate's aides promised that Nixon would adopt policies helpful to black Americans, but he later regretted his embrace.

As his term progressed and tensions mounted in the South, Kennedy showed more concern for civil rights and for the safety of demonstrators. In the spring and summer of 1963, Kennedy got more aggressive than ever. At first, Kennedy and the Reverend Martin Luther King Jr. felt no personal connection to each other, and the young president kept the increasingly influential young civil rights leader at a distance. Kennedy didn't trust King and wasn't sure where the black leader's commitment to mass protests in addition to lobbying and lawsuits would lead.

In the spring of 1963, Kennedy grudgingly agreed to meet with King, head of the Southern Christian Leadership Conference, but he told aides it was like "inviting Karl Marx to the White House." Kennedy preferred to deal with the more predictable and conventional black leaders Roy Wilkins, executive director of the NAACP, and Whitney Young, president of the National Urban League.[25]

That April, King began his relentless campaign to desegregate Birmingham, Alabama, the largest segregated city in the country. Police Chief Eugene "Bull" Connor allowed his men to beat protesters and use cattle prods, high-pressure hoses, and police dogs on them. Kennedy privately told associates at the White House that these scenes on the TV news made him sick.[26]

On May 2, for example, Kennedy saw newspaper photos and television images of dogs turned by Connor on demonstrators in Birmingham during a peaceful protest.[27] Kennedy was impressed by the demonstrators' courage and horrified by the viciousness of Connor's deputies. When he saw a photo of a dog in the process of biting a young man in the stomach, the president told aides he was particularly disgusted.

The following month, in June 1963, Alabama Governor George Wallace tried to block a schoolhouse door when African American students sought to enter the University of Alabama at Tuscaloosa. This, coupled with more violence in Birmingham, prompted Kennedy to give a strong speech condemning the oppression of blacks a hundred years after the

Emancipation Proclamation and asking Congress to enact the most comprehensive civil rights law in history.

Privately, Kennedy aides had been very busy in Alabama, paving the way for the public actions in Washington. They persuaded state officials, trustees, and faculty members to support desegregation, and nearly 100 corporations in the area agreed to hire African Americans as a gesture of conciliation. Kennedy again federalized the National Guard, and he made it known that U.S. troops from Fort Benning, Georgia, were on alert to be helicoptered in if things got out of hand. Wallace backed off.

That evening, Kennedy described civil rights as a moral issue, the first modern president to do so. "It is as old as the Scriptures and as clear as the Constitution," he said in a national address.[28] "The heart of the question is whether . . . we are going to treat our fellow Americans as we want to be treated." Kennedy described the abuses endured by blacks and asked other Americans if they would accept similar treatment for long. He promised to send major civil rights legislation to Congress within a week, and that bill became the landmark Civil Rights Act of 1964, enacted under President Lyndon Johnson after Kennedy's assassination in November 1963. The measure was designed to end segregation in all public places nationwide and to give the attorney general the power to sue on behalf of black children to desegregate white schools.

Meanwhile, King and his allies began organizing a massive march on Washington to pressure Congress, and Kennedy grew concerned that the march would alienate legislators who felt that they were being backed into a corner and that they needed to stand up to what their constituents might consider a political threat. So Kennedy asked King and other organizers to the White House to talk things over and perhaps postpone the march until the political atmosphere was less volatile.

On June 22, 1963, Preston Bruce, an African American doorman, met the black leaders at the North Door of the White House and took them to the Red Room to meet with Kennedy to discuss the upcoming march. They included King, Whitney Young of the Urban League, A. Phillip Randolph of the Brotherhood of Sleeping Car Porters, James Farmer of the Congress of Racial Equality, and Roy Wilkins and Clarence Mitchell, leaders of the NAACP. "In the Red Room," Bruce recalled, "A. Phillip Randolph, Whitney Young, and Clarence Mitchell came up to me and we talked for fifteen minutes. They wanted to know if, in my personal opinion, John F. Kennedy was a fair and sincere man. Or was he just another false politician saying things he didn't really mean? I told them I had had only fair treatment from the president and that I believed both he and his brother cared heart and soul about justice for black people."[29]

Kennedy then appeared and escorted the black leaders to the Cabinet Room for their meeting. After the president expressed his doubts about whether the march was a good idea, he said, "We want success in Congress, not just a big show at the Capitol."[30] But the leaders insisted that the march should go forward. Martin Luther King Jr. said that even though Kennedy might think the march was "ill-timed," he felt that, "Frankly, I have never engaged in any direct action movement which did not seem ill-timed." King added that the protest "could also serve as a means of dramatizing the issue and mobilizing support in parts of the country which don't know the problems at first hand. I think it will serve a purpose."

Finally, Kennedy accepted the idea that the march should proceed. "This is a very serious fight," he told the black leaders. ". . . What is important is that we preserve confidence in the good faith of each other. I have my problems with the Congress: You have yours with your own groups. We will undoubtedly disagree from time to time on tactics. But the important thing is to keep in touch."[31]

After the meeting, the leaders said the march would end at the Lincoln Memorial rather than the Capitol, so that members of Congress wouldn't feel they were under siege. And Kennedy announced his support for this "peaceful assembly."

In the end, nearly 250,000 people gathered at the Memorial on August 28, 1963, for the march, in which King gave his most iconic speech calling for racial justice. "I have a dream that on the red hills of Georgia the sons of former slaves and the sons of former slave owners will be able to sit together at the table of brotherhood," he said.

Bruce said Kennedy left the Oval Office early that day and asked Bruce to accompany him to the third-floor solarium in the residence. They stood together at the window, and even though they couldn't see the crowd through the trees they heard the massive group sing "We Shall Overcome." Kennedy's voice "choked," Bruce recalled, and he said, "Oh, Bruce, I wish I were out there with them."[32]

In a televised address to the nation after the march, Kennedy said, "One hundred years of delay have passed since President Lincoln freed the slaves, yet their heirs, their grandsons, are not fully free. They are not yet freed from the bonds of injustice. They are not yet freed from social and economic oppression, and this nation, for all its hopes and all its boasts, will not be fully free until all its citizens are free."

*   *   *

BEHIND THE SCENES, Preston Bruce was a mainstay of the household staff for many years, with extensive duties in running the residential East Wing of the White House, and he saw many contrasts between Kennedy and his predecessors. "The Eisenhowers had stuck to a schedule that could be depended on," Bruce wrote in his memoirs. "Every night at ten o'clock when I'd go to up to secure the house, they'd be settled into bed for the night, their bedroom doors safely closed. But the Kennedys were night owls, and I never knew what to expect. Several times as I came down the East Hall I interrupted the President and Mrs. Kennedy, in skimpy nightclothes, scampering back and forth across the hall to each other's bedrooms. I was embarrassed even though they didn't seem to mind."[33]

Bruce resolved to mention the problem to the first couple when the moment seemed right. One evening, when they returned from a dinner party, Bruce met them at the East Entrance and he later described them as "very lovey-dovey, kissing and hugging each other." He accompanied them upstairs to the residence in their private elevator, according to custom, and decided this was the moment. As they left the elevator and started walking down the hall, he nervously raised the issue of their privacy.

"Perhaps I shouldn't ask you this, but I'd be very happy if you'd tell me how I should secure the lights in your section of the house."

Kennedy asked, "Well, how did you do it before?"

Bruce answered, "We turned the lights out at ten o'clock each night in all the rooms that can be seen from the outside of the house."

Kennedy said, "Well, you do it just the way you've always done it."

Then Bruce finally got to the point. "When it comes to your area, should I come in there to put them out?"

"Yes, sure, come right ahead," Kennedy replied.

But Mrs. Kennedy, with what Bruce described as "a twinkle in her eye," finally spoke up. "Don't worry, Bruce," she said. "We know you're married too." From then on Bruce went upstairs and turned out the lights at 10 p.m. He didn't say what he observed there, but presumably the Kennedys didn't feel the need to be more discreet in front of their married staffer.[34]

Bruce got to know Kennedy so well that they developed a little ritual.[35] Several times a week, the president would ask Bruce to borrow his comb, would groom himself with it, and would then put the comb in his pocket. Bruce thought it was a strange quirk but he made sure to keep a supply of fresh combs at the ready at all times.

*　*　*

YET KENNEDY'S RELATIONSHIP with his black staff was not a profile in courage. "The largely African American household staff admired the first lady's manners and her restoration of the mansion they revered," writes historian Michael Beschloss.[36] "If the truth be told, they were less comfortable with her husband. This was not because they found the president laggard on civil rights. Most of the southern blacks who had served the White House for years were anything but firebrands. They were disconcerted by his complex private life, which was foreign to them and made them feel like accomplices against the first lady they respected. Kennedy's attitude was that a president's private relationships should be off limits, even to historians. When an Oxford friend once nattered about the mistress of some past leader, [Kennedy] cut him off: 'Not at all a way to treat a great man.'"[37]

But there were a few positive signs. At a news conference in late April 1961, President Kennedy was criticized by a reporter for *Jet,* an African American–oriented magazine, for planning to attend an awards banquet scheduled for May 19 and sponsored by the all-white White House Photographers Association.[38] Kennedy was uncharacteristically thrown off balance. His faced reddened and he said with some embarrassment that he would investigate the situation. His aides said he might not attend unless the group added a black photographer in its membership immediately. The association accommodated him and hastily granted membership to Maurice Sorrell, then a photographer for the Afro-American Newspapers group in Washington.[39]

Kennedy was probably prodded to take this stand by his wife, Jacqueline, who seemed more sensitive to racial issues than he did, especially at the start of his presidency. In fact, *Ebony* magazine reported that Mrs. Kennedy had more African Americans as social guests at the White House during the three years of her husband's presidency than at any other span of time. "Mrs. Kennedy completely changed the White House social pattern by simply including Negroes on virtually every guest list she prepared," said *Ebony.* "As a result more Negroes were White House guests than throughout the years since the venerable mansion was built."[40]

The magazine said Mrs. Kennedy's friendships with blacks predated her marriage to John F. Kennedy and that she learned to be a photographer from Robert Scurlock, a black man who operated a photo studio in the capital. She learned the trade after college in order to work as an inquiring photographer for the *Washington Post.*

"Mrs. Kennedy did not forget the man who started her on her brief journalistic career and rewarded Scurlock later by letting him take exclusive photos of her husband and herself," *Ebony* said. The magazine praised Mrs. Kennedy for including blacks "in a part of American life, which most of her predecessors had considered the exclusive domain of whites"—the social life of the White House.

Among the black entertainers invited to the White House by Mrs. Kennedy was mezzo soprano Grace Bumbry, who performed selections from Richard Strauss, Henri Duparc, and Aaron Copeland and sang a spiritual called "Out in Fields with God" at a state dinner in February 1962. And Mrs. Kennedy insisted that "the racial makeup of the honor guard that accompanied the president's body at his funeral [in November 1963] must at all times be integrated," *Ebony* reported.

* * *

ON POLICY, President Kennedy's aggressiveness on civil rights came too late. As Kennedy biographer Nick Bryant writes, "Kennedy had become president at a turning point in American history. By the end of the 1950s, many segregationists had come to accept the vulnerability of their position. Southern blacks looked forward to the day—just around the corner it seemed—when they would finally enjoy first-class citizenship. An optimistic civil rights movement remained resolutely committed to the idea of nonviolent, peaceful change. A majority of Americans were favorably disposed toward racial reform. At the time of his presidential victory, Kennedy had a unique opportunity to secure a peaceful transition toward a more integrated and equitable society."[41]

Kennedy, like Washington, Jefferson, and Andrew Johnson, missed a historic opportunity to advance the civil rights of blacks. Kennedy developed a new commitment to help African Americans only after the violent clashes between the white power structure in the South and civil rights demonstrators in 1963, but by then it was too late. Kennedy squandered more than two crucial years when he did not adopt stronger policies that might have calmed fears and closed divisions. Instead, as Bryant argues, he failed to act decisively, a huge failure that allowed Southern resentments to fester, encouraged white supremacists, and pushed thousands of black demonstrators to be even more confrontational.[42]

CHAPTER NINE
THE BREAKTHROUGH

Blacks made enormous strides under Lyndon B. Johnson, both in the larger society and at the White House itself. Johnson embraced the Kennedy agenda on civil rights and other issues, pushed it quickly through Congress as a tribute to the martyred president, and then built on it in fundamental ways.

Johnson was not a stranger to civil rights advocacy. For years, the Texas Democrat and loyal backer of Franklin Roosevelt's New Deal had believed that his own support for black advancement, although limited, was a way to establish himself as a national figure. Johnson didn't want to be known as just another bigoted, parochial Southern politician as he prepared to move from Congress to the presidency. "As a congressman and a senator, he had helped black farmers, provided low-cost housing to blacks and Hispanics, and slightly reduced legal roadblocks to black voting in the South through the 1957 and 1960 civil rights laws," writes historian Robert Dallek, who argues that Johnson over the years had developed a "sense of fairness and compassion" toward blacks as a disadvantaged minority.[1]

During the 1940s and 1950s, Johnson repeatedly warned that the patience of blacks was wearing thin. "The Negro fought in the war, and … he's not gonna keep taking the shit we're dishing out," Johnson told a friend. "We're in a race with time. If we don't act, we're gonna have blood in the streets."[2]

During his vice presidency under John F. Kennedy, he served as chairman of the Committee on Equal Employment Opportunity

(CEEO), which was designed by Kennedy advisers to help blacks gain access to more jobs. Johnson felt it was a way to broaden his appeal in the North, especially among liberals whom he feared might try to block any presidential bid he might begin for 1968. On the other hand, he was also concerned that chairing the CEEO might hurt him with Southern conservatives who felt he was moving too fast. He tried to steer the panel in a moderate direction that didn't anger any faction. As a result, there were some employment gains for blacks, Dallek says, "Yet these CEEO gains barely made a dent in black unemployment or satisfied the demand for comprehensive civil rights legislation that would challenge the whole Jim Crow system of segregation across the South."[3]

*   *   *

AS SOON AS he became president after Kennedy's assassination in November 1963, Johnson saw a heightened commitment to civil rights as not only the right thing to do, but also a way to make his presidency historic. Within two weeks, he met with black leaders, including Roy Wilkins, executive director of the NAACP, and Whitney Young, president of the National Urban League, to coordinate strategy. Both were moderates. A bit later, he hosted the controversial Reverend Martin Luther King Jr. of the Southern Christian Leadership Conference and an advocate of non-violent confrontation and mass action. It was a signal to the country that the new president was on the side of African Americans and was ready to move fast. It also marked the start of a turbulent relationship with King, in which Johnson would work closely with the black leader but privately allow the FBI under J. Edgar Hoover to gather intelligence purportedly showing that King was linked to communists and was an adulterer. This was done in case Johnson needed embarrassing information to use against King at some point.[4]

Johnson and King would meet periodically at the White House or talk strategy on the phone. Johnson, always eager to exert his mastery over others, was the dominant partner and totally in control, but the sessions were conducted with mutual respect and a recognition that they were making history together and needed each other to be most effective in reaching their goals.

An illustration of their symbiotic relationship came on January 15, 1965, when the president phoned King to mark the civil rights leader's thirty-sixth birthday. King was in Selma, Alabama, organizing a voter registration drive and Johnson was challenging Congress to approve a vast agenda of social activism. "The president and the civil rights leader—the politician and the preacher—were bouncing ideas off each other like two old allies in a campaign strategy huddle, excited about achieving their dreams for a more just society," writes author Nick Kotz. "Here was Johnson, never an admirer of King's direct-action tactics, now advising King about how to put pressure on Congress for voting rights. And King, never quite sure of Johnson's motives, was advising Johnson on how to get re-elected in 1968."[5]

King told Johnson it was important for the president to name the first African American to the cabinet. "It would really be a great step forward for the nation, for the Negro, and for the national image," King said.[6] "I am sure it would give a new sense of dignity and self respect to millions of Negroes." Johnson agreed, and said he hoped to select Robert Weaver, the federal housing administrator, to be the first secretary of housing and urban development, heading a new department.

Johnson urged King to help him win passage for Medicare, federal aid to education, and funds to aid the poor, in addition to a voting rights bill to guarantee the vote to blacks and abolish poll taxes. "There is not going to be anything, Doctor, as effective as all voting," Johnson said. "That will give you a message that all the eloquence in the world won't bring."

King replied, "You're exactly right about that. It's very interesting, Mr. President, to notice that the only states that you didn't carry in the South [in the 1964 election]—the five southern states—had less than 40 percent of the Negroes registered to vote. So it demonstrates that it is so important to get Negroes registered to vote in large numbers; it would be this coalition of the Negro vote and the moderate white vote that would really make the New South."

Johnson exclaimed, "That is exactly right!"

Eventually, their relationship soured when King pursued his strategy of confronting authorities, which in Johnson's view alienated many Americans and members of Congress because the showdowns sometimes led to violence. Another source of deep friction came when King began to attack Johnson's escalation of the war in Vietnam.

* * *

DESPITE THE SHAKINESS of the Johnson-King partnership, the civil rights issue had become personal with the president, in large part because of the experiences of a black member of his household staff. Johnson told friends and legislators how Zephyr Wright, his college-educated, African American cook, had a few years earlier driven then-Vice President Johnson's official car with her husband from Washington to Texas, and they weren't allowed to use the restrooms at gas stations. Relating the story to the powerful Senator John Stennis of Mississippi, a segregationist, Johnson said, "When they had to go to the bathroom, they would ... pull off on a side road, and Zephyr Wright, the cook of the Vice President of the United States, would squat in the road to pee." Johnson added: "That's wrong. And there ought to be something to change that. And it seems to me that if people in Mississippi don't change it voluntarily, that it's just going to be necessary to change it by law."[7]

Wright also figured prominently in another incident that appalled both Johnson and his wife, Lady Bird.[8] While Johnson was a senator in the 1950s, ambulance companies in Washington refused to pick Wright up after she fell on an icy sidewalk and broke her leg. Johnson finally managed to get medical attention for her but he and his wife always remembered the racial discrimination that they observed in this incident. As a Southerner who had thrived in politics by adjusting to segregation, Johnson at first seemed like an unreliable civil rights advocate. And, as with John F. Kennedy, Dwight Eisenhower, Harry Truman, and Franklin Roosevelt, sometimes his private attitudes came to the surface. In January 1964, he told a Texas friend, "I'm gonna try to teach these nigras that don't know anything how to work for themselves instead of just breedin'; I'm gonna try to teach these Mexicans who can't talk English to learn it so they can work for themselves ... and get off of our taxpayer's back."[9]

Johnson's racial attitudes often were dominated by his sense of what would do him the most good politically. On June 11, 1967, he met with Larry Temple, a Texas lawyer he was courting for a job in the White House counsel's office. "I have a Supreme Court appointment coming up," Johnson said. "Who would you recommend?" When Temple suggested Judge A. Leon Higginbotham, an African American whom Johnson had earlier named to federal court in Pennsylvania, Johnson replied crudely, and possibly to impress his guest with his toughness, "Larry, the only two people who ever heard of Judge Higginbotham are you and his momma. When I appoint a nigger to the bench, I want everyone to know he's a nigger."[10]

At the same time, Johnson resolved to overcome his condescension and racist feelings and pull the electorate along toward enlightenment on race. "I'm going to be the president who finished what Lincoln began," he said on more than one occasion.[11]

To that end, he called Senator Richard Russell of Georgia, a segregationist, into the White House a few days after becoming president and said he was intent on passing a massive civil rights bill as soon as possible. In typically blunt terms, Johnson added, "Dick, you've got to get out of my way. I'm going to run over you. I don't intend to cavil or compromise." Russell replied, "You may do that. But by God, it's going to cost you the South and cost you the election." Johnson said, "If that's the price I've got to pay, I'll pay it gladly."[12] After signing the Civil Rights Act of 1964, he told aides "We have just lost the South for a generation."[13]

That was at least partly true, but on balance it was smart politics. It brought millions of black voters, in the South and other parts of the country, more firmly into the Democratic fold—and into Johnson's camp. Of course his civil rights stance wouldn't cost him the 1964 presidential election, either. In fact, Johnson defeated Republican conservative Barry Goldwater by a landslide.

Johnson also felt at first that he could find common ground with Martin Luther King Jr.[14] He came to agree with King adviser Clarence Jones, who said the president and the civil rights leader shared a common Southern heritage and sensibility regarding poverty, racial divisions, religion, food, music, and speech, and they could communicate much more easily than Kennedy and King ever could.

*   *   *

FROM THE START OF his presidency, Johnson moved with dizzying speed to win passage for social legislation, including the Civil Rights Act of 1964 and the Voting Rights Act of 1965, and to take the high road on race. He gave many speeches espousing his strong support for civil rights and justice for African Americans. As he had suggested to Dr. King, he named Robert Weaver, the administrator of the Housing and Home Finance Agency, as the first black cabinet member—secretary of the new Department of Housing and Urban Development. He appointed Gerri Whittington as his secretary, thereby integrating his personal staff.[15] Later, in 1967, he named Thurgood Marshall, the famous civil rights lawyer and federal judge whom Johnson had earlier named Solicitor General of the United States, as the first black justice on the Supreme Court. He considered these appointments justified in their own right, since his black choices were superbly qualified. But he also believed his nominations would elevate Weaver and Marshall to the status of role models for young African Americans, who could now see that they could achieve great things if they applied themselves.

He was capable of dramatic personal gestures that left a lasting impact. Among Johnson's many African American guests at the White House was singer Sarah Vaughan, who performed at a state dinner to enthusiastic applause. But then she vanished from the event. Bess Abell, the White House social secretary, found Vaughan sobbing in an office that had been provided as a dressing room. Asked by Abell what was wrong, Vaughan replied, "There's nothing wrong. This is the most wonderful day of my life. When I first came to Washington, I couldn't get a hotel room, and tonight, I danced with the president."

When Secretary of State Dean Rusk offered to resign because his daughter planned to marry a black man, Johnson said no.[16] Rusk feared that an interracial marriage within the family of a cabinet member would draw criticism to Johnson. But the president wasn't bothered at all and graciously congratulated Rusk on the impending wedding. Family friends said the incident showed how enlightened Johnson was becoming.

Despite his past as a senator from segregated Texas, Johnson's rhetoric and his actions became sensitive to the black struggle. Addressing a joint session of Congress on January 8, 1964, for his first State of the Union address, he declared, "Let this session of Congress be known as the session which did more for civil rights than the last hundred sessions combined. As far as the writ of federal law will run, we must abolish not some but all racial discrimination, for this is not merely an economic issue or a social, political, or international issue. It is a moral issue—and it must be met by the passage this session of the [civil rights] bill now pending in the House."[17]

Johnson added: "All members of the public should have equal access to facilities open to the public. All members of the public should be equally eligible for federal benefits that are financed by the public. All members of the public should have an equal chance to vote for public officials and to send their children to good public schools and to contribute their talents to the public good.... Today, Americans of all races stand side by side in Vietnam and Berlin. They died side by side in Korea. Surely they can work and eat and travel side by side in their own country."[18]

He felt he had become a savior to many blacks. During a 1964 campaign stop in Texas he said, "When I get out of that car you can just see them light up and feel the warmth coming up at you ... those Negroes go off the ground. They cling to my hands like I was Jesus Christ walking in their midst."[19]

And if such assessments were overblown, his rhetoric and his actions did set his presidency apart on racial matters. In a June 4, 1965, commencement speech at Howard University, a historically black school in Washington, DC, Johnson won the admiration of civil rights leaders when he said American Negroes were "another nation: deprived of freedom, crippled by hatred, the doors of opportunity closed to hope" and he said freedom was no longer enough.[20] "You do not take a person who, for years, has been hobbled by chains and liberate him, bring him up to the starting line of a race and then say, 'you are free to compete with all the others,' and still justly believe that you have been completely fair. Thus it is not enough just to open the gates of opportunity. All our citizens must have the ability to walk through those gates. This is the next and the more profound stage of the battle for civil rights. We seek ... not just equality as a right and a theory but equality as a fact and equality as a result."

The iconic baseball star Jackie Robinson, who had fought against racism as the first African American in the major leagues, was won over by Johnson after having endorsed Republican Richard Nixon in the 1960 presidential race (which he later regretted). "I wasn't always happy with President Johnson in the White House, of course, but I have to admit that he did a courageous job of translating into hard legislation some of the key issues of the civil rights movement," Robinson wrote in his memoirs. "... [T]here's something really unusual about a southerner who was once a dyed-in-the-wool states' righter and who, for whatever reason, changes his mind. Somehow it seems that those from below the Mason–Dixon Line who come over to the liberal cause bring with them a firmness and sincerity that northern liberals don't have. Harry Truman displayed some of this and President Johnson even more."[21]

But Johnson's attempts to guarantee equality of result—instead of equality of opportunity—angered many white voters who felt that the president was attempting to give blacks unfair advantages. Just as important, many blacks were angry that they remained second-class citizens in many ways, and there were numerous incidents of urban unrest.

*   *   *

BEHIND THE SCENES, African Americans had a powerful ally in the president's wife, Lady Bird Johnson, in a repetition of the pattern with Eleanor Roosevelt. Historian Carl Sferrazza Anthony traces her support for civil rights to "her childhood friendship with a servant's daughter. Although Johnson had herself been victimized—she was spat upon when speaking of civil rights during the 1960 presidential campaign and was denigrated in a John Birch Society publication because she had held hands with African-American women at her receptions—she marched on."[22]

"When President Lyndon B. Johnson signed the 1964 Civil Rights Act," Anthony adds, "Lady Bird Johnson was the only woman present— seated in the first row. During the 1964 campaign, she took a train trip throughout the southern states, emphasizing the need for integration. Threatened by the Klan and signs like 'Fly Away Black Bird,' she nevertheless persisted in her espousal of civil rights."[23]

She also helped to get Walter Washington, an African American, appointed as the District of Columbia's first mayor under home rule.[24] Mrs. Johnson made a practice of driving through poor areas in Washington to determine which schools, parks, and neighborhoods were most in need of help.

*   *   *

DESPITE THE EFFORTS of Johnson, Lady Bird, and Dr. King, the nation's racial climate became stormier and more violent. The promise of reconciliation seemed strong when Johnson held a televised ceremony to sign the Civil Rights Act of 1964 on July 2, just in time for Independence Day. The law voided the Jim Crow laws that had denied African Americans access to voting booths, public schools, and public accommodations for so many generations. But later that summer there would be a dozen bombings of black churches, homes, and businesses, and racial tensions rose across the country.[25]

Less than a week after Johnson signed the Voting Rights Act of 1965, a huge riot devastated the overwhelmingly black Watts section of Los Angeles, long afflicted with high rates of crime and unemployment. The riot erupted on August 11 when white police officers arrested a black man for drunk driving.[26] Over the course of six days, 34 people were killed, nearly 900 were treated at hospitals for injuries, 4,000 were arrested, and millions of dollars were lost in damage from arson and vandalism. An estimated 14,000 national guardsmen were sent in to help the Los Angeles police restore order.

"In retrospect, the Watts riot marked a fateful watershed for the Johnson administration and the Great Society," writes historian Hugh Davis Graham.[27] "In the euphoria of signing the Voting Rights Act, Johnson could legitimately bask in the knowledge that the momentum of the Great Society was producing a cornucopia of achievement for 1965: the Voting Rights Act, Medicare, federal aid to education, urban mass transit, the new Department of Housing and Urban Development, clean air and water pollution programs, immigration reform, national endowments for the arts and the humanities. Johnson's popularity ratings were soaring, and the media had grown respectful of the political genius of the former 'cornpone' vice president. Johnson had achieved a White House intimacy with Martin Luther King Jr., Roy Wilkins, and Whitney Young, and he even seemed to enjoy a surprising rapport with the university-based community of intellectuals with whom he had always been uncomfortable."

But over the three summers of 1965–1967, riots in many cities resulted in 225 deaths, 4,000 wounded, and $112 billion in property damage.[28] Racial hostility appeared to be spinning out of control.

Martin Luther King Jr., who was brilliantly organizing protests around the country, criticized Johnson for not doing enough to help black people in the ghettoes, and Johnson was offended. At one point in 1965, after the Watts riot, Johnson was standing in the elevator with doorman Preston Bruce, and asked him, "Bruce, do you think I am doing all I can for black people?"

"Yes, I do, Mr. President, unless there is some way you can go inside each person's mind and change that," replied Bruce.

"Well, damn it, did you read what Martin Luther King Jr. just said about me?" Johnson asked angrily.

Bruce said "Yes, I read all that, Mr. President, but I don't agree with him. I wish he knew as much about what you've done as I do."

Johnson answered, "Thanks, Bruce. You are one of the dearest friends I have."[29]

The relationship between Johnson and King got worse. Not only did King keep up the pressure on Johnson to move faster on civil rights and economic justice, he also stepped up his criticism of the administration over the Vietnam War. And as the decade of the sixties unfolded, urban riots became more and more common.

Black nationalists were radicalizing once-mainstream organizations such as the Student Non-violent Coordinating Committee (SNCC) and the Congress of Racial Equality (CORE), moving them from interracial coalitions to separatism. More and more blacks were rejecting King's methods of nonviolence as ineffective and weak. The confrontational "black power" movement captured the media's attention. "Within a year of the explosion in Watts, the stereotypical image of black America in the national media had been transformed—from nonviolent victims of Klan terrorism, to looting rioters crying, 'Burn, baby, burn,'" says Graham.[30] ". . . White Americans were shocked by the Watts riot and resented the surge of black separatist rhetoric from the leaders of SNCC and CORE."

A Harris poll in mid-1966 showed that 75 percent of white voters believed that blacks were moving too fast, up from 50 percent in 1964. A new administration civil rights bill, aimed at ensuring fairness in housing, was rejected by Congress in 1966. That November, the white backlash resulted in the Republicans' capturing from the Democrats eight governorships, three Senate seats, and forty-seven House seats. The civil rights coalition had evaporated.

*　*　*

ON JANUARY 18, 1966, the hostilities of the era suddenly broke into the genteel atmosphere of the residential East Wing.[31] Lady Bird was hosting a group of "Women Doers" in the upstairs family dining room to talk about how to control crime. But Eartha Kitt, an African American singer and an invited guest, suddenly stood up and addressed the first lady. "Boys I know across the nation feel it doesn't pay to be a good guy," Kitt said. "They figure with a record they don't have to go off to Vietnam. We send the best of the country off to be shot and maimed. . . . They don't want to go to school because they are going to be snatched from their mothers to be shot in Vietnam. . . . You are a mother, too. I am a mother and I know the feeling of having a baby come out of my guts. I have a baby and then you send him off to war. No wonder the kids rebel and take pot. And, Mrs. Johnson, in case you don't understand the lingo, that's marijuana!"

Mrs. Johnson, her voice trembling, replied, "Because there is a war on, that doesn't give us a free ticket not to try to work for better things—against crime in the streets, and for better education and better health for our people. I cannot identify as much as I should. I have not lived the background that you have, nor can I speak as passionately or as well, but we must keep our eyes and our hearts and our energies fixed on constructive areas and try to do something that will make this a happier, better educated land."[32]

* * *

IN THE PRIVACY of the White House, the notoriously hot-tempered Johnson was just as ornery and abusive to his black household staffers at the White House as he was to everyone else.

Preston Bruce, the longtime doorman, felt Johnson's wrath from the start. On December 7, 1963, Johnson and his family moved into the White House, still draped in black after Kennedy's funeral less than three weeks earlier, and the trouble began.

Johnson held a big reception in the family quarters for more than 200 people to bring his own staff and the remaining Kennedy staff together for a social occasion. But holding it in the out-of-the-way family quarters at the last minute was a strain on Bruce and the rest of the household staff. As the guests were leaving, Bruce was escorting one batch after another out of the residence when he noticed the light on the president's elevator blinking.

"The moment the elevator door opened upstairs, there was big, tall Lyndon B. Johnson," Bruce recalled.[33] "His craggy face was beet red and he seemed to fill up the whole doorway. He bore down on me, yelling at the top of his lungs, 'Where have you been? I've been *waiting* and *waiting* for this elevator!' He stuck out his chest and stomach and moved in on me as if he would run me right over."

Bruce was furious at the abuse, and he stood his ground, explaining, "Mr. President, I've been trying to get your guests out of the house. I know how to do it, but I must have time."

Johnson said, "If you don't have someone to help, tell them to hire someone!"

"Well, Mr. President," Bruce replied coldly, "if *you* call the Usher's Office, I'm sure they'll be delighted to do that."

Bruce left the White House that night considering whether to quit. He doubted that he could work for someone as inconsiderate and hot-tempered as the new president. And there was the possibility that he would be fired. But the next evening, when he saw Johnson, the president was all smiles. "Well, here's my old friend Bruce. How ya doin' Bruce? Howdya feel tonight?"

The tempest had passed, and Bruce remained on staff. Things didn't get any easier, but at least Bruce and his colleagues gradually came to understand that Johnson would fly into fits of temper or rudeness, but become gracious and polite a bit later. It was his personality, and he treated everyone that way. And Bruce became an admirer of Johnson's social policies, especially his aggressive and successful efforts to guarantee and expand civil rights.

*   *   *

ON A MORE mundane level, tensions were rising on the household staff. Johnson and Lady Bird preferred the meals of Zephyr Wright, their long-time black cook, to the food prepared by Rene Verdon, a sophisticated French chef who had been in charge of the kitchen under Kennedy and was retained by Johnson.

"Most of the time," wrote Chief Usher J. B. West, "Zephyr cooked upstairs, turning out meals for four to fourteen, the way she'd done for years. She knew their likes and dislikes so well that she rarely even asked Mrs. Johnson what to cook. Every now and then, though, the Johnsons would hold a more formal dinner party in the second-floor dining room ... with Rene preparing the food."[34]

A showdown erupted over Wright's salary. She had been cooking for the Johnsons while LBJ was vice president, for $500 a month.[35] But when Johnson became president in November 1963, Wright realized that the French chef was making three times her salary, and she demanded pay equal to Verdon's. She was told that Verdon was the official White House chef, and had substantially greater responsibilities, being in charge of a large staff and running important official events, such as state dinners. Wright argued that this was not fair, that she also cooked for official events and often had to accommodate the president's late-night dining habits with guest lists of twenty people. Wright's salary was raised, after consultations with the first lady, to $650 per month and eventually to $750 per month, more than she was originally paid but still much less than Verdon's salary.

Tensions remained. Wright had an advantage in knowing the Johnsons' favorite foods and being an expert in their preparation. When she whipped up platters of chili con queso, a Tex-Mex cheesy dish that was one of the president's favorites, Verdon nicknamed it "chili con-crete."[36] Johnson once sent the Frenchman's version of tapioca back to the kitchen with instructions to ask Wright for her superior recipe, and Verdon fumed. The friction got so bad between the cook and the chef, with the Johnsons siding mostly with their longtime employee, that the dapper Frenchman left. A new French chef, Henri Haller, whom the Johnsons renamed Henry, was soon hired, but it was clear that Wright was a force to be reckoned with and retained the first family's loyalty.

Wright knew that the best way to get respect from Lyndon Johnson was to stand up to him, even when he got overbearing and demanding over menus, times of meals, and the burdens he put on his cook and household staff over his seemingly endless rounds of socializing. "Zephyr was not a bit intimidated, gave as good as she got," recalled Chief Usher Rex Scouten.[37]

*   *   *

OVER TIME, Preston Bruce became a confidant for Johnson because the president needed to unburden himself and knew his doorman wouldn't talk out of school. Bruce felt that he had a special bond with the commander in chief and was able to comfort him amid the savage criticism of his policies in the Vietnam War, which was going badly. It was the simple kindnesses that Johnson seemed to appreciate the most. Some aides thought Bruce was able to calm the president down better than anyone else. "I didn't do all that much," Bruce recalled.[38] "I'd just let him storm for a bit, then I'd say, 'Now, Mr. President, could I get you some coffee? Would you like something?' and he'd quiet down and say 'Yes, Bruce. That's a good idea.'"

Bruce's theory was that he and Johnson came from poor rural backgrounds and respected each other for prospering despite their early disadvantages. At one point, Johnson asked, "Didn't you grow up on a farm?" and Bruce allowed that he had. Johnson said he and his family had endured hard times when he was a boy, and he never forgot what it was like to be poor.

As the antiwar protests grew in size and ferocity through the election year of 1968, the opposition took on a more anti-Johnson tone. One particularly nasty chant was, "Hey hey LBJ, how many kids did you kill today?" Johnson took it to heart, and became demoralized. As Senators Eugene McCarthy of Minnesota and Robert Kennedy of New York gathered momentum in their bids to challenge him for the Democratic presidential nomination, he announced on March 31 that he would not run again.

Four days later, Martin Luther King Jr. was killed by a sniper in Memphis, Tennessee, triggering some of the worst rioting in American history, including deadly disturbances in Washington, DC.

Then disaster struck again. On the night of June 5, when he won the California presidential primary, Kennedy was shot and killed after he gave a victory speech at the Hotel Ambassador in Los Angeles. The country seemed to be having a nervous breakdown. That November, the voters, sick of the turmoil and the failure in Vietnam and seemingly endless chaos at home, elected Richard Nixon as president based on his promises to end the Vietnam War with honor, impose law and order, and heal the nation's wounds.

Just before he left the White House that winter, Johnson made a surprise gesture honoring Preston Bruce.[39] It happened after the president invited the doorman to a reception one evening. Bruce met Johnson in the Oval Office and they shared a limousine ride to the Sheraton Carlton Hotel in downtown Washington, where a large group of black officials were waiting to honor Johnson for appointing so many African Americans to government positions. Johnson brought his loyal aide to the dais and told the crowd, "I came over tonight with one of my dear friends. His name is Preston Bruce. He was born a year after I was born. He has been in the White House faithfully serving many, many presidents. Outside of my wife and family, who give me great comfort in moments of need, this great American gentleman, Preston Bruce, has kept me going."

Bruce felt moved by the president's words. But what he had done was not unusual. It was, in fact, fully in keeping with the pattern set by so many other African Americans who had provided comfort and solace to presidents since the beginning of the Republic.

Chapter Ten
Mixed Results in a Conservative Era

Richard Nixon

The years from 1968 to 1992 marked what many black leaders considered a series of setbacks for civil rights and for race relations.[1] Many white Americans felt that their own advancement was being hindered by government programs for blacks enacted under Lyndon Johnson. The assassinations of Martin Luther King Jr. and Robert Kennedy in 1968 demonstrated a virulent streak of anger and hatred permeating American life. Race riots underscored and intensified the polarization. The election of Republican Richard Nixon in 1968, based on his Southern strategy and a "law and order" message that divided whites from blacks, set the stage for more racial hostility and opened a particularly wide gap between working-class white America and black America.

Nixon had never associated much with blacks and largely avoided racial issues for most of his political career as a U.S. representative, U.S. senator, and vice president.[2] But that changed in his 1968 campaign for president when he developed a "Southern strategy" of siding with conservative whites on a broad swath of issues that pitted them against blacks, including tough stands on crime and public demonstrations and an implicit commitment to slow down civil rights enforcement. This was designed to divide America, play upon white fears and resentments, and forge a new political majority based on bringing to the GOP as many previously Democratic white voters as possible.

In his losing campaign against John F. Kennedy in 1960, Nixon had carried 32 percent of the African American vote. But in the 1968 campaign, his approach to racial issues hardened, and his support among blacks plunged to 12 percent.[3] At first, he positioned himself as a centrist alternative to the more liberal Nelson A. Rockefeller and the more conservative Ronald Reagan, two of his main competitors for the Republican nomination.[4] But he moved decisively toward the conservative side and toward racial polarization when he convinced Southern delegates that he would be less aggressive in enforcing civil rights measures than would Rockefeller or the Democrats. In exchange for the support of leaders such as Senator Strom Thurmond of South Carolina, Nixon signaled that he would appoint more conservative judges and slow down school desegregation.

However, political scientist Alvin Felzenberg points out that, "Among the ironies of Nixon's presidency was that it was he who officiated over the final dismantling of segregation in the American south. Early in his administration, Nixon set out to achieve full implementation of the *Brown v. Board of Education* decision. Working through Secretary of Labor George P. Shultz, Nixon's advisers set up biracial panels in each affected state to devise and implement plans to desegregate. In public, Nixon generally shied away from taking credit for his achievement. In private, and occasionally in public, he signaled to his southern supporters that the cost of their non-cooperation would entail more court orders, which he would enforce."[5]

Political scientists Hanes Walton Jr. and Robert C. Smith agree, noting that, "Although Richard Nixon was a white supremacist and his 1968 campaign was based on a strategy of attracting the white racist vote in the South, as the first post–civil rights era president he presided over the successful desegregation of southern schools, the renewal of the Voting Rights Act in 1970, implementation of Executive Order 11246 establishing affirmative action, and the appointment of scores of blacks to high-level positions in the government. In addition, Nixon proposed a far-reaching, material-based reform—the Family Assistance Plan—that would have guaranteed an income to all families with children. Although this change was defeated by an odd coalition of blacks and liberals (who thought the income guarantee was too low) and conservatives (who wanted no guarantee at all), if it had passed it would have substantially raised the income of poor families, many of whom were black. Historians are unclear as to why Nixon took such a strong civil rights policy stance (especially on affirmative action), but the political climate in the late 1960s probably made such positions seem politically expedient."[6]

Another big issue during the Nixon administration was "benign neglect." White House adviser (and later Democratic Senator from New York) Daniel Patrick Moynihan used those words to describe his theory about how it might be time for the federal government to step back from helping African Americans in order to encourage them to take more responsibility for their own lives, families, and communities. "We may need a period in which Negro progress continues and racial rhetoric fades," Moynihan wrote in a widely quoted internal memorandum to Nixon. "... The time may have come when the issue of race could benefit from a period of 'benign neglect.' The subject has been too much talked about."[7] This perfectly reflected Nixon's own views.

In personal terms, there was a duality to Nixon. He used pejorative racial terms about blacks in private (as he did about other social groups, including Jewish Americans). He sometimes called black people "niggers" and said some Africans were "just out of the trees."[8] On January 22, 1973, reacting to the Supreme Court's *Roe v. Wade* decision legalizing abortion, Nixon told an aide, "There are times when an abortion is necessary. I know that—when you have a black and a white. Or a rape."[9]

Earlier, when he was vice president, his condescending attitude emerged when he asked a question of White House butler John Pye, who was black, after a dinner.[10] "Boy, what are y'all going to do with the rest of the food?" Nixon queried. He wanted Pye to put some aside for the vice president to take home. Pye resented being called "boy" but politely replied that the extra food would be donated to charity.

Despite all this, Nixon was the first president to host a black couple for an overnight at the White House when entertainer Sammy Davis Jr. and his second wife, Altovise, stayed in the Queen's Bedroom in 1973. On another occasion, Nixon inspired Davis to get a bit carried away, and Davis literally embraced Nixon at a rally. It didn't help Davis's reputation in the African American community, which was largely anti-Nixon, but it showed that Nixon would associate with blacks in public if it suited his political goals of the moment—in this case, seeming conciliatory and friendly.

Davis felt that Nixon had deceived him. In an interview with *Ebony* magazine, the entertainer said, "I was made a lot of promises by the Nixon Administration. Not for me personally, but things that were going to be done for my people if I gave my commitment. You see, the Democrats have always hurt me. I supported John F. Kennedy, I did everything I could for him, and then I was told not to come to the White House because it would embarrass the president.... So here I am being treated as an outcast by the Democrats and being treated as a human being by a man named Bob Brown, and Bob Brown, as you know, was one of Nixon's top advisors."[11]

Still, Davis had a surprising influence on Nixon in at least one instance, and it had nothing to do with race. Davis suggested that Nixon hold a gala on the White House lawn to honor returning prisoners of war who were being released from Vietnam.[12] It was held on May 24, 1973, and Nixon described it as "the largest and most spectacular White House gala in history." The entertainers included Davis, John Wayne, Bob Hope, and a variety of singers, actors, and actresses, as well as 1,300 guests, including the POWs and their wives and families. Songwriter Irving Berlin concluded the evening by leading everyone in the patriotic anthem "God Bless America."

On the other hand, Nixon had a falling-out with the only black member of the U.S. Senate, Republican Edward Brooke of Massachusetts. Elected in 1966 as the first black to be sent to the Senate by popular ballot, he campaigned for Nixon in 1968. But Brooke opposed Nixon's nomination of Clement Haynsworth to the Supreme Court and was instrumental in Haynsworth's defeat in 1969. He also opposed G. Harrold Carswell, whose nomination to the court failed in 1970. In each case, Brooke argued that the nominees were too conservative on civil rights, racial equality, and other issues. In January 1970, Brooke argued that the administration had not moved strongly enough to desegregate the public schools and attacked the administration's decision not to seek an extension of the 1965 Voting Rights Act as a step backward on civil rights.

In March 1970, Brooke complained that the Nixon White House had made a "cold, calculated political decision" to slow down progress for blacks and instead to pursue the "Southern strategy" of courting Southern whites to win reelection in 1972.[13] Over time, Brooke also became increasingly opposed to Nixon's pursuit of the Vietnam War. And on November 4, 1973, Brooke became the first Republican senator to publicly call for Nixon's resignation because of the Watergate scandal.

*   *   *

NIXON'S RESIGNATION IN August 1974 sent shock waves through the country, and also through the household staff at the White House. The day he left office was "one of the saddest days of my life," said Preston Bruce, a longtime doorman.[14] "At about ten o'clock," Bruce continued, "the President left the Oval Office and walked over to meet me at the elevator. He looked terribly upset. The doors closed, the elevator started, and for the first time I saw Richard Nixon cry. He and I held onto one another. I, too, wept, as I had with Mrs. Kennedy and Robert."

"I said, "Mr. President, this is a time in my life that I wish had never happened."

Nixon replied, "I have in you a true friend"—almost the exact words that Lyndon Johnson had spoken to Bruce as he prepared to leave office in the winter of 1968.

Gerald Ford

When he replaced Spiro Agnew as vice president in 1973, Gerald Ford realized that he was joining an administration that had polarized the country along racial lines. "The Nixon administration had closed the door to minorities, particularly blacks," he admitted later.[15] But he swallowed his concerns and took the number-two job.

Ford tried to at least show sensitivity to racial issues, but was mostly rebuffed. As President Nixon prepared to give his State of the Union address in 1974, then–Vice President Ford suggested that Nixon make some positive comments about the need to guarantee civil rights for black citizens and praise African Americans for their contributions to the country. Ford thought some uplifting words on race might help reduce black-white tensions. But the request, made by Ford aide Stanley Scott, was turned down because Nixon aides argued that it demonstrated weakness and might erode Nixon's hold on white voters and white members of Congress from the South. Nixon was especially eager not to stir the pot because he needed all the support he could get in the growing confrontation with Congress over the Watergate scandal.

Later, Ford asked for permission to attend the funeral of Martin Luther King Jr.'s mother, but Nixon's staff rejected it, and Betty Ford, the vice president's wife, ended up attending instead.

After he became president, Ford met with civil rights leaders several times (Nixon had avoided them, fearing that they might embarrass him by using such an occasion to criticize him publicly). Ford named Philadelphia lawyer William T. Coleman as the first black Secretary of Transportation.

On busing for school integration, however, Ford kept to Nixon's strategy of opposing the practice. This put him on the opposite side of the issue with many blacks, who were often in favor of busing so they could send their children to superior schools. Meanwhile, many whites, especially working-class parents, opposed it as unfair and burdensome for their children.

Ford wanted to replicate for every child the benign experience he had enjoyed in Grand Rapids, Michigan, neighborhood schools as a boy.[16] Of course that wasn't possible given the racial divisions in the country and the disparities in funding schools, where poor areas were badly shortchanged.

Ford tried to take a middle-of-the-road position. He condemned the courts for imposing more busing on local school districts. But he also enforced the law and would not support a constitutional amendment to ban busing.

And as president, Ford tried to be even-handed and made some important symbolic moves, such as inviting the Congressional Black Caucus and other black leaders to meet with him at the White House shortly after he took office. And he did ask Congress for another five-year extension of the Voting Rights Act. But this did little to ease racial tensions.[17]

"I wanted these groups to know that I could be—and really wanted to be—point man for them in their dealings with the government," he said. But there was rarely any follow-through when Ford made proposals on racial policy, and he came across as ineffectual.[18]

Ford also endured a huge setback with blacks when his agriculture secretary, Earl Butz, made a vulgar racial comment that resulted in his resignation late in the 1976 presidential campaign. Butz, referring to blacks as "colored," said they wanted only three things—good sex, loose shoes, and a warm bathroom, only he used far more shocking terms.[19] [Note: His exact words, not reported in many family newspapers, were: "The only thing the coloreds are looking for in life are tight pussy, loose shoes, and a warm place to shit."][20]

In personal terms, Ford exhibited well-meaning decency during his tenure. The president and his wife, Betty, were gracious to everyone. As

RELIGION, AFRICAN AMERICANS, AND THE PRESIDENCY

Religion has sustained both presidents and African Americans from the founding of the nation, both in terms of providing personal solace and, later, as a foundation for achieving social justice. Here, President Barack Obama prays with Christian leaders in the Blue Room of the White House prior to an Easter prayer breakfast on April 6, 2010. His bond with church-going African Americans has deepened because of their mutual commitment to the precepts of Christianity. (Copyright Pete Souza/The White House/Corbis)

"THE PECULIAR INSTITUTION" OF SLAVERY

An artist's rendering of George Washington with his slaves at his plantation at Mount Vernon, Virginia. Most of the earliest presidents owned slaves, a clear violation of the values of the new republic and a contradiction of the Declaration of Independence. (Library of Congress)

The brutal reality of slavery was the subject of much soul searching by America's first presidents, but they did little or nothing to end what was called "the peculiar institution." (Slaves Build Capitol: Library of Congress)

African Americans as Advisors and Private Confidants to Presidents

A depiction of Abraham Lincoln and abolitionist Sojourner Truth marking the occasion when Truth presented the president with a Bible from the African American residents of Baltimore on Oct. 29, 1864. Many blacks revered Lincoln as a quasi-religious figure. (Library of Congress)

Elizabeth Keckley, a seamstress at the White House, impressed President Lincoln and his wife, Mary Todd Lincoln, with her discretion and personal dignity. She became a confidante of both the president and first lady. (Photo courtesy of Wilson Special Collections Library, UNC Chapel Hill)

Taking Up the Cause of African Americans

Eleanor Roosevelt presents the NAACP's Springarn Medal for achievement by an African American to contralto Marian Anderson in Richmond, Virginia. Mrs. Roosevelt angered Southern segregationists when she arranged for Anderson to perform at the Lincoln Memorial after the Daughters of the American Revolution refused to allow the singer to appear at Constitution Hall in Washington because of her race. (Library of Congress)

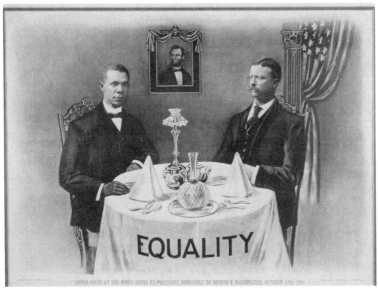

An artist depicted a controversial dinner between President Theodore Roosevelt and Booker T. Washington at the White House on Oct. 17, 1901. Segregationists were upset because TR invited the famous educator for a social get-together. (Copyright David J. & Janice L. Frent Collection/Corbis)

RECOGNIZING THE CIVIL RIGHTS MOVEMENT AS A MORAL AND POLITICAL FORCE

President John F. Kennedy met at the White House with African American leaders on June 21, 1963. It was the largest gathering of such leaders at the White House until that time. (Washington State Historical Society)

President Lyndon Johnson discussed racial issues, including the Voting Rights Act, with civil rights leader Martin Luther King Jr. in 1965. Johnson achieved many legislative breakthroughs for African Americans while King kept up the pressure with his aggressive campaign for equality. (Hulton Archive/Getty Images)

AFRICAN AMERICANS AS FRIENDS
AND CLOSE ASSOCIATES OF PRESIDENTS

Entertainer Sammy Davis Jr. hugs President Richard Nixon at a youth rally on Aug. 22, 1972. Davis' support of Nixon drew considerable criticism from other African Americans who considered Nixon an opponent of equal rights. (AP Photo/Jim Palmer)

President Ronald Reagan and his wife Nancy with Eugene Allen, who worked as a White House butler of thirty-four years and served eight presidents. Allen continued a long tradition in which African Americans played an integral role in running the White House. (Photo by Kevin Clark/The Washington Post/Getty Images)

President George W. Bush announces a plan for peace in the Middle East on June 24, 2002, as key advisers Condoleezza Rice, Colin Powell, and Donald Rumsfeld listen to his remarks in the Rose Garden of the White House. Rice was national security adviser and Powell was secretary of state, making them the highest-ranking African Americans to serve in the U.S. government until that time. (Photo by Alex Wong/ Getty Images)

President Barack Obama wipes his face with a cloth provided by White House butler Von Everett in the Blue Room following a meeting with business leaders. Such personal moments have led to close bonds between the presidents and the household staff members who have gotten to know them well over the years. (Copyright Pete Souza/The White House/CNP/Corbis)

BARACK OBAMA WITH LINCOLN, ADMIRED PREDECESSOR

As president-elect, Barack Obama speaks at a "We Are One" rally at the Lincoln Memorial in Washington on Jan. 18, 2009, two days before his inauguration. Obama has been attempting to move beyond the race-centered debates of the past. (Copyright Jim Young/Corbis)

Betty once recalled, "I think the staff was taken aback by our friendliness at first. I'd say a cheerful 'good morning,' for example, and the help was stunned. At first I thought no one liked me because no one was talking to me. Later I discovered it was just a matter of getting used to our style after the Nixons. Something else no one seems to expect is for a first lady to sleep with the President! We are the first president and first lady to share a bedroom in an awfully long time."[21]

Betty counted as one of her closest friends Clara Powell, who was black and helped care for the Ford children for many years. "She and I brought up the children together," Betty said.[22] They spent a lot of time together when the kids were young and did chores in tandem. Sometimes they got down on all fours to scrub the floor side by side as Betty loudly sang along with a favorite song, "Get Out on Your Knees and Pray," on the record player.

President Ford's personal attitudes were uncomplicated and inclined toward simple justice. In personal reflections he recorded in lengthy handwritten notes for his memoir, *A Time to Heal,* he described his views on "What I've learned from blacks and other minorities." In a neat scrawl, he wrote:

> Blacks and other minorities have shown me that a majority among them have a harder time in our society than whites as a whole. Their job opportunities, both in getting and advancing in employment are less. Housing opportunities were and to some extent are now more limited.
>
> On the other hand blacks and other minorities have shown me that a growing percentage, when given equal educational opportunities, can advance up the economic and social ladder in competition with whites.
>
> Blacks and other minorities have demonstrated to me that an overwhelming majority are committed to domestic tranquility, morality, and obedience to the law.
>
> I'm convinced the responsible leadership in these groups recognizes that welfare in perpetuity is not the answer but job opportunity plus education, housing; equality before the law are the answer.[23]

Beyond such positive attitudes on racial matters, he could also be brutally honest about his own standing in the black community. When he ran for president in 1976, he realized that blacks hated and distrusted Nixon so much that, as Nixon's former vice president, he could never win them over. "Most blacks wouldn't vote for me no matter what I did," he said during that campaign. In the end, Jimmy Carter received nearly 90 percent of the black vote as part of his victorious coalition.[24]

Ronald Reagan

Ronald Reagan's rollback of government activism and cuts in the growth of federal spending put a more conservative cast on racial issues from 1981 to 1989. Yet under Reagan, America saw the ascendancy of Colin Powell as the most successful and popular African American leader until Barack Obama won the White House in 2008.

Reagan, the oldest president in American history at sixty-nine when he took office in January 1981, is best known for his role in helping to defeat communism and end the Soviet empire. Historians will long debate precisely how much Reagan had to do with those achievements, but it is clear he was at least a catalyst in hastening the unraveling process.

On domestic issues, Reagan is remembered for his argument that the federal government had grown too large and intrusive and his success in changing the terms of debate in Washington to focus on ways to restrain government's power.

In his personal life, he had never demonstrated racism. His tolerance had nothing to do with ideology but instead was based on the sense of fair play instilled by his parents and Reagan's loyalty to those in his circle. He recalled that one of his formative experiences was when his father, Jack, forbade him as a thirteen-year-old boy to see *Birth of a Nation,* the film about Reconstruction by D. W. Griffith, because of its anti-black message. His parents, Jack and Nellie Reagan, preached tolerance, racial and religious.

He credited his participation in team sports and the exposure it provided him to African Americans for what he considered his enlightened racial views. He believed that among those he felt were causing the most racial strife in the mid-1960s, black and white, none had participated in a sport on an integrated team. He played football for Eureka College beside William Franklin "Burgy" Burghardt, the starting center and an African American. During one trip, the team was to stay overnight near Dixon, Illinois, Reagan's hometown, and work out on Reagan's old high school field. But when the time came to check into a local hotel, the owner would not allow Burghardt and another African American player, Jim Rattan, to rent rooms. Eureka coach Ralph McKinzie decided that the entire team would sleep on the bus rather than submit the two black players to this humiliation. But Reagan came up with a solution—he would take the two African Americans home with him for the night, and the white players would stay at the hotel. His parents welcomed the players and "didn't even blink or act as if anything had happened that was not a daily occurrence," Reagan said later.[25]

He believed that the best way to help everyone, even those on the bottom rung of the economic ladder, was to enlarge the economy through the free market. But that was little comfort to African Americans, who were often left behind, especially the average black family, whose real income was declining markedly in relation to whites'. Poverty also rose rapidly in the inner cities during Reagan's administration.

As governor of California and as president, Reagan wasn't oblivious to the problems of blacks, but he refused to see government as the answer. "The declining living standards in the inner cities and the poverty of the increasing number of children born to unwed mothers were occasional topics of discussion in the 'issue luncheons' held with Reagan on many Mondays in the White House," reports Reagan biographer Lou Cannon. "And Reagan could be affected by individual stories of poverty and hardship." But he preferred to leave the solutions to individuals, states, charities, and the free market. He argued that government programs created "a new kind of bondage" for African Americans. Even on a matter as fundamental as civil rights, Reagan opposed the use of federal power to guarantee African Americans the voting rights and other basics that had been denied to them by Southern states since Reconstruction. Part of this was no doubt because of his convictions, but it also was part of his political strategy to appeal to Southern whites. Making matters worse for him in his relationship with the black community, for most of his presidency, until the ascension of Colin Powell to national security advisor, he had no African American as a member of his inner circle.[26]

This was clear from an incident early in his presidency. At a reception for mayors and other local officials, many of whom were black, Reagan didn't recognize his own Secretary of Housing and Urban Development, an African American named Samuel Pierce. "How are you, Mr. Mayor?" Reagan asked brightly. "I'm glad to meet you. How are things in your city?" The incident was widely reported and caused considerable embarrassment for the White House.

Yet Reagan was upset when black leaders criticized him for racial prejudice or insensitivity. In a letter to NAACP President Benjamin Hooks on January 19, 1983, Reagan wrote, "A short time ago you were quoted as having told the press that no administration in 30 years has 'demonstrated as much determination as President Reagan to roll back hard-won gains of black Americans.' You then described 1982 as the worst year in recent memory for blacks because of my budget policies. Ben, there are no facts to substantiate such charges and they are a distortion of the actual record as well as of my own position on these matters."[27]

Reagan went on to defend his racial and economic policies. He concluded, "Ben, if only it were possible to look into each other's hearts and minds, you would find no trace of prejudice or bigotry in mine. I know that's hard for you to believe and that's too bad because together we could do more for the people you represent than either of us can do alone. Prejudice is not a failing peculiar to one race, it can and does exist in people of every race and ethnic background. It takes individual effort to root it out of one's heart. In my case, my father and mother saw that it never got a start. I shall be forever grateful to them."

Reagan was just as emotional and defensive in a March 23, 1983, letter to Leonard Kirk, a black, unemployed Vietnam veteran who had sent Reagan a telegram supporting his defense policy but calling him "a closet racist and friend of the rich." Reagan wrote, "I appreciate very much your support of my defense policy. I believe I also can understand why you think me a 'closet racist.' Certainly there has been a constant drumbeat of propaganda to that effect ever since I took office. Some leaders of black organizations have joined in this whether to enhance their own stature by arousing the membership to anger or not I don't know." Reagan continued that, "I was raised from childhood by my parents who believed bigotry and prejudice were the worst things a person could be guilty of. My father once slept in his car during an Illinois blizzard rather than stay in a hotel that wouldn't allow Jews. He was Irish Catholic. As a sports announcer broadcasting Big League baseball in the middle '30s I campaigned against the rule that prohibited blacks from playing in organized ball. As governor of California I appointed more blacks to executive and policy making positions than all the previous Governors of California put together. I too have a dream, a dream that one day whatever is done to or for someone will be done neither because of or in spite of their race. We are all equal in the sight of God—we should be equal in the sight of man. By the way, I was raised in poverty."[28]

Frank Donatelli, who was Reagan's White House political director, told me, "Reagan was very much a libertarian in terms of race—and gays, for that matter.... He was distressed that he was viewed so negatively by the civil rights movement. True, he was not for affirmative action or quotas but I remember him being very perplexed at the opposition and the fact that he didn't have much black support." Reagan was hurt when he was booed by some at an NAACP convention when he spoke to the group, and he later told his staff, "I don't understand why I can't make more headway there."[29]

Cannon says, "In discussing racial prejudice, Reagan often cited his opposition, as a sports broadcaster, to the long and shameful practice of barring blacks from major league baseball." His staff referred to it as "the Jackie Robinson story," noting the Brooklyn Dodger who in 1947 became the first black to play in the major leagues. "Reagan invariably told it when he met privately with any group of blacks," Cannon reports. "[Media adviser Michael] Deaver was not overly fond of the story, which Reagan told to demonstrate his support for baseball integration and his opposition to racism but which also suggested that he had not done much lately for the cause of civil rights."[30]

But as president, Reagan did not have a particularly strong interest in racial issues except as a longtime opponent of affirmative action, according to presidential scholars.[31] Reagan was often criticized for backing away from a strong federal role in civil rights enforcement, and when he entered office he opposed affirmative action programs. And he got off to a bad start, according to his critics, by starting his 1980 campaign as the GOP nominee for president on a bitter note. He appeared on August 3, 1980, at the Neshoba County Fair in Mississippi and declared his commitment to states' rights.[32] This was, at minimum, an extremely insensitive choice for a major campaign event because it was only a few miles away, at Philadelphia, Mississippi, where three civil rights workers, James Chaney, Andrew Goodman, and Michael Schwerner, had been murdered in the summer of 1964. Democrats charged that Reagan was sending a message to Southern white racists to signal that he would not uphold the civil rights of minorities or that he would not aggressively prosecute civil rights violations.

After he took office, he retreated from strict enforcement, at least as the Democrats wanted it pursued, and he focused on enhancing states' rights. He was also criticized for expressing doubts about the value of affirmative action programs that gave blacks an advantage in some hiring and educational situations to make up for past injustices. None of this should have come as a surprise because it was what he had promised to do in the campaign. And in the name of reducing the size and power of government, Reagan succeeded in cutting or slowing the growth of programs that had benefited blacks over the years, such as welfare and enforcement of civil rights laws and regulations. Reagan also remade the federal judiciary by appointing conservatives to many judgeships over eight years. And he named a host of conservatives to the bureaucracy.[33]

Another controversial policy was his "constructive engagement" with the apartheid regime in South Africa. Reagan argued that diplomacy and quiet pressure would do more to undermine the racist white government than isolation or confrontation, such as the use of economic sanctions. In this, he was following the pattern of his predecessors since the 1950s by keeping close ties to the South Africa regime as an anti-communist bulwark in the region. But attitudes in the United States were changing and the Democrat-controlled Congress was increasingly outraged by the white South African government's strict system of racial separation for the entire country, known as apartheid. When Congress approved a wide-ranging series of economic sanctions against South Africa in 1986, Reagan vetoed the bill, but he was overridden. His opposition further alienated him from blacks in the United States.

But Reagan did show some flexibility. He said the renewal of the Voting Rights Act of 1965 was unnecessary but he approved it anyway. He opposed the establishment of a legal holiday to honor Dr. Martin Luther King Jr. but signed a measure creating that holiday into law, bowing to the will of Congress. In 1982, he initially supported tax exemptions for Bob Jones University, a religion-based conservative institution in Greenville, South Carolina, that prohibited interracial dating. Reagan at first saw it as a case of an overbearing federal government (in the form of the Internal Revenue Service, which had denied Bob Jones the tax exemptions for violating civil rights guidelines authorized by Nixon in 1970) trying to regulate and interfere with religion. But amid a firestorm of criticism that Reagan seemed anti-black, he changed his mind and disallowed the exemptions after meeting with African Americans serving in his administration.[34] He also named Colin Powell as his White House national security advisor, making him the highest-ranking African American in the history of the U.S. government up to that time.

And there were examples of personal tolerance, such as when Nancy Reagan invited Eugene Allen, a longtime butler at the White House, as a guest at a state dinner for German Chancellor Helmut Kohl.[35]

George H. W. Bush

George Herbert Walker Bush, who had been Reagan's vice president and succeeded him in the 1988 election, essentially continued Reagan's racial policies. Bush and his wife, Barbara, had not been particularly attuned to the civil rights movement, and as president Bush's concerns were mainly focused on foreign policy. He had, after all, served as U.S. envoy to China, U.S. ambassador to the United Nations, and director of central intelligence, and had specialized in foreign affairs as Reagan's vice president for eight years.

But in their personal lives, the president and his wife were paragons of fairness. "I was fortunate to grow up in a home where prejudice of any kind was not tolerated," said Bush in an e-mail interview with the author of this book. "Yet, I lived a very protected childhood and had little exposure to people of different backgrounds. All that ended when I joined the Navy at age 18. I met kids from all different kinds of backgrounds, from all over the country. I learned a lot from them. When we were out to sea, one of my jobs was to censor mail going off the ship. I learned even more from reading those letters home."[36]

Bush also said, "In 1968, when I was a congressman from Houston, I took a lot of heat for voting for the Open Housing Bill, which was an extension of the 1964 Civil Rights Bill. My constituents were largely opposed to the measure. But I had just come back from Vietnam where I saw young boys of all races and backgrounds fighting for and dying for their country. And then when they came home we were going to tell them where they could or couldn't live?"[37]

In an interview with *Ebony* in 1989, her husband's first year as president, Mrs. Bush discussed her first encounter with racism, in 1957. It happened when Mrs. Bush was driving three of her children and two black women, family housekeeper Julia Mae Jackson and babysitter Otha Taylor, from

Texas to the family estate in Kennebunkport, Maine. The group was repeatedly turned away from hotels and restaurants that did not serve blacks. "Things went like that most of the way," recalled Mrs. Taylor in a separate *Ebony* issue. "Mrs. Bush got so frustrated. She would go in a place and if they said we couldn't come in too, she would walk right back out. Julia Mae and I told her we could eat or stay somewhere else but she said it wasn't right. She said we should stay together."[38]

When they were turned away in Oklahoma City, Mrs. Bush phoned her husband, then an oil company executive in Texas, and George spoke with the hotel manager and arranged for the group to stay together in the hotel. But they weren't allowed to eat in the dining room together and they had to leave before dawn "so no one could see us," Mrs. Taylor said.[39]

In the *Ebony* interview, Mrs. Bush's temper flared when she recalled the incidents so many years later. "I was just sick," she said. "We had those babies with us. You know, Little Rock had happened in the middle of the trip so it polarized people. It was disgusting." They ended up staying mostly in Howard Johnson's, which had started allowing blacks to rent rooms and dine there.[40]

Assessing the progress made since then, Mrs. Bush said, "Oh, I think we've made wonderful progress, wonderful progress, so much so that I now worry about many of my black friends who have made it out of the problems and who don't go back to help other people. I worry about that because I know that I can't go into a black housing area or a Hispanic housing area or an Asian one, and say this is what you must do because that—you know, white-haired, white lady isn't going to do it. But a young, positive, successful role model can do it. And we've got to get more people going back into their own neighborhoods and helping someone else out."[41]

She added: "Of course, I see room for improvement in white neighborhoods. I mean, a lot of room for improvement. We have got to help people who can't help themselves, and we've got to help them not only by setting a good example—and of course we have to help them financially. But do you realize how much we help people financially, and that is not the whole answer. We have got to go back and train them for jobs and we've just got to educate our people. We've got to educate our children—all races—about promiscuous sex. . . . We've got to tell those people who are down and out that if you get a good education you can do anything, and if you cop out— go off, have babies, quit school—you don't have anything."[42]

Citing the civil rights pioneer Frederick Douglass, Mrs. Bush said, "I consider him an inspiration and I'm always appalled that I don't see more of [the story of] Frederick Douglass being told to people because he really taught himself to read and he just fought the most extraordinary battles and became an adviser to five presidents and spoke foreign languages and edited a newspaper. He was just an amazing man."[43]

Former President Bush said that when he was in office he tried to be race-neutral, including on his personnel appointments. "As for choosing people for key roles, race did not play a role at all," he told me. "I did not choose Clarence Thomas [for the Supreme Court] because he was black. Or Colin Powell [chairman of the Joint Chiefs of Staff]. Or Louis Sullivan [secretary of Health and Human Services]. I thought they were the best person for the job at hand. I just didn't look at it that way. Maybe I was supposed to, but I didn't."[44]

He didn't mention it, but his wife, Barbara, also made history by hiring an African American, Anna Perez, to work on the first lady's senior staff as her press secretary in 1989. Perez would return to government as the chief press officer for National Security Advisor Condoleezza Rice under George W. Bush in 2001. Mrs. Bush said she wanted Perez for the job not only because she was highly qualified but because she would serve as the first lady's most visible staff member. "I hope that sends a message ... that, you know, we care about race," Mrs. Bush said during her first year as first lady.[45] She showed admirable sensitivity and compassion when she cradled a five-month-old African American baby with AIDS during a 1989 visit to a pediatric AIDS center in Washington, to show that people couldn't contract the disease through casual contact.[46]

Former President Bush also said, "I had a good relationship with civil rights leaders behind closed doors but they often slammed me in public. It was just sort of how it worked. Our disagreements were about politics, not race, but it was not always viewed that way."

When I asked him what were his most important decisions on the issue of race, the former president said, "No memory." And when I asked him who were his most important advisers on race, he replied, "I am not sure how to answer that. I don't even remember asking anyone for specific advice on 'race.'"

But his critics (and some supporters, including Colin Powell) point out that, in his successful 1988 campaign, he inflamed white fears by underscoring the case of Willie Horton, a convicted murderer who ran away from a weekend furlough and assaulted a man and his fiancée. Since Horton was black and the victims were white, the potential for a divisive issue was huge. And Bush fanned the flames, attacking his Democratic opponent, Massachusetts Governor Michael Dukakis, for approving the furlough program and being soft on crime.

"George Bush's administration was ... characterized by ambivalence on civil rights," write political scientists Hanes Walton Jr. and Robert C. Smith. "In 1990 he vetoed the Civil Rights Act (designed to overturn several Supreme Court decisions that made it difficult to enforce employment discrimination laws), calling it a 'quota bill,' but in 1991 he signed essentially the same bill he had vetoed a year earlier. Bush also appointed the second black to the Supreme Court, but the appointee was a man described by most black leaders as an 'Uncle Tom' and a 'traitor to the race.' Justice [Clarence] Thomas was also accused by Anita Hill, a former black female employee, of sexual harassment. Additionally, Bush rejected proposals by his aides for new antipoverty programs, arguing that they were too expensive and too liberal."[47]

The Clarence Thomas furor caused Bush serious harm with black voters. At first, Thomas looked like he could be a strong choice for the high court. His personal story was compelling. A descendant of slaves, Thomas had overcome poverty in his hometown of Pin Point, Georgia, graduated from Yale Law School, and became assistant secretary of education for the U.S. Office of Civil Rights in 1981. The following year, Reagan named him chairman of the Equal Employment Opportunity Commission (EEOC), and Thomas quickly became known as an opponent of affirmative action laws, school busing, and other liberal programs designed to promote integration and equality. During his confirmation hearings, Thomas attacked his critics for unfairly pillorying him for his conservative views and conducting a "high-tech lynching for uppity blacks." As chairman of the EEOC, Thomas was relatively slow to act on discrimination complaints and had only a few months of experience on the District of Columbia Circuit Court. His minimal legal credentials offended many, partly because he was chosen to fill the seat that had been held by the only black justice in history, Thurgood Marshall, who resigned in June 1991. A firestorm erupted when Anita Hill, a black law professor at the University of Oklahoma, charged Thomas with sexual harassment when she worked with him at the EEOC. This led to a vicious series of charges and countercharges against both

Thomas and Hill. In the end, Thomas was confirmed by the Senate 52–48, but Bush's reputation with many black voters was tarnished.

"A month later," writes historian Sean Wilentz, "Bush sealed his doom with black voters when he signed a piece of civil rights legislation that permitted employers to avoid charges of discrimination if their racial disparities in hiring could be justified as a business necessity. Above all, Bush appeared to be stubbornly placing his own sense of loyalty to a nominee above any reasonable assessment of competence or any sense of political wisdom. Standing by his man Thomas, Bush put the nation through a televised, emotional trauma while allowing himself to look inept."[48]

Another low point occurred when riots erupted in Los Angeles in the spring of 1992 after a Simi Valley jury acquitted police officers who had assaulted a black man, Rodney King. The attack was captured on video by a citizen and played endlessly on television. The riots left 54 people dead, 2,000 injured, and $1 billion in property damage.[49] Bush's response was slow, but he eventually sent in U.S. troops to restore order.

Powell, then chairman of the Joint Chiefs of Staff, talked to President Bush about race only rarely, when he felt he needed to make a special point.[50] One such occasion arose because of those 1992 Los Angeles riots. It was the worst racial episode of the Bush presidency, and the commander in chief ordered Powell to send in soldiers and marines to keep order. Powell felt the military should have been sent in sooner, because people's lives were in such danger. But he felt the need to give Bush a larger explanation of the problems in the black community that gave rise to the crisis, such as harassment and improper arrests of blacks by the police. In the end, such views made little difference, however, because Bush, facing reelection that fall, was intent on taking a tough law-and-order stand, not showing sympathy for the rioters. Bush ended up losing the election.

But Bush did show a personal commitment to racial fairness. For example, he named Dr. Louis Sullivan, former president of the Morehouse Medical School in Atlanta, Georgia, as secretary of the Department of Health and Human Services, Bush's only black cabinet member. More important and symbolic was Bush's choice of Powell as chairman of the Joint Chiefs of Staff, the highest-ranking soldier in the American military. As such, Powell helped direct the successful military campaign to push Iraq out of Kuwait in the first Persian Gulf War and became a national role model for whites and blacks as an iconic modern soldier.

Powell summed up his patron this way: "The George Bush I served was a patrician born to privilege in New England, yet made it on his own in Texas oil fields; a well-bred gentleman who was also full of mischief and fun to be around. He was fair-minded in his judgment and treatment of individuals, yet seemed unmindful of the racial polarization being caused by the far right wing of his party. He had given America proud victories in Panama and the Persian Gulf, presided over the end of the Cold War, and left a world safer from nuclear catastrophe. He had sensed the public pulse on these issues just as he had missed it on America's domestic concerns. He was honored for the one and penalized for the other. As for my personal relationship with George Bush, he had entrusted me with heavy responsibility and respected my judgments. He had also shown me kindness, loyalty, and friendship. I thought the world of him and always will."[51]

Chapter Eleven
Three Southern Presidents

Beyond Lyndon Johnson, three other modern presidents with Southern roots stand out. Jimmy Carter, Bill Clinton, and George W. Bush all came from communities where segregation was considered normal during their early lives, yet as adults and political leaders they overcame their backgrounds. Their presidencies produced some positive results for African Americans, and their dealings with black advisors and staff were on the whole productive and positive.

Jimmy Carter

When Jimmy Carter, a peanut farmer who promised not to lie, was elected president in 1976, he was considered a racially enlightened leader. He had run for governor of Georgia in 1966 and lost, partly because many white voters considered him too liberal on civil rights. When he ran for governor again in 1970 and won, he was hailed by many national commentators and political figures as a model for a new type of racially tolerant and savvy leader in the "New South."

He seemed deeply sensitive to racial issues and the need for equality, largely because he had embraced a form of born-again Christianity that emphasized compassion and social justice, and the belief that the rich and the privileged had a special responsibility to help the less fortunate. He moved decisively toward a broader populism. This became clear in his inaugural address as governor in January 1971, when he declared not only that "the time for discrimination is over"—a campaign theme—but also that "no poor, rural, weak, or black person should ever again have to bear the additional burden of being deprived of the opportunity for an education, a job, or simple justice."[1] There was no small amount of self-righteousness in his beliefs, which put off many other politicians as well as many voters during his public career, but his beliefs were genuine.

Carter's long-shot presidential campaign was a testament to his perseverance and grit. He surprised the experts and defeated Gerald Ford in 1976 by 2.1 percentage points in the popular vote and a 297–240 margin in the Electoral College. Carter largely owed his victory to the fact that African Americans gave him the winning margin in twelve states.[2]

Black voters were impressed with his benign and even courageous racial history. Carter was much more familiar with blacks on a personal level than any of his predecessors. Unlike Nixon and Ford, whose growing-up associations stretched no further than football fields, Carter spoke of a childhood in the predominantly black hamlet of Archery, Georgia. In a community of twenty-five households only the Carters and one other family were white,[3] and legalized segregation and inequality known as Jim Crow held sway.

"All my playmates were black," Carter wrote in his memoir, *Why Not the Best?*[4] "We hunted, fished, explored, worked and slept together.... We ran, swam, rode horses, drove wagons, and floated on rafts together. We misbehaved together and shared the same punishments. We built and lived in the same tree houses and played cards and ate at the same table. But we never went to the same church or school."

The black children, following custom, let Jimmy win at sports and in their other games, so there was no true equality. "I was literally a grown man before I was thrown into social situations in which I routinely met and talked with black men and women on an equal basis," Carter wrote.[5] At home, black women cooked for his family and acted as nannies for the children while their mother, Miss Lillian, went off to work as a registered nurse.[6]

Carter recalled how the blacks kept their feelings to themselves, even in the company of the relatively tolerant Carter family. "All our black neighbors came to see Daddy when the second Joe Louis–Max Schmeling fight was to take place," Carter wrote.[7] "We propped the radio up in the open window of our house, and we and our visitors sat and stood under a large mulberry tree nearby." When the fight ended with a Louis knockout of Schmeling, "there was no sound from anyone in the yard, except a polite, 'Thank you, Mr. Earl,' offered to my father. Then, our several dozen visitors filed across the dirt road, across the railroad track, and quietly entered a house about a hundred yards away out in the field. At that point, pandemonium broke loose inside that house, as our black neighbors shouted and yelled in celebration of the Louis victory."

As a young man, Carter refused to join the White Citizens Council in the hamlet of Plains, Georgia, which had become his home, even though his peanut business was threatened with a boycott (which never materialized).[8] However, during his 1976 campaign for the White House, in discussing busing, Carter warned about "black intrusion" into white areas.[9] Carter said that "interjecting into [a community] a member of another race" or "a diametrically opposite kind of family" or a "different kind of person" posed a threat to what Carter called "ethnic purity," an inflammatory phrase that reminded some of the Third Reich. And there is little doubt that Carter used the term to attract white ethnic voters in Democratic primaries in Pennsylvania and Michigan and white voters in Texas, Missouri, and Georgia. He succeeded.

As president, he initially inspired high hopes. "Basing their assumption upon his compassion for the less privileged and his view of society as unjust, many thought that he would promote a liberal agenda of social reforms," writes Carter biographer Kenneth E. Morris.[10] "He did not. Although he approved of compassionate policies that mitigated the harshest consequences of a free market system, he remained essentially an economic conservative. As governor, his chief accomplishment was to reorganize state government—precisely the kind of reform that appealed to the business class—and, as president, he championed conservative causes like economic deregulation."

Carter named some blacks to important jobs, including civil rights activist Andrew Young, a former aide to Martin Luther King Jr., as the U.S. ambassador to the United Nations, followed later by another African American for the same post, Donald F. McHenry, a State Department veteran. He chose three black women for other key roles, Juanita Kreps as secretary of commerce, Patricia Roberts Harris as secretary of housing and urban development, and Eleanor Holmes Norton to run the EEOC. He appointed Vernon Jordan, president of the National Urban League, and civil rights activist Marian Wright Edelman as part of a group that assessed cabinet appointments for Carter. "No previous administration had come close to this inclusiveness, which boosted Carter's standing among blacks and white liberals," says historian Sean Wilentz.[11]

But black leaders wanted more, and Carter seethed at what he considered their disloyalty. "Whereas [former Democratic presidential nominee] Adlai Stevenson once expected black gratitude because he was not Eisenhower, Carter expected the same because he was not Nixon," writes historian Kenneth O'Reilly.[12] "He never quite understood that civil rights leadership expected much more out of his administration in the first place" on job-creation programs, civil rights, law enforcement, and other issues. Carter also tried to find a middle ground by awkwardly and confusingly supporting affirmative action while attacking quotas, which alienated all sides.[13]

Carter fired Young for a series of provocative remarks and actions, including his unauthorized conference in July 1979 with Zehdi Terzi, the chief U.N. representative of the Palestine Liberation Organization (PLO). Dismissing Young angered many black leaders and voters, which in turn reduced their commitment to turn out for Carter in the 1980 election.

Throughout his presidency, Carter tried to connect his commitment to civil rights for blacks to a larger series of policy formulations and causes, including gender equality and opposition to barriers of opportunity based on region, class, and physical or mental disability.[14] At the University of Notre Dame on May 22, 1977, Carter linked his foreign policy to the U.S. civil rights movement.[15] He said Martin Luther King Jr.'s "I Have a Dream" speech showed the power words have to promote human rights. Carter then posited that Lincoln's argument that the nation could not exist "half slave and half free" was a forerunner of his own belief that a peaceful world cannot long exist "one-third rich and two-thirds hungry."

Carter also supported the Supreme Court's 5–4 ruling in the *Bakke* case, in which the Supreme Court ruled in 1978 that would-be student Allan Bakke had been unfairly denied admission to the medical school at the University of California at Davis because he was white. Bakke claimed that he was discriminated against because blacks with grades and aptitude tests lower than his were admitted. The court specifically said race could be a factor in university admissions but that the California program was unconstitutional because it imposed a percentage quota for minorities. Thus, the high court watered down the overall concept of affirmative action, defined as using government programs to compensate for previous injustices in hiring, education, and government benefits to minorities, but preserved it at the same time.

However, Carter rejected an ambitious proposal by his African American Housing Secretary Patricia Roberts Harris for a new urban antipoverty program, and supported only a weakened version of the Humphrey-Hawkins full employment bill.[16]

Rosalynn Carter, the first lady, reinforced her husband's instincts on civil rights. "Rosalynn Carter's sense of racial equality reaches deep into her Georgia childhood, which spurred her early on to speak out against whites on behalf of civil rights," writes historian Carl S. Anthony.[17] "On several occasions she and her family were threatened because they espoused racial equality. As first lady, when Carter learned that local white ministers had refused to preside at a funeral for a young white man because his family lived in a racially integrated neighborhood, she privately shamed a Baptist minister into performing the service. Besides that, her achievements on behalf of African Americans [were] numerous. She addressed the women of the Congressional Black Caucus, held a special reception for 1,000 members of a Blacks in Government conference, was awarded a Doctor of Humane Letters from Morehouse College, and hosted the first White House musical festival honoring African Americans."

*   *   *

IN THEIR EVERYDAY LIVES, the Carters were quite at home with black people. In his diary for inauguration day, January 20, 1977, Carter wrote: "We had the first of a very relaxed and informal series of meals with our family. Earlier, when Rosalynn was visiting the White House, some of our staff asked the chef and cooks if they thought that they could prepare the kind of meal which we enjoyed in the South, and the cook said, 'Yes, Ma'am, we've been fixing that kind of food for the servants for a long time!'"[18]

He did have the best of intentions. Little known to people outside the White House, the Carters brought in a black ex-convict to care for their nine-year-old daughter, Amy. Carter explained:

> One of Amy's best and closest friends while we lived at the governor's mansion had been Mary Fitzpatrick, who had worked for us while a convict from the Georgia penitentiary near Atlanta. After I was elected President, I contacted the Georgia Pardon and Parole Board and asked if she might be allowed to come to Washington to take care of Amy.

She would be paid as a regular employee, and we would be responsible for her good behavior. They agreed to these terms.

As a visitor to a small south Georgia town, Mary had been involved in a street fight in which a man she had never seen before had been killed. Without adequate legal counsel, she had been convicted of murder, and although we were convinced that she was innocent of this charge, she was serving out her life sentence. Hers was a story all too common among the poor and the black before some of the legal reforms were imposed on our nation by the Supreme Court and Congress in the 1960s.

Mary Fitzpatrick lived in a small room on the third floor of the White House and performed her duties in an exemplary manner. Very close to Amy, Mary proved to be of special help during the times when both Rosalynn and I had to be away from home. She became a valuable member of our White House family and, at the same time, worked hard to be a good citizen. There was some initial criticism and a few ugly letters because we let a 'criminal' work in the White House, but we benefited as much as Mary from the arrangement. Much later, because of her good work and obviously complete rehabilitation, she was given a full pardon by the State of Georgia. One of her proudest days was when she registered to vote.

Yet in the end, Jimmy Carter's presidency was another lost opportunity for blacks. "His heart was in the right place," said civil rights icon Thurgood Marshall, "but that's the best I can do with him."[20]

Bill Clinton

Bill Clinton was a child of segregated Arkansas. One of his most vivid memories was of the integration at Little Rock's Central High School by nine black students in 1957, which was angrily opposed by local whites and Governor Orval Faubus, who tried to block the nine with the National Guard. But the integration was enforced when President Eisenhower sent in U.S. Army troops to ensure safety and order. It was a searing moment of division that Clinton never forgot.

"President Dwight Eisenhower federalized the troops to protect the students, and they went to school through angry mobs shouting racist epithets," Clinton recalled.[21] "Most of my friends were either against integration or apparently unconcerned. I didn't say too much about it, probably because my family was not especially political, but I hated what

Faubus did.... The Little Rock Nine became a symbol of courage in the quest for equality." Thirty years later in 1987, as governor of Arkansas, Clinton invited the nine black students to the Governor's Mansion to honor them. He traced his lifelong commitment to equal rights to his desire to avoid the inhumanity shown by the white power structure in the Central High crisis.[22]

As a boy, Clinton got a personal insight into black culture from "Odessa, a black woman who came to our house to clean, cook, and watch me when my grandparents were at work. She had big buck teeth, which made her smile only brighter and more beautiful to me," he wrote in his autobiography.[23] "I kept up with her for years after I left Hope [Arkansas]. In 1966, a friend and I went out to see Odessa after visiting my father's and grandfather's graves. Most of the black people in Hope lived near the cemetery, across the road from where my grandfather's store had been. I remember our visiting on her porch for a good long while. When the time came to go, we got in my car and drove away on dirt streets. The only unpaved streets I saw in Hope, or later in Hot Springs when I moved there, were in black neighborhoods, full of people who worked hard, many of them raising kids like me, and who paid taxes. Odessa deserved better."

In another revealing moment, Clinton was inspired by the famous Baptist preacher Reverend Billy Graham, when as a boy in 1958 Clinton went to hear Graham preach in Little Rock's War Memorial Stadium. Local segregationists had suggested that Graham allow only whites to attend, but the preacher refused and said he would cancel his appearance rather than preach to a segregated audience. The segregationists backed down and Graham went ahead with his event, which included having people come down to the football field to dedicate their lives to Jesus Christ. Hundreds of blacks and whites came down the aisles together, stood together, and prayed together, Clinton wrote. "It was a powerful counterpoint to the racist politics sweeping across the South," he added.[24] "I loved Billy Graham for doing that. For months after that I regularly sent part of my small allowance to support his ministry."

But perhaps his most formative experience on racial matters came from his grandfather, James Eldridge Cassidy, who ran a small grocery store in Hope, Arkansas, along with his wife, Edith Grisham Cassidy. The couple cared for young Bill while his mother was studying nursing in New Orleans. "[A] lot of my grandfather's customers were black," Clinton said.[25]

"Though the South was completely segregated back then, some level of racial interaction was inevitable in small towns, just as it had always been in the rural south. However, it was rare to find an uneducated rural southerner without a racist bone in his body. That's exactly what my grandfather was. I could see that black people looked different, but because he treated them like he did everybody else, asking after their children and about their work, I thought they were just like me. Occasionally, black kids would come into the store and we would play. It took me years to learn about segregation and prejudice and the meaning of poverty, years to learn that most white people weren't like my grandfather and grandmother, whose views on race were among the few things she had in common with her husband. In fact, Mother told me one of the worst whippings she ever got was when at age three or four she called a black woman 'nigger.' To put it mildly, Mammaw's whipping her was an unusual reaction for a poor southern white woman in the 1920s."

Political scientists Hanes Walton Jr. and Robert C. Smith contend that "Bill Clinton was arguably the first authentically non-racist, non-white-supremacist president in American history. American presidents are a product of the culture and socialization process of their time, and Bill Clinton was the first president to come of age in the nominally non-racist, non-white-supremacist post–civil rights era. By all accounts, Clinton was as free of racist and white-supremacist thinking as any white person can be. Yet, to win the presidency, Clinton ran on a strategy of deliberately distancing himself from black voters in order to win over the so-called Reagan Democrats who had voted Republican because of the Democrats' close identification with African Americans."[26]

But Clinton had a strong understanding of black history and culture, including the importance of the black church. Thurgood Marshall Jr., who worked in the Clinton administration as a government lawyer, recalled how President Clinton impressed him at the funeral for his father, the former Supreme Court justice, in February 1993.[27] Clinton not only sang the first part of an old black spiritual, "Lift Every Voice and Sing," but he knew multiple verses and he boomed them out, one after another. "The man knew every word," Marshall said. He obviously had gone to many services in African American communities and had taken an interest in their traditions.

Clinton had numerous black friends, genuine social intimates and not simply advisors or associates, which set him apart from his predecessors.

His circle included Ernie Green, one of the Central High School Nine; Democratic activist and later Clinton's Commerce Secretary Ron Brown, and, standing above all others, Washington power broker Vernon Jordan, who remained an intimate throughout Clinton's eight years as president.

Jordan was a deal-maker, a Washington insider, and a veteran of the civil rights movement. The tall, suave lawyer declined any job in the administration, preferring to advise Clinton informally and avoid media scrutiny. He was so intent on preserving his privacy that he quietly turned down Clinton's offer to name him attorney general, one of the most prestigious jobs in government.[28] But Jordan had a personal relationship of trust and friendship with Clinton that few people have ever had with any president.

He often gave advice, going back to Clinton's time as governor of Arkansas when in 1982 he urged Bill's wife, Hillary, to take her husband's last name rather than offend traditional voters in a tough upcoming campaign.[29] "He was a southerner and older than we were by enough years to understand why the name issue mattered," Clinton recalled. From then on, she was Hillary Rodham Clinton instead of Hillary Rodham.

Jordan represented Clinton many times on official matters, including talks with independent presidential candidate Ross Perot on whether Perot would reenter the 1992 campaign; he also served on Clinton's transition planning board after he won his first term and scheduled get-acquainted dinners with other Washington power brokers. Jordan arranged for the Clinton family's accommodations during their first extended presidential vacation in August 1993 at Martha's Vineyard, Massachusetts.

His influence increased during Clinton's eight years in the White House. Jordan was a frequent companion for Clinton on the golf course, at social events, and on vacation in Martha's Vineyard. He and his wife, Ann, hosted many parties and dinners for the Clintons. And Jordan was at Clinton's side to provide advice and solace during some of the president's roughest times, including the worst of the public disclosures about his affair with former White House intern Monica Lewinsky. When Clinton's lies about the affair resulted in his impeachment by the House of Representatives and a sensational trial in the Senate, which acquitted him, Jordan stood by his friend.

Questions were also raised about Jordan's role in finding a job for Lewinsky, with critics wondering if this was done to keep her quiet, but Jordan always denied any impropriety and his reputation was so strong that the issue quickly faded. Summarizing his feelings about the sex-and-lies scandal and how he had let so many people down, Clinton wrote in his memoirs, "I also felt bad that Vernon Jordan had been caught up in the maelstrom. We had been close friends for so long, and time and again I had seen him help people who needed it. Now he was being targeted because of me. I knew he hadn't done anything wrong and hoped someday he would be able to forgive me for the mess I had gotten him into."[30]

He was similarly apologetic to Betty Currie, his black personal secretary who facilitated his trysts with Lewinsky out of loyalty to the president and was widely criticized for it.[31]

But Clinton was so sensitive to blacks that the African American writer Toni Morrison famously called him the first black president. Morrison wrote that "Clinton displays almost every trope of blackness: single-parent household, born poor, working-class, saxophone-playing, McDonald's-and-junk-food-loving boy from Arkansas."[32]

His ongoing connections in the African American community "sent a message that his comfort level was very, very high" with black people, and "he was deeply trusted by the black community," said Bill Galston, a former White House advisor to Clinton and now a political scientist.[33] "There was a kind of intimacy that can develop between black and white southerners," many of whom live and work in relatively close proximity day to day and want to avoid the harsh collisions of the past.

"This guy didn't and couldn't look down his nose at other people," says one of Clinton's confidants. "He was not a supercilious northern liberal."

In his first term, Clinton appointed many blacks to high-level positions, including 25 percent of his cabinet, and to the courts.[34] Among his choices were Jesse Brown as secretary of veterans' affairs, Ron Brown as commerce secretary, Mike Espy at agriculture, Hazel O'Leary at energy, Drew Days as solicitor general, and Joycelyn Elders as surgeon general.

In terms of policy, he enhanced his popularity among African Americans by refusing to support the elimination of affirmative action and by using military force to restore the democratically elected president to office in Haiti.[35] He also became the first U.S. president to make state visits to several African countries. Further adding to his luster among blacks was Clinton's attempt to pass legislation guaranteeing health care to all Americans, which would have helped many poor and lower-middle-class African Americans. The measure failed but blacks respected Clinton for trying.

Clinton was a student of America's lingering racial inequality. In discussing the issue of affirmative action, he reminded aides that white men still held 95 percent of the top management jobs in corporate America, and black unemployment was twice white unemployment. Clinton publicly argued that affirmative action had been beneficial for the country, but he knew that many white voters would object if he pushed the issue too hard.[36]

During the 1992 campaign, Clinton pledged to "end welfare as we know it" by imposing a two-year time limit on eligibility for Aid to Families with Dependent Children.[37] During his first two years in office, the Democratic majority in Congress refused to act on Clinton's welfare bill, fearing political retribution from black voters. When the Republicans took control of Congress in the 1994 election, they enacted a more sweeping proposal to abolish the sixty-year-old New Deal guarantee of welfare as a federally mandated right. Clinton vetoed two versions of this bill, but as his 1996 reelection campaign approached, he decided that signing such a measure would help him with conservative and centrist voters, and he signed another version in July of 1996.

*   *   *

ON JUNE 12, 1995, in a 5–4 ruling, the Supreme Court decided in *Adarand v. Pena* that affirmative action was constitutional only if "narrowly tailored" and if it served a "compelling governmental interest."[38] Ever the practical politician seeking to remain popular and deprive his adversaries of ammunition, Clinton used this opportunity to find a middle ground on this very contentious issue. Clinton could now endorse the court decision and its theory of affirmative action in a limited form. He called his approach "Mend it, don't end it." And in a speech at the National Archives, he described his approach to affirmative action as middle of the road: "No quotas in theory or practice; no illegal discrimination of any kind, including reverse discrimination; no preference for people who are not qualified for any job or other opportunity; and as soon as a program has succeeded it must be retired." Clinton added: "But let me be clear: affirmative action has been good for America."

As journalist John F. Harris wrote, "The long-awaited pronouncement on affirmative action was correctly viewed as far more a defense than a critique of the status quo. As a practical matter, the administration made little effort, except as required by legal challenges, to either mend existing programs or end ones that had outlived their usefulness. [White House advisor Christopher] Edley [a senior black official], though he cheered the result, reflected later that such a process could just as easily have produced a retreat from affirmative action as an affirmation. 'The whole thing was very much a jump ball,' he said."[39]

*   *   *

IN ADDITION, Clinton overruled members of the Congressional Black Caucus and most civil rights and civil liberties groups by signing an anti-crime bill that included mandatory sentences for first-time drug offenses and other crimes and in some cases the punishment of juveniles as adults, life in prison for people convicted of three felonies (called the "three strikes and you're out" provision), and expansion of the death penalty to cover more than fifty federal crimes.[40]

Despite his disagreements with African American leaders and activists, Clinton remained popular with blacks throughout his presidency. In his last year in office, for example, 70 percent of African Americans approved of Clinton's job performance (compared with 30 percent for Jimmy Carter at a comparable time).[41] And his decision to establish his post-presidential office in the black community of Harlem added to his luster among African Americans.

*   *   *

IN THE SPRING of 1997, the race issue weighed heavily on Clinton. He could see the end of his presidency approaching, in January 2001, and wanted to make a lasting mark as a progressive who had believed in civil rights all his life. He and his advisors, including pollster Mark Penn, came up with the idea of creating a seven-member, blue-ribbon advisory board to study race relations, modeled on Truman's Civil Rights Commission and the Kerner Commission of 1968, which analyzed the causes of racial violence and racial attitudes across America after a series of lethal urban riots. The more Clinton thought about it, the more ambitious he wanted his commission to be, and he broadened its scope from black-white issues to immigration and relations among other races. The board's report was scheduled for completion in the summer of 1998.

"For the next fifty years, many thinkers expected the nation's worst problems to come from entitlement programs, or the environment, but Clinton believed they would stay centered in race," writes historian Taylor Branch, who met with Clinton regularly throughout his presidency as the president's in-house chronicler. "We needed, and other countries would welcome, a blueprint for interracial democracy refined from the unique experiences of the United States. The president conceded that critics would belittle the mission as both unneeded and impossible, Pollyannaish, or redundant. He said evasion was a proven symptom of racial discomfort, as he and I knew from our youth, and dismissed fears that his commissioners might split into factions. Even if they did, the effort was worthwhile."[42]

Clinton named black historian John Hope Franklin to chair what became known as the Advisory Board on Race, and included a large array of diverse thinkers, leaders, and activists that guaranteed internal argument and raised questions about whether the panel could find consensus on its direction, let alone agree on any findings. But privately, Clinton told Branch, a longtime confidant who had written brilliantly about the civil rights movement, that he had high hopes. "President Clinton welcomed conflict and questions, recalling civil rights as the driving lesson of his public life," Branch said.[43] "He traced the stubborn roots of the human compulsion to define greatness by subjugation of different peoples, as in Bosnia, Rwanda, or the old Soviet Union, and challenged the board to refine different standards. Diversity must be upgraded, for instance, from 'being nice' to an essential strength for the interdependent world."

For weeks, Clinton prodded the race board to avoid being timid and to overcome concerns among its members that it might be taking on too much. He referred to an August 1997 incident in which a Haitian immigrant named Abner Louima was arrested in New York on the periphery of a bar fight, beaten by police, and sodomized at Brooklyn's 70th Police Precinct station with a broomstick. Clinton told his advisory board to use the disgraceful episode as an example of how much prejudice remained in American society. They began to do so.

Throughout his presidency, Clinton exhibited the same interest in America's racial climate that he showed in following the Louima case. In the winter of 1999, he was impressed by the conviction of the first of four defendants in Jasper, Texas, for the murder of James Byrd Jr., a black man who was stripped and dragged for three miles behind a pickup truck in 1998. In a discussion with Branch, Clinton saw it as a sign of racial progress that a mostly white jury in Texas had convicted white supremacists for killing a black man.[44]

That winter, Clinton also was following the case of Amadou Diallo, an immigrant from Guinea who lived in the Bronx and was shot repeatedly by police outside his apartment. Police said he matched the description of a serial rapist and they thought he pulled a gun, which turned out to be his wallet. Clinton feared that the case would lead to more polarization. Clinton's keen interest in the case was all the more remarkable because he was at that time being impeached for his affair with former White House intern Monica Lewinsky, and was fighting for his political life.[45]

At a private meeting with chronicler Branch that winter, Clinton expressed satisfaction with his pardon of Henry O. Flipper, the first black graduate of the U.S. Military Academy at West Point, in the class of 1877.[46] Clinton exonerated Flipper on his conviction for "conduct unbecoming an officer and gentleman" in a racially charged dispute with a superior over alleged embezzlement of government funds. The president also hosted a number of Flipper's descendants at the White House, and afterward, Clinton said, black maids, butlers, and other members of the household staff had formed a line to thank the president when he returned to the residence upstairs after the pardon ceremony.

Yet the race-relations board was turning into a chaotic mess. Christopher Edley Jr., a Harvard law professor who joined senior advisor George Stephanopoulos in helping to lead the White House's review of race relations, provided the president with a stack of articles and speeches by supposed experts on racial issues.[47] But the reading didn't make matters any easier. After perusing the material, Clinton declared: "Most of these people don't know what the hell they're talking about." Clinton felt that he knew best, with his personal experience growing up in the South and as governor of Arkansas and a man who had studied racial history all his life. He thought he had a better sense of reality than the so-called policy experts. Most Americans, Clinton believed, wanted to promote racial equality, but their emotions were easily manipulated by demagogues and special interests. "The definition makes all the difference," he told Stephanopoulos. "Preferences we lose; affirmative action we win." But he couldn't settle on an overall approach to racial justice that could be summed up by the board and implemented by the government.

He was, in formulating a position on affirmative action and so many other issues, always willing to conduct one more review, get one more perspective, in his penchant for flexibility and his desire to find new solutions and fresh compromises. As writer Sally Bedell Smith has said,

Clinton could talk eloquently about the need for racial reconciliation, but he lacked the discipline needed to move "beyond talk to action."[48]

But perhaps the biggest problem for the race panel was keeping the president's attention amid the Monica Lewinsky sex-and-lies scandal, which diverted him and the nation from other concerns just when the race initiative was being launched. The final report, issued in September 1998, disappointed civil rights activists who felt it was filled with platitudes, such as calling for more efforts to educate Americans on the importance of racial diversity. Edley said at the time that most members of Congress had put legislation to help minorities "on hold."[49]

The race initiative did generate some moments of high symbolism.[50] In May, Clinton issued a formal apology on behalf of the nation for the federal government's sponsorship of the egregious "Tuskegee experiment," in which black men were allowed to suffer from advanced syphilis so that scientists could study the effects of the untreated disease. In September, Clinton returned to his home state for an anniversary ceremony honoring the Little Rock Nine.

"Such events had their value," writes Harris.[51] "Increasingly, however, they served only as reminders of how the race initiative hurtled off into abstraction and substantive irrelevance. The effort had bogged down earlier on organization issues: Should the campaign focus on race alone or include such questions as treatment of gays and the physically disabled? (Clinton eventually settled on a narrower focus.) Should the president appoint a high-profile body like the Kerner commission of the 1960s to issue a report to the nation? (He chose instead a lower-profile advisory board, whose recommendations were made directly to him.) These logistical tussles only skirted the larger problem: What was Clinton really trying to achieve? By the end of 1997, even before the nation was introduced to the charms of Monica Lewinsky and public attention moved to other subjects, the race initiative was a dawdling and aimless exercise that was drawing criticism even from participants on Clinton's advisory board."

In the end, the race initiative amounted to very little.

In March and early April 1998, as official investigations were accelerating into his affair with Monica Lewinsky, Clinton made the longest trip of his presidency: a visit to Africa that included six countries in eleven days and a tumultuous welcome in Accra, Ghana. "At home," wrote author Harris,[52] "Clinton was being systematically disrobed in the most personally embarrassing investigation in American political history. Here, he was revered. The throbbing mass of Ghanaians understood that in taking this trip, Clinton was showing himself as a different kind of leader, possessed of a larger vision, who wanted to take American diplomacy—and America's reputation among common folk around the world—in new directions."

It was a harbinger of the message that Barack Obama would try to send as the first African American president during his first year in office, in 2009.

Clinton had also been considering for months whether to issue, on behalf of the nation, an apology to African Americans for slavery. Some black leaders favored the symbolic gesture. Others wanted financial reparations to the descendants of slaves. Clinton ultimately decided against either course, judging that it would be too divisive.

*   *   *

RELATIONS BETWEEN THE Clintons and the household staff started off awkwardly. Not accustomed to a twenty-four-hour staff of servants, the Clintons couldn't quite figure out what the household workers were supposed to do, and they weren't sure they could trust employees who had served Republican Presidents Ronald Reagan and George H. W. Bush. And Hillary Clinton was more hard-charging than any other first lady in the household staff's experience. Not only was she immersed in policy, such as health-care reform, but she insisted on changing many of the East Wing traditions, ranging from the type of food served (she preferred more flair and less of the conventional French cooking that previous presidents had wanted) to the rooms where the household staff could go. The Clintons didn't like the idea of the workers, all of them strangers to the new first couple, walking through the family quarters at all hours to perform chores such as closing doors or switching off the lights. The Clintons were so suspicious of the staff and what they thought were their excessive loyalties to the Bushes and the Reagans, that the new first lady fired an assistant head usher, Chris Emery, because he accepted too many phone calls from former first lady Barbara Bush. Emery tried to explain that he was trying to help Mrs. Bush operate her new computer, but Mrs. Clinton felt he was telling tales out of school to her predecessor.

"Mrs. Clinton was very demanding," recalls Emery.[53] "Everyone was at her beck and call" and staff members would gather around the White House simply awaiting her orders because they weren't sure how to anticipate her wishes. But eventually, everyone adapted, and after several months, the Clintons and the household staff got along fine.

George W. Bush

The pattern of blacks playing a key part in the presidency continued with George W. Bush during his two terms. In fact, among his first acts, he appointed Colin Powell as secretary of state and Condoleezza Rice as White House national security advisor, making them the highest-ranking blacks ever to hold federal office. Both had served in national security positions in the administration of his father, George H. W. Bush.

Bush had come from a privileged background. His parents had inherited considerable wealth but they moved their young family to the Midland, Texas, area while the father made his own way in the oil business. "Dubya" recalled how a local high school was segregated in those days, as was much of the larger community. But he said his parents "did not tolerate bigotry." His wife, Laura, related in her memoirs how his mother "smacked him" as a child when he used a racial epithet.[54] And he developed friendships with African Americans in the schools he attended. He also worked in an inner-city poverty program after college, which exposed him to another side of life. He continued to maintain friendships with African Americans through his adult life, and his longtime spiritual advisor was Kirbyjohn Caldwell, the black pastor of Windsor Village United Methodist Church in Houston.

But as governor of Texas Bush wasn't known for making much of a political outreach to black voters and he entered the White House with minimal support from African Americans, less than 10 percent. Many black leaders and voters questioned the legitimacy of his election because of a disputed vote count in Florida in which many blacks were apparently disenfranchised. Partly as a result, Bush attempted to appeal to the black community in a variety of ways. For example, he made an extended visit to several African countries.[55] On Goree Island in Ghana (where enslaved Africans began their horrendous and often-lethal passage to America), he did not formally apologize for slavery (as Clinton also refused to do on his visit), but he described slavery as "one of the greatest crimes of history." Bush also hosted half of Africa's leaders at a Washington summit and held one of his rare state dinners for the president of Uganda. Among other symbolic gestures, Bush hung a portrait of Martin Luther King Jr. in the White House, laid a wreath at King's tomb, hosted Thomas Jefferson's black relatives at the White House, and signed legislation creating a National Museum of African American History and Culture.

The biggest setback to Bush's reputation among blacks was his administration's inept handing of Hurricane Katrina and his personal insensitivity to the storm's aftermath, which caused disproportionate harm to the poor black community of New Orleans. When Katrina hit a broad swath of the Gulf Coast in August 2005, Bush was completing a five-week vacation at his Texas ranch. He paid scant attention to the initial news reports of the devastation, even though the horrendous conditions were receiving saturation coverage in the media. Bush's aides say he rarely read newspapers or watched TV news, and his staff didn't keep him adequately informed of the crisis that had hit.

Two full days after Katrina struck, Bush finally cut his vacation short and returned to Washington to oversee the lagging rescue and recovery efforts. The following day, he visited the Gulf Coast and told Michael Brown, director of the federal crisis-management agency FEMA, "Brownie, you're doing a heck of a job." Most observers believed Brown was doing a very poor job, and Bush's comments made him seem hopelessly out of touch. When the president visited hard-hit New Orleans, where thousands of black residents were stranded without adequate food and water in the local football stadium, he joked about how much he loved to party in the city as a young man. Bush was widely lambasted for insensitivity and ineptitude. Rap singer Kanye West told a nationally televised fund-raiser for hurricane victims that, "George Bush doesn't care about black people."

Such comments offended Bush. "One of the most hurtful things during my administration was to hear some say that the federal response to Katrina was flawed because of race," Bush told me later.[56] "The truth is that Katrina was one of the largest, deadliest, and costliest storms in history. It impacted an entire region, and government at all levels failed to respond adequately. As I said to the press at the time, 'The storm didn't discriminate, and neither did the recovery effort.' When those Coast Guard choppers were pulling people off roofs, they didn't check the color of a person's skin."

With polls showing Americans appalled at the federal effort and Bush's seeming indifference, the president fired Brown and apologized for the government's "unacceptable" slow response in evacuating victims and failure to get needed supplies to the desperate residents of New Orleans.

He also announced a major program of long-term federal assistance to rebuild the damaged areas, create jobs for people in the region, and provide other help. But the Republican-controlled Congress, while it approved billions of dollars in aid, ignored many of his recommendations for a comprehensive rebuilding of the hurricane-ravaged region. Bush also enlisted Condoleezza Rice, by then his secretary of state, to publicly defend her boss's racial sensitivity. But the Katrina fiasco was a lasting blemish on Bush and his presidency.

Bush's record on racial policy was mixed. He issued guidelines banning racial profiling by federal law enforcement agencies (except for cases involving terrorism and national security), proposed to Congress a program to increase low-income and minority home ownership, and proposed a "Faith-Based Initiative" to allow churches, including those in hard-pressed African American communities, to provide social services to the poor. One of his proudest accomplishments was pushing through Congress the No Child Left Behind Act, which was designed to raise the performance of low-income and minority students by measuring students' success on standardized tests as a way of holding schools accountable.

Bush told me that No Child Left Behind "was the most significant piece of civil rights legislation since the Voting Rights Act of 1965. It challenged a status quo that tended to move African American kids through schools without measuring whether they could add, subtract, read, or write."[57]

In foreign policy he dispatched a special envoy to mediate the Sudanese civil war, sent a small U.S. peacekeeping force to Liberia, and proposed substantial increases in funds to combat AIDS in Africa. However, over the vigorous objections of the Congressional Black Caucus and other African American leaders, Bush brought about the removal of Jean-Bertrand Aristide, the democratically elected president of Haiti.

During the Clinton administration, U.S. forces were used to restore Aristide to office after he had been overthrown in a military coup. But the Bush administration, charging that Aristide was corrupt and engaged in drug trafficking, cut off all U.S. aid to Haiti and encouraged the World Bank and the International Monetary Fund to do the same. As insurgents threatened to take over the country, the United States told Aristide that if he did not leave Haiti it could not guarantee his safety. African American leaders had urged the United States to intervene to preserve Aristide's presidency (charging the insurgents were "thugs" and "terrorists"). Instead, Bush blamed Aristide for the crisis and forced him into exile in

Africa. Later, Secretary of State Powell threatened to prosecute Aristide on corruption charges in U.S. courts.[58]

African American leaders opposed the central goal of Bush's domestic policy agenda—his tax cuts—because they benefited mainly rich whites.[59] These leaders also objected to his foreign policy, especially the war on Iraq, which they felt diverted money from needed social programs. And black leaders opposed a series of Bush proposals to cut funding for housing, Head Start, and Medicaid and to increase the hours parents on welfare had to work, as well as shift control over health and welfare programs to the states.

Then the issue of affirmative action returned with full force. It erupted when the administration began to focus on what position to take in two lawsuits challenging the University of Michigan's affirmative action programs. These two cases were the most important on the issue since the Supreme Court's landmark 1978 ruling in *Regents of University of California v. Bakke.*

The Bush administration was divided on what position to argue before the Supreme Court.[60] Conservatives favored asking the court to overrule *Bakke* and declare that the Fourteenth Amendment prohibited any consideration of race in university admissions. Solicitor General Theodore Olson, the official responsible for writing the brief, was insistent that this hard line be taken; it was, after all, Olson who in 1996 had persuaded the 5th Circuit Court of Appeals in *Hopwood v. Texas* to overrule *Bakke.* Moderates in the administration, including Alberto Gonzalez, the president's counsel, urged President Bush to avoid the constitutional question of whether race could ever be used in admission decisions. Instead, this faction said the administration should simply ask the court to declare the Michigan programs unconstitutional because they constituted racial quotas. Olson was reportedly furious at the internal opposition to his views and threatened to go public with his objections until he received a call from Vice President Dick Cheney telling him to cool off and keep his objections private.

In a late-afternoon speech, Bush adopted the position of Gonzalez and the other moderates, saying that while he supported "diversity of all kinds," the Michigan programs were fundamentally flawed because they constituted racial quotas.[61]

* * *

THE RELATIONSHIP between the Bushes and the household staff was warm and friendly. George and Laura, his wife, knew how the East Wing residence was supposed to operate since they had visited so often when George's father was president. And they were on a first-name basis with many members of the staff from day one. "Laura and I were very close to the White House residence staff," Bush told me.[62] "They are family to us, and always will be."

In addition, while the staff may have preferred Clinton's progressive social policies, they did appreciate Bush for his personal habits and the consideration he showed toward them. For one thing, Bush was nearly always on time, while Clinton was habitually late. This made a serious difference in the planning of meals and other events because with Bush the staffers could rely on him to maintain a schedule, enabling them to get home to their families with predictability. The Bushes also were un-failingly polite and pleasant, which was much appreciated.

Colin Powell and Condoleezza Rice

As mentioned earlier, two particularly bright spots in racial progress emerged with the rise of Colin Powell and Condoleezza Rice. Their stories deserve special attention.

General Powell enjoyed an illustrious career in the Army, and was named by Ronald Reagan as the White House national security advisor, one of the most important jobs in the government. After that, President George H. W. Bush appointed Powell as chairman of the Joint Chiefs of Staff, making him the most powerful person in the military. In that job, Powell helped direct the successful first Persian Gulf War against Iraq. In 2001, he became secretary of state for President George W. Bush's first term.

Powell did have his resentments. He wrote in his autobiography, *My American Journey,* that he was occasionally asked how he felt about the Willie Horton TV spot used by supporters of George H. W. Bush (but not by Bush's campaign) against Democratic nominee Michael Dukakis in the 1988 presidential campaign. Horton, a black felon, had sexually assaulted a woman and stabbed her boyfriend while on a weekend pass from a Massachusetts prison while Dukakis was the state's governor. "Was the ad depicting this incident racist? Of course," Powell wrote.[63] "Had it bothered me? Certainly. Republican strategists had made a cold political calculation: no amount of money or effort could make a dent in the Democratic hold on the black vote, so don't try. Some had gone even further—if the racial card could be played to appeal to certain constituencies, play it. The Horton ad served that purpose. It was a political cheap shot."

"I nevertheless tried to keep matters in perspective," Powell added.[64] "I had been given responsibility at the highest level in a Republican administration. National security advisors to presidents are not chosen as tokens. The job is real, demanding, and critical. Never in the two years I worked with Ronald Reagan and George Bush did I detect the slightest trace of racial prejudice in their behavior. They led a party, however, whose principal message to black Americans seemed to be: lift yourself by your bootstraps. All did not have bootstraps; some did not have boots. I wish that Reagan and Bush had shown more sensitivity on this point. I took consolation, nevertheless, in the thought that their confidence in me represented a commitment to the American ideal of advancement by merit."

Powell wrote: "My career should serve as a model to fellow blacks, in or out of the military, in demonstrating the possibilities of American life. Equally important, I hoped then and now that my rise might cause prejudiced whites to question their prejudices, and help purge the poison of racism from their systems, so that the next qualified African American who came along would be judged on merit alone."[65]

Powell's and Rice's roles in the younger Bush's Iraq war led Harry Belafonte, an African American entertainer and human rights advocate, to attack them as "house slaves" doing the work of their white master.[66] Many black leaders criticized Belafonte for his attack, but most blacks were turning against the war. A poll in April 2003 found that only 39 percent of blacks supported the war, compared with 81 percent of whites and 61 percent of Hispanics.

*   *   *

CONDOLEEZZA RICE WAS an unusual woman in many ways. A former figure skater, trained classical pianist, and brilliant intellectual (whose first name is based on an Italian expression for "with sweetness," *con dolcezza*), she overcame the prejudices of her hometown of Birmingham, Alabama, in the segregated 1950s and 1960s, and adopted her parents' belief in education as a way up the social and economic ladder. She specialized in Russian history and caught the attention of Brent Scowcroft, President George H. W. Bush's national security advisor, who became her mentor as she was promoted to the position of chief Russian expert on the National Security Council staff. This was an especially important job during the demise of the Soviet Union, which occurred during Bush's presidency from 1989 to 1993.

She left government and served as provost of Stanford University during the eight years of Bill Clinton's presidency, and then became the chief national security advisor to George W. Bush, the earlier president's son, during his successful 2000 presidential campaign.

In 2001, she returned to government service as Bush's White House national security advisor, working with Colin Powell at the State Department. While Powell's pragmatic views were sometimes disregarded by Bush in favor of the more hard-line, military-oriented approach of Vice President Dick Cheney and Defense Secretary Donald Rumsfeld, Rice tried not to alienate anyone while siding with the hard-liners. She also became popular with the news media, as was Powell, because of her accessibility and her ability to clarify complex policy issues in succinct and compelling ways.

Rice rose to the very top during the latter part of George W. Bush's presidency. Not only did Rice move from national security advisor to secretary of state in his second term (becoming the first African American woman to hold both those jobs), she also became a confidant of Bush. She accompanied him and his wife to the presidential retreat, Camp David, on weekends, and spent many weeks during the couple's vacations at their ranch in Crawford, Texas. White House aides said she became like a sister to Bush and was deeply loyal to him and his policies, including the controversial invasion and occupation of Iraq and his belief in waging "preventive war" to stop terrorism.

In this loyalty, she followed in the footsteps of innumerable black advisors and members of the presidential household staff over the years. She was not only one of the most influential blacks ever to serve in government, she was also one of the most influential national security and foreign policy advisors in the nation's history.

Bush told me that he counted on Rice (and Powell) for advice on foreign policy and national security, and "they were not special advisors on race. However, occasionally they did talk to me about programs related to making sure African Americans had access to the American dream. I specifically recall getting good advice from Condi on the Michigan case."[67] He declined to elaborate.

But Bush added that, "Prior to my running for president, Condi and I discussed whether or not I would focus on Africa. I agreed with her that Africa would be an important part of my agenda. Once we focused on Africa, it became clear that HIV/AIDS had to be addressed. In many countries, virtually an entire generation was in danger of being wiped out. Tragically, the treatments existed that would save lives, but the aid programs were failing miserably. Money was being spent, but often it was stolen by corrupt governments or wasted by ineffective international organizations."

He went on to recount the program his administration established in 2003, called PEPFAR, "based on a new model of aid that treated foreign governments as partners and measured success by the number of lives saved rather than by the number of dollars spent. By the end of my administration, we had helped bring life-saving treatments to more than 2.1 million people and care for more than 10 million people around the world."

* * *

ONE OTHER OVERARCHING point about Powell and Rice needs to be made. As with so many other African Americans at the White House, they felt a constant need to prove themselves not only as individuals but as black role models. When he named Powell secretary of state, Bush didn't mention race, but Powell discussed the idea in depth in accepting the nomination. "I want it repeated because I hope it will give inspiration to young African Americans coming along—but beyond that, all young Americans coming along—that no matter where you belong in this society, with hard work and with dedication and with the opportunities that are presented by this society, there are no limitations on you. And I also want to pay tribute to so many people who helped me reach this position in life: African Americans who came before me who never could have risen to this position because the conditions weren't there and we had to fight to change those conditions."[68]

In separate remarks at the Powell announcement, Rice also referred to race, although less expansively. "If I may close with just a personal note," she said, "this is an extraordinary time for America because our values are being affirmed, and it's important to always remember what those values are at home. And I grew up in Birmingham, Alabama. I did not go to integrated schools until I was in 10th grade and we moved to Denver, Colorado."[69]

Over their tenures, neither Powell nor Rice would overtly use their race as a part of their jobs, either inside the administration or in public. They didn't allow their African American identities to define their public roles.[70] But at the same time, they didn't try to escape from their heritage. Rice, for example, told the National Association of Black Journalists in 2003, "When the founding fathers said 'We the People,' they did not mean us. Our ancestors were considered three-fifths of a person."[71] [This is a reference to Article 1, Section 2.3 of the Constitution.] And she also made sure to speak, as did Powell on similar occasions, of the enormous advances made by blacks over the years.

Chapter Twelve
The First Black President

Barack Obama was the unlikeliest of presidents. A one-term senator from Illinois, he had little national or international experience and faced a formidable array of opponents, led by New York Senator and former first lady Hillary Rodham Clinton, who also sought the Democratic nomination in 2008. Beyond his purely political disadvantages, the race issue also loomed large. The son of a black man from Kenya and a white woman from Kansas, Obama would test the idea of whether America was ready for an African American president.

But the lure of making history was irresistible for Obama. In a candid discussion with his advisers in December 2006, in the Chicago conference room of senior strategist David Axelrod, his wife Michelle asked him what he exactly he thought he could achieve by becoming president. "Well," Obama replied, "there are a lot of things I think I can accomplish, but two things I know. The first is, when I raise my hand and take that oath of office, there are millions of kids around this country who don't believe that it would ever be possible for them to be president of the United States. And for them the world would change on that day. And the second thing is, I think the world would look at us differently the day I got elected, because it would be a reaffirmation of what America is, about the constant perfecting of who we are, I think. I can help repair the damage that's been done."[1]

Obama went on to announce his candidacy on February 10, 2007.

He had to pass two specific tests: First, he needed to prove that, as a Harvard Law School–educated apostle of conciliation, he could hold the support of black voters, potentially the core of his support in the big cities and in the large, diverse swing states such as Florida and Ohio. Many of them, especially older voters, were accustomed to black candidates who emphasized their fierce commitment to civil rights and confronting the white establishment. Second, Obama had to persuade white voters to make a leap of faith and believe that he was a different kind of black presidential candidate, one who would be even-handed in considering racial issues and could understand their lives and finds ways to solve their problems.

He managed to combine both appeals—as a bridge builder. It was what most voters wanted in their leader after eight years of polarization under Republican President George W. Bush. His desire to be a healer came through in many ways, including his admiration of Abraham Lincoln as one of his heroes. Not only was Lincoln also from Illinois and a man with a minimal record as a national politician, but Obama also saw Lincoln as a person who came from humble beginnings and rose to the highest level of politics as a principled compromiser, just the way Obama saw himself.

During the campaign, he said in an interview:

> What I admire so deeply about Lincoln—number one, I think he's the quintessential American because he's self-made. The way Alexander Hamilton was self-made or so many of our great iconic Americans are, that sense that you don't accept limits, that you can shape your destiny. That obviously has appeal to me, given where I came from. That American spirit is one of the things that is most fundamental to me, and I think he embodies that.
>
> But the second thing that I admire most in Lincoln is that there is just a deep-rooted honesty and empathy to the man that allowed him to always be able to see the other person's point of view and always sought to find that truth that is in the gap between you and me. Right? That the truth is out there somewhere and I don't fully possess it and you don't fully possess it and our job then is to listen and learn and imagine enough to be able to get to that truth.
>
> If you look at his presidency, he never lost that. Most of our other great presidents, there was that sense of working the angles and bending other people to their will, [Roosevelt] being the classic example. And Lincoln just found a way to shape public opinion and shape people around him and lead them and guide them without tricking them or

bullying them, but just through the force of what I just talked about—that way of helping to illuminate the truth. I just find that to be a very compelling style of leadership. It's not one that I've mastered, but I think that's when leadership is at its best.[2]

Obama would spend much of the 2008 campaign and, later, the early part of his presidency, putting these theories to the test.

*   *   *

OBAMA ENTERED THE campaign with a clear idea about how far the country had come in dealing with race, and how far it still had to go. He had not always been so understanding and conciliatory. In his memoir, *The Audacity of Hope*, he wrote about how, like so many other young black men, he had felt anger at white society during his late teens and twenties, and confusion about his place in white-dominated America. As he matured, he realized that, as the product of a mixed marriage and raised by a white mother and white grandparents, he had much in common with whites as well as blacks. His natural tendency was to avoid confrontation and to find areas of agreement, whether as president of the *Harvard Law Review*, as a community organizer in Chicago, or as a state legislator and, later, U.S. Senator from Illinois.

As a presidential candidate, he was in some ways a political Rorschach test, a way for Americans to project their hopes and dreams and, for the more traditional or bigoted, their fears and resentments, on a single individual. And he played the positives to his advantage, while managing to minimize the negatives. On balance, his personal biography, coupled with his refusal to get too far ahead of public opinion on racial issues and other major concerns, and together with his gauzy and inspirational rhetoric, propelled his success.

In *The Audacity of Hope*, Obama demonstrated a clear understanding of his personal appeal as a harbinger of change, often a popular theme in American politics, and a person who reflected and embodied the nation's ideal of diversity. He wrote, accurately, that many Americans felt a strong connection to the most memorable line from his speech to the 2004 Democratic National Convention: "There is not a black America and white America and Latino America and Asian America—there's the United States of America." Emphasizing his personal story, Obama went on to write that, "In a sense I have no choice but to believe in this vision of America. As the child of a black man and a white woman, someone who was born in the racial melting pot of Hawaii, with a sister who's half Indonesian but who's usually mistaken for Mexican or Puerto Rican, and a brother-in-law and niece of Chinese descent, with some blood relatives who resemble Margaret Thatcher and others who could pass for Bernie Mac, so that family get-togethers over Christmas take on the appearance of a U.N. General Assembly meeting, I've never had the option of restricting my loyalties on the basis of race, or measuring my worth on the basis of tribe."[3]

This formulation is no doubt a genuine expression of Obama's feelings. But it was also astute politically in that it blended the thread of black and white relationships with a broader sense of diversity in the country. As he made clear in the campaign, Obama does not see America solely through the lens of black and white, but with a larger perspective of racial, ethnic, gender, and other differences. In the campaign, this greatly widened his appeal and helped to remove him from the divisive band of angry black politicians such as Jesse Jackson and Al Sharpton, who have unsettled whites and who, by 2008, had lost much of their appeal to both younger blacks and affluent African Americans. It was also clever and poignant that Obama dedicated his best-selling memoir to "the women who raised me," his mother and his maternal grandmother. Both were white. (His father abandoned the family, returning to Kenya, when Obama was a boy.)

Obama said he wasn't trying to forget "the sins of our past," such as slavery and segregation, but felt that the country had moved a long way toward fairness and tolerance. His own elections, first as a U.S. senator and, most dramatically, as president, confirmed how much the racial climate had changed for the better.

For years, Obama shied away from any massive government efforts to help African Americans—which would generate white animosity and limit his own appeal—in favor of general programs that, he believes, would lift everyone. But he has felt that something must be done, as he said vaguely in his book,[4] to address "the deteriorating condition of the inner-city poor."

His answers have been, and remain, well within the mainstream of political thought and some of his ideas are quite conservative. He wrote that, "We could begin by acknowledging that perhaps the single biggest thing we could do to reduce such poverty is to encourage teenage girls to finish high school and avoid having children out of wedlock."[5] And this, he says, is mostly the job of "school- and community-based programs," and parents, clergy, and community leaders. For years, he has also called for creating jobs in the inner cities, improving the availability of child care and health care, increasing numbers of police, and establishing better schools.

It was a good-hearted series of prescriptions, but nothing new or particularly bold. It identified Obama as a liberal but not a radical, a man who did not threaten the majority of voters, at least not in 2008.

*   *   *

AS THE 2008 presidential campaign began, Obama and his advisers understood better than Hillary Clinton and her team the mechanics of the Democratic nominating process—especially the role of caucus states. The caucuses emphasized direct and public participation by relatively small numbers of committed activists in choosing delegates, as opposed to states that used primaries, where people voted anonymously and en masse. More important, Obama understood that after eight years of government by Republican George W. Bush, the party and the country were eager for a big change and that he represented a vivid break from the past in the mold of John F. Kennedy in 1960. He played up his generational differences with Clinton and other candidates and welcomed the media's arguments that, as a young newcomer with strong charisma and a message of transformational change, he would take the torch of leadership from the older generation, as Kennedy did.

And in the end, no change would be bigger in the minds of voters than electing the first African American as president—not even electing the first woman.

In retrospect, Obama had some crucial advantages that no other black presidential candidate had ever had. He was, after all, the product of an interracial marriage, the kind of relationship that was illegal in many states for generations and that black men could have been lynched for a century earlier. But in 2008 this was actually an advantage because his mixed heritage reinforced his carefully calibrated image as an unusual candidate who brought a fresh perspective to racial issues. Obama's goal as a candidate was always to move beyond the history of slavery, segregation, and racial bitterness and find a new way of looking at relations between blacks and whites that celebrated common values such as tolerance, opportunity, and the work ethic. But dealing with race remained one of Obama's most important challenges during the campaign, especially in the view of many working-class whites in big swing states such as Ohio and Missouri. They feared that Obama couldn't understand their problems and that he might be biased in favor of fellow blacks.

* * *

ON THE OTHER side of the racial ledger, Obama saw his race as a way to inspire blacks, especially black men, to abandon some of their more self-destructive tendencies. One was the lack of commitment of some young African American men to their children and to the concept of family.

In a speech on Father's Day in June 2008 Obama told the Apostolic Church of God in Chicago, a mostly black congregation: "Of all the rocks upon which we build our lives, we are reminded today that family is the most important. And we ... recognize and honor how critical every father is to that foundation.... If we are honest with ourselves, we'll admit that too many fathers also are missing—missing from too many lives and too many homes. They have abandoned their responsibilities, acting like boys instead of men. And the foundations of our families are weaker because of it."[6]

Obama added: "We need fathers to realize that responsibility does not end at conception. We need them to realize that what makes a man is not the ability to have a child—it's the courage to raise one." He noted that his own father had left the family when Obama was a child, leaving his mother to raise him. "I know what it means to have an absent father," he said, emphasizing that he had resolved "that if I could be anything in life, I would be a good father to my children."

One hurdle that Obama needed to overcome was the reluctance of black voters to take him seriously as a presidential contender. This was accomplished when he won the overwhelmingly white state of Iowa in the caucuses of early 2008, the first big test of the nominating cycle. But he had another, equally important obstacle to the fullest possible level of black support. Time and again, African American voters told me and other reporters that they were worried about the potential for Obama's assassination. Michelle Obama addressed this issue directly very early in the campaign when asked by Steve Kroft of *Sixty Minutes* if she feared for her husband's life. "As a black man, Barack could be shot going to the gas station," the future first lady replied.[7] It was a blunt statement about everyday life for American black men, who are ten times more likely than white men to be victims of homicide. But it also was a signal to black Americans that if the Obamas weren't overly worried about assassination, they shouldn't be either.

* * *

THE MOST IMPORTANT racial issue in the campaign, and one that could easily have undermined Obama's entire strategy, erupted over the inflammatory, racially charged remarks of the candidate's pastor in Chicago, the Reverend Jeremiah Wright. Not only was Wright the spiritual mentor for the Obama family who had officiated at Barack and Michelle's wedding and baptized their two daughters, Sasha and Malia, he was also a personal friend and important link to many movers and shakers in the Chicago black community. Wright, in short, had been essential to Obama's rise in Illinois politics, from his days as a community organizer to his service in the state Senate and U.S. Senate.

What caused the furor were videotapes of Wright sermons in which he berated whites for racism, condemned the United States as a nation with the declaration of "God damn America," and said white Americans couldn't be trusted to deal fairly with the black community. The story broke in March 2008 when ABC News reported on Wright's sermons. One videotape, widely broadcast on television, showed Wright, shortly after the terrorist attacks of September 11, 2001, shouting from the pulpit at his Trinity United Church of Christ, "We bombed Hiroshima. We bombed Nagasaki. And we nuked far more than the thousands in New York and the Pentagon—and we never batted an eye. We have supported state terrorism against the Palestinians and black South Africans and now we are indignant because the stuff we have done overseas is now brought right back into our own front yards. America's chickens are coming home to roost!"[8]

Suddenly, Obama was forced to confront the race issue head-on, which threw off his carefully calibrated strategy of billing himself as something unique in American history—the black presidential candidate who was, in policy and attitude, race-neutral. He realized that the Wright furor threatened to reopen all the old wounds and suspicions and enmities between black and white. And now he had to walk through a minefield. He could easily come across as a turncoat or a toady to blacks or an untrustworthy racial zealot to whites.

Obama decided to talk about the Wright issue—and race in America—directly and candidly. In a dramatic speech delivered in Philadelphia that spring, Obama summoned all his powers of eloquence and charisma. He said both blacks and whites had made mistakes in dealing with each other in the past and he tried to explain the role of incendiary rhetoric in black churches as a way to boost black self-esteem. "I thought it was very important at that point for me to help translate the experiences both of Reverend Wright," Obama recalled later, "but also how the ordinary white American might feel in hearing Reverend Wright and how both sets of experiences were an outgrowth of our history and had to be acknowledged and dealt with instead of just papered over or reduced to a caricature. And I think that the speech in Philadelphia succeeded in doing that."[9]

Obama said Wright had a "profoundly distorted view of this country—a view that sees white racism as endemic, and that elevates what is wrong with America above all that we know is right with America."[10] Obama said he couldn't give up on his pastor. "I can no more disown him than I can disown the black community. I can no more disown him than I can my white grandmother," who had expressed racial attitudes "that made me cringe." He went on to call for racial understanding and declared, "This union may never be perfect. But generation after generation has shown that it can always be perfected."

Obama's speech was widely praised for promoting a spirit of reconciliation. But Wright wouldn't disappear. In a speech at the National Press Club on April 28, he refused to retract or modify his anti-white comments and gave another angry performance similar to the earlier one. This time, Obama denounced Wright, disavowed him, and announced that he and his family would leave Wright's church. "His comments were not only divisive and destructive," Obama said, "but I believe that they end up giving comfort to those who prey on hate, and I believe that they do not portray accurately the perspective of the black church. They certainly don't portray accurately my values and beliefs."[11] He said Wright's comments were "outrageous" and "ridiculous."

"He's a great preacher," Obama observed later.[12] "... But Reverend Wright remained rooted in the rhetoric of the Sixties.... What he was saying was not considered in any way exceptional in the African American community for his generation. He never updated or refreshed that world view to accommodate the changes that were taking place in America. And what you were seeing in Reverend Wright and those statements were not only offensive to everybody in many ways, but it also showed an anger and bitterness ... that may be more acceptable in some circles in the African American community but is never acceptable in mainstream America. And so you had that sudden, really volatile potential clash of visions."

In the end, Obama's balanced approach eased racial suspicions enough for him to move beyond the Wright controversy, and he pivoted to broader themes, especially his pledges to heal the troubled economy, end the war in Iraq, pursue the war in Afghanistan, and bring a new era of change and cooperation to Washington. He won the election by holding onto the traditionally Democratic black vote, pivotal in big states including Ohio and Florida, which he captured. He also managed to reassure enough white voters that he understood their problems and had better ideas than Senator John McCain, his Republican opponent, about ending the economic downturn. He won 53 percent of the popular vote—nearly 69.5 million to McCain's nearly 60 million, the highest for any Democrat since Lyndon Johnson in 1964. In the process, he won 375 electoral votes to McCain's 163, a very solid majority. Beyond that, Obama got 43 percent of the white vote, 95 percent of the black vote, 67 percent of the Latino vote, and 62 percent of the Asian vote. This racial divide was not specific to Obama, however. No Democratic president since Lyndon Johnson in 1964—not Jimmy Carter, not Bill Clinton, not Barack Obama—has won a majority of white votes. But among younger white voters aged eighteen to twenty-nine, Obama won by 54 percent to 44 percent, a good sign for Obama's future.

America had lived up to its ideals at last. The country had elected an African American president more than 140 years after African Americans had been slaves and four decades after the civil rights movement had forced changes in American law to give blacks the right to vote and ensure legal equality across the land.

*   *   *

THE DAY HE was sworn in, on January 20, 2009, Obama toured the almost-bare Oval Office, a forty-seven-year-old commander in chief (the fifth-youngest president in history) who looked even younger than his years, and stood under the famous portrait of George Washington by Rembrandt Peale, which hangs over the fireplace. David Axelrod, one of his senior advisers, told me later that it was an emotional time for those, like "Axe," who had been with him from the start of his ascent to the presidency and who had believed in him for many years. It seemed the realization of a dream—the first African American president taking over, in front of the backdrop of the first president, who had owned slaves and who brought them with him to the White House.

Even Obama's critics were impressed. As former President George H. W. Bush told me, "Obviously we have come a long way. It's unimaginable to think there was a time when not everyone went to the same school, or sat together on the bus, or drank out of the same water fountain. But of course there is still such a long way to go. There are still too many stereotypes and prejudices and just plain ignorance. It would be nice to think that the election of our first African American president would mean the end of racial issues forever. Certainly, President Obama's election was a major step forward. I hope we get there someday."[13]

Princeton historian Cornel West captured the euphoria of Obama's supporters, especially the black community, when he wrote in November 2008: "For the first time in the history of American civilization, a black man will occupy the White House and lead the nation. The shattering of this glass ceiling has a symbolic gravity difficult to measure—here and around the world. On one election day and one January morning, the self-image of America undergoes a grand transformation. In the eyes and hearts of young people of all colors, the sky is now the limit." West, an African American, also argued that "Obama's glorious victory brings to a close the age of Reagan, the era of conservatism, the epoch of the southern strategy. The economics of greed, the culture of indifference to the poor, the politics of fear have run their course."

This assessment would prove premature. But to some extent, Obama shared West's view that the nation might at least be starting to move into a post-racial phase. In April 2009, while visiting Turkey, Obama was asked at a town hall meeting why Americans had become proud of their country again since his election. Obama said, "I come from a racial minority; my name is very unusual for the United States. And so I think people saw my election as proof, as testimony that although we are imperfect, our society has continued to improve, that racial discrimination has been reduced, that educational opportunity for all people is something that is still available."[14]

Obama was confident that he had established himself as a unique individual above all, not a black man or a liberal or a machine politician from Chicago. "He has become individuated," said Cornell Belcher, an African

American who was an Obama pollster during the campaign.[15] "He is not so much a black man as an extraordinary individual." Belcher compared Obama to basketball star Michael Jordan, a black man whose amazing talents transcended race, whose personality was widely appealing, and who became almost universally popular throughout the country. Belcher argued that Obama had inoculated himself from racial stereotypes. That premise, which was widely shared in the White House and by Obama himself, would be tested repeatedly during Obama's time in office.

* * *

MORE THAN SEVEN out of ten voters approved of Obama's job performance during his first few months as he moved aggressively to save the financial system from a meltdown, and persuaded Congress to enact a $787-billion plan to stimulate the economy. His coverage in the news media was overwhelmingly positive, and he pleased the sometimes-fawning journalists by granting dozens of interviews, holding an average of one prime-time news conference per month at the start (which in his second year would happen much more rarely), and giving many well-received speeches that made news. Meanwhile, his rhetoric about working in partnership with other nations lifted the United States' reputation in many foreign countries.

He immediately began a campaign to overhaul the health-care system, which became his top domestic priority—and Americans at first told pollsters that they trusted him to do the right thing. For African Americans, it appeared that he could do no wrong. He enjoyed nearly unanimous support from black voters, according to Cornell Belcher. And this popularity among blacks came despite the fact that Obama was staying away from "black issues" as much as possible, trying to avoid the perception among whites that he was giving preferential treatment to African Americans.

But at about the six-month mark, Obama's honeymoon with the country and the media began to evaporate, and the reasons had nothing to do with race. Most Americans, especially independent voters not allied with either major party, concluded that charisma and goodwill weren't enough. Increasingly, pollsters said, non-black voters were asking, What has this new president done for me? Has he ended the recession? Has he reduced unemployment? Has he made my retirement more secure? Is he able to end partisanship in Washington, as he promised, and get the government moving again? In short, was he living up to his campaign slogan, "Yes, We Can"? To increasing numbers of voters, the answer was no. His approval rating began a gradual decline, and by August, barely half the country thought he was doing a good job.

*   *   *

IN KEEPING WITH his largely positive start, Obama managed for the first six months to keep racial concerns and sensitivities on the back burner. In fact, it looked as if the situation might turn out to be like John F. Kennedy's. During the 1960 campaign, Kennedy caused considerable fear that his Roman Catholic faith would lead him to follow the pope's orders and put Protestants at a disadvantage. The Massachusetts senator felt compelled to give a memorable speech in Houston, to Baptist ministers, in an effort to reassure Protestant voters that he would govern in a secular way and wouldn't let his religion affect his policy decisions. To some extent, it worked. There was still plenty of residual skepticism and outright opposition to installing a Catholic in the White House, but Kennedy allayed enough concerns that he was able to defeat Republican Vice President Richard Nixon in an extremely close general election. After becoming president, however, little was said about Kennedy's Catholicism. The issues facing the country, especially the ongoing confrontation with Soviet communism, were considered far more important than religious concerns.

In Obama's case, the problems facing the country in the winter and spring of 2009 crowded out racial concerns. True, he selected a number of blacks for his inner circle, including former Clinton administration lawyer Eric Holder as attorney general and Chicago confidant Valerie Jarrett as senior White House adviser. The new first couple also made a habit of holding high-visibility events highlighting blacks from the entertainment industry, sports, education, and other fields. But by and large he didn't raise white voters' concerns that he was favoring blacks and unfairly elevating African American culture because his policies weren't overtly race-based. Democratic pollster Stan Greenberg told me in July 2009 that Americans were on the alert for preferential treatment by Obama toward blacks but they had concluded that Obama and his White House were "race neutral."

Obama gave two important speeches on race during his first six months: one during his trip to Ghana, and the other to the NAACP in New York on the civil rights organization's 100th anniversary. In each case, he argued that Americans needed to move beyond the old enmities, stereotypes, and suspicions over race and unite around their central values such as tolerance, justice, and community.

He took his first opportunity to send a conciliatory message about racial matters on his trip to Ghana on July 11, 2009. "I do not see the countries and peoples of Africa as a world apart," he told the Ghanaian Parliament after a tumultuous reception in Accra, complete with people in native garb joyously celebrating with cheers and traditional dances.[16] "I see Africa as a fundamental part of our interconnected world—as partners with America on behalf of the future that we want for all our children."

He added: "It is easy to point fingers, and to pin the blame for these problems on others. Yes, a colonial map that made little sense bred conflict, and the West has often approached Africa as a patron, rather than a partner. But the West was not responsible for the destruction of the Zimbabwean economy over the last decade, or wars in which children are enlisted as combatants. . . . In my father's life, it was partly tribalism and patronage in an independent Kenya that for a long stretch derailed his career, and we know that this kind of corruption is a daily fact of life for far too many." He went on to call for individual Africans to take responsibility for their governments, for their economies, and for their personal lives to advance their education, promote public health, and reduce disease.

The following week, on July 16, he addressed the NAACP in New York at the civil rights organization's 100th anniversary, enhancing his reputation as a conciliator. Thanking the group for its service and its courage over the years, he drew thunderous applause repeatedly, and at times he adopted the preacher-like cadences of the black church, a cornerstone of the civil rights movement.

Obama tried to focus fresh attention on some of America's most grievous sins—slavery, segregation, and racial prejudice—while at the same time trying to move black-and-white relationships into a new era that celebrated common values and shared virtues.

He recalled his tour the previous week of Cape Coast Castle, where Africans were kept in wretched conditions before they were transported to the Americas in bondage. "I was reminded of all the pain and all the hardships, all the injustices and all the indignities on the voyage from slavery to freedom," he told the civil rights activists. "But I was also reminded of something else. I was reminded that no matter how bitter the rod or how stony the road, we have persevered. We have not faltered, nor have we grown weary. As Americans, we have demanded, strived for, and shaped a better destiny."[17] But he refused to dwell on the past. He went on to call for a new spirit of reconciliation. He said bigotry still existed, but added: "There's probably never been less discrimination in America than there is today." He called on black Americans to take responsibility for their own success. "Yes, government must be a force for equality," he declared. "But ultimately, if we are to be true to our past, then we also have to seize our own destiny, each and every day" and he urged parents to help their children with homework and put them to bed early, rather than let them play endless video games. "That mother of mine gave me love, she pushed me, and cared about my education, she took no lip and taught me right from wrong," Obama said. "Because of her, I had a chance to make the most of my abilities. I want all the other Barack Obamas out there, and all the other Michelle Obamas out there, to have that same chance—the chance that my mother gave me, that my education gave me. That's how our union will be perfected and our economy rebuilt."[18]

He wanted, above all, to avoid portraying the race issue solely in terms of an aggrieved black minority seeing itself as the perpetual victim of the white Establishment in the United States. Instead, he aimed to find a broader human context for America's racial past and future.

In a separate interview with *Washington Post* columnist Eugene Robinson the day after his NAACP speech, Obama gave one of his most detailed analyses of the state of black America, and he emphasized that the aggressive anti-Establishment campaigns of the civil rights era appeared to be no longer necessary.[19] Discussing a "generational shift" in the black community, he said, "If we haven't already reached this point, we're getting close to reaching it, where there are going to be more African Americans in this country who never experienced anything remotely close to Jim Crow than those who lived under Jim Crow. That, obviously, changes perspectives."

Obama added: "One of the ways that I think that the civil rights movement … weakened itself was by enforcing a single way of being black—being authentically black. And, as a consequence, there were a whole bunch of young black people—and I fell prey to this for a time when I was a teenager—who thought that if you were really 'down' you had to be a certain way. And oftentimes that was anti-something. You defined yourself by being against things as opposed to what you were for. And I think now young people realize, you know what, being African American can mean a whole range of things. There's a whole bunch of possibilities out there for how you want to live your life, what values you want to express, who you choose to interact with."

Robinson, who is black, wrote on the following Sunday, July 19, after his interview with Obama: "The real news wasn't in the content but the visuals: the nation's leading black civil rights organization being addressed by the nation's first black president. Obama could have read nursery rhymes and the event still would have been noteworthy. In his six months in office, Obama has taken few occasions to confront the issue of race head-on. This moment was inescapable. But his words about the deficits that still plague black Americans were delivered to a room full of NAACP convention delegates who are, by and large, highly educated and comfortably affluent— men and women who already have high expectations for their children and know how to hold their elected officials accountable. Missing was the too-large segment of the black community that has been left behind."

Obama was effectively walking a tightrope. He was attempting to keep faith with the history of the African American civil rights community and at the same time not scare majority white voters on whom he depended for his reelection. He no doubt was expressing his genuine feelings about the need for a new, less confrontational approach on the part of blacks. He was also making a nuanced appeal to white voters that he wasn't just a black president, that he has a broader purview that was less threatening than the harsh black leaders of the past, such as Malcolm X, Louis Farrakhan, Jesse Jackson, and Al Sharpton, and innumerable other black firebrands at the local level.

Then came the Cambridge incident, which threw Obama off balance and showed how close to the surface of American life racial sensitivities remained.

*　　*　　*

ON JULY 16, 2009, the same day as Obama's NAACP speech, Harvard Professor Henry Louis Gates Jr. returned to his Cambridge, Massachusetts, home from a trip to China and found himself locked out. His key wouldn't work, and Gates and his driver, both African Americans, forced open the door and went inside.

Meanwhile, a neighbor called police and reported a suspected break-in. The white officer who responded to the call, Sergeant James Crowley, entered the house and asked Gates for identification. Gates produced his Harvard ID, but it didn't contain an address. Crowley radioed for verification from the Harvard campus police, and an argument ensued that resulted in Gates being handcuffed, arrested, and taken to the police station. He was charged with disorderly conduct, but the allegations were dropped a few days later.

The incident made a few headlines around the country. Gates was, after all, a renowned African American scholar. But what generated a furor were Obama's comments at his news conference on July 22. Asked about the incident, he appeared to be aware that Gates, a longtime friend of the president's, had accused the police of racial profiling and the president sided firmly with the professor. "Now, I don't know, not having been there and not seeing all the facts, what role race played in that," the president said. "But I think it's fair to say, number one, any of us would be pretty angry; number two, that the Cambridge police acted stupidly in arresting somebody when there was already proof that they were in their own home." He also said: "What I think we know, separate and apart from this incident, is that there's a long history in this country of African Americans and Latinos being stopped by law enforcement disproportionately. That's just a fact."

His comment that the police "acted stupidly" set off angry reactions across the country, especially among the police and their supporters. What perplexed and troubled Obama's friends and supporters was the fact that his words seemed so blunt and unwisely chosen, far from the nuanced approach he usually took on complex or divisive issues. White House advisers pointed out that he considered himself an expert on racial profiling, having sponsored legislation to limit the practice as an Illinois state legislator. And the pattern of trouble between the police and African American men had special relevance to him as one of those men. He had spoken from the heart as a black man who had in his youth experienced his share of unfair attention from the police, his friends said.

But the debate over the incident quickly got out of hand, White House advisers told me privately. Obama was coming across as precisely what he was trying not to be—a partisan for African Americans and a critic of white folks. Just as important, the advisers said, his racial comments were crowding out news coverage of his plans to overhaul the health-care system, just as Congress was focusing on the issue in a series of make-or-break decisions. The whole episode was becoming a huge distraction.

Three days later, Obama decided to address the issue again. He came to the White House briefing room, unannounced, and told reporters he had gone too far at his news conference. Now Obama was repentant. He said both the professor and the policeman were probably guilty of "over-reaction." He added that "race is still a troubling aspect of our society" but said all sides should step back and try to find ways to get along.

And he delivered a mea culpa. "Because this has been ratcheting up—and I obviously helped to contribute to ratcheting it up—I want to make clear that in my choice of words I think I unfortunately gave an impression that I was maligning the Cambridge Police Department or Sergeant Crowley specifically—and I could have calibrated those words differently." He added: "To the extent that my choice of words didn't illuminate but rather contributed to more media frenzy, I think that was unfortunate." He said he had phoned Gates and Crowley separately that afternoon, expressed the hope that they could smooth over their differences, and invited each to the White House for beers.

When he hosted the pair at a picnic table on the South Lawn a few days later, along with Vice President Joe Biden, the media billed it as the "beer summit" and gave the event considerable attention. But nothing much came of it, except for a photo of the four men sipping brews on a pleasant summer afternoon.

And Americans weren't very impressed. Many voters told pollsters, including Republican Kellyanne Conway and Democrat Stan Greenberg, among others, that they didn't see why Obama had gotten involved in a local matter and that he seemed to be wasting his time.[20]

But White House officials told me the event revealed a significant part of Obama's character. It showed that, at heart, he was a conciliator. For many white voters, however, Obama had resurrected concerns from the 2008 campaign. He had seemed to depart, in knee-jerk fashion, from his even-handedness and openly side with a black man from Harvard against a white cop, even though he knew little about what had actually happened.

The incident showed how far America still was from the "post-racial" society that Obama supporters had envisioned when he took office six months earlier.

*   *   *

AS HIS FIRST year progressed, the race issue occasionally bubbled up and diverted Obama from other concerns. Many commentators detected a strain of anti-black prejudice in the angry protests staged in the summer of 2009 at Democratic legislators' town-hall meetings across the county. To some extent these demonstrations extended beyond the health-care issue and served as a coalescing point for a broader anti-Obama movement. White House aides such as Press Secretary Robert Gibbs disputed the idea that race was involved, but to others it was a clear trend. For one thing, the protesters were almost universally white. For another, some of their signs and comments—"I want my country back," and signs portraying Obama as a witch doctor—seemed, at minimum, racially tinged. And the effort by anti-Obama forces to undermine his legitimacy—by arguing, falsely, that he was actually born in Kenya and was not a U.S. citizen, and by claiming that he was at heart a socialist and a tyrant—struck many as racial at its core.

Former President Jimmy Carter, who had always been sensitive to racial issues going back to his years as governor of Georgia, agreed that the anti-Obama trend was troubling. "I think an overwhelming portion of the intensely demonstrated animosity toward President Obama is based on the fact that he is a black man," Carter said that September.[21]

Carter added: "That racism inclination still exists. And I think it's bubbled up to the surface because of the belief among many white people not just in the South but around the country, that African Americans are not qualified to lead this great country. It's an abominable circumstance, and it grieves me and concerns me very deeply."[22]

Then the polarization got worse. Representative Joe Wilson, a South Carolina Republican and member of the Sons of Confederate Veterans, interrupted Obama's address to a joint session of Congress on September 9, 2008, with the shouted outburst, "You lie!" He quickly apologized for his emotional breach of congressional decorum but not for the content of what he said. This prompted accusations of racism. "Fair or not, what I heard was an unspoken word in the air: 'You lie, boy!'" wrote Maureen Dowd, a *New York Times* columnist, the following Sunday.[23] ". . . Wilson clearly did not like being lectured and even rebuked by the brainy black president presiding over the majestic chamber." Dowd added that she had previously resisted the conclusion that the anti-Obama protests of the summer were racially motivated. "But Wilson's shocking disrespect for the office of the president—no Democrat ever shouted 'liar' at W. when he was hawking a fake case for war in Iraq—convinced me: Some people just can't believe a black man is president and will never accept it," Dowd said. ". . . Now he's at the center of a period of racial turbulence sparked by his ascension. Even if he and the coterie of white male advisers around him don't choose to openly acknowledge it, this president is the ultimate civil rights figure—a black man whose legitimacy is constantly challenged by a loco fringe."

Authors Barbara Ehrenreich and Dedrick Muhammad made similar points amid what seemed to be a rising anti-Obama environment on the political right. "What do you get when you combine the worst economic downturn since the Depression with the first black president? A surge of white racial resentment, loosely disguised as a populist revolt," Ehrenreich and Muhammad wrote.[24] "An article on the Fox News Web site has put forth the theory that health reform is a stealth version of reparations for slavery: whites will foot the bill and, by some undisclosed mechanism, blacks will get all the care. President Obama, in such fantasies, is a dictator and, in one image circulated among the anti-tax, anti-health reform 'tea parties,' he is depicted as a befeathered African witch doctor with little tusks coming out of his nostrils. When you're going down, as the white middle class has been doing for several years now, it's all too easy to imagine that it's because someone else is climbing up over your back."

They went on to report, however, that it was the black community that was actually suffering disproportionately from the economic hard times, with high levels of unemployment and mortgage foreclosures. Ehrenreich and Muhammad called it the gradual "destruction of the black middle class" that started under George W. Bush and that Obama was doing little or nothing to relieve.

Privately, White House advisers conceded that these critics had a point: Obama was not interested in pigeonholing himself as a "black president." He wanted to represent everyone. But this also meant that he was very reluctant to take steps to relieve the disproportionate suffering of the African American community brought on by the recession.

Obama and his senior aides argued that the most important objective was to strengthen the economy for everyone. Since blacks were disproportionately hurt by many of our society's problems, such as unemployment and subpar public schools, the president's reasoning went, improving these areas would automatically help blacks. "I think everyone appreciates that his role as president is by definition for all Americans," said Obama confidant Valerie Jarrett, a senior adviser at the White House and an African American.[25]

Obama told several TV interviewers in September 2009 that Americans weren't very concerned about the color of his skin and that the objections to his policies were based on fear that he was bringing change too fast or that he was too liberal and too committed to activist government. "Are there some people who don't like me because of my race? I'm sure there are," he told ABC News in an interview with George Stephanopoulos on September 20, 2009. "Are there some people who voted for me only because of my race? There are probably some of those, too."

In private, the president told aides he was pleased with how accepting most Americans had been of him and his policies. David Axelrod, White House counselor and Obama's chief political strategist, told me, "I think what he is struck by, what all of us are struck by, is as you travel the country, there's so many people who offer their support and good wishes. There is not this sense of harsh division. And I'm always mindful of the fact that, especially in today's age, the loudest, angriest voices tend to get outsized attention because they make for better TV." Axelrod referred to a *Washington Post* poll in early September 2009 showing that "two-thirds of the people polled have warm and positive feelings about him, regardless of what they thought about his policies. I think he's got a great relationship with the American people. There are always going to be some angry voices out there, and the story really isn't about the angry voices. The story is how much people have embraced him."[26]

Still, Democratic pollster Geoff Garin said race was "a piece of the puzzle for some voters. I think in some cases it may add to the emotional power of some of the opposition to Obama.[27]

This would prove to be a prescient analysis as Obama's presidency proceeded and Obama realized that his uniqueness as a black president was causing him political problems. During an interview with me in the Oval Office for this book,[28] Obama said, "I think that every president should feel an obligation to deal with not only issues of discrimination but also the legacy of slavery and segregation that has been such a profound part of our history. You know, obviously it's hard for me to engage in a mind experiment and say, well, if I weren't African American would I feel less strongly about it or more strongly about it—and I know I feel strongly about it. I do come to this issue with personal experiences that are unlike any previous presidents'."

*   *   *

ONE OF THE barometers of Obama's success was support from the black community, the firmest pillar of his support in the 2008 election. In his first autumn as president, that support seemed to be holding up well.

Not only did he have overwhelming backing from black voters—nearly 100 percent in some Democrat-sponsored polls—he also remained very popular within the forty-two-member Congressional Black Caucus. At the group's annual banquet in Washington on September 26, 2009, the greeting was effusive, with Obama receiving jubilant ovations during his speech.[29]

But there were signs of trouble with African Americans on Capitol Hill. Obama was taking some positions that were at odds with the liberal views of most black members of Congress. Even though he signed legislation to provide more pay equity for women, expand health care for children, and increase spending on education, which were popular within the caucus, he had disappointed members in other ways. He seemed to be wavering in his support of government-sponsored health insurance to compete with private insurers, which many black legislators supported. And he escalated the war in Afghanistan, a move that many black legislators opposed. When he announced in early December that he would send in 30,000 more troops, increasing the U.S. contingent to 100,000, black legislators were deeply frustrated.

Many black leaders were concerned because the unemployment rate for blacks in November 2009 was 15.6 percent, while the national rate was 10 percent and the rate for whites was 9.3 percent.[30] They pointed to a big achievement gap between whites and blacks in public schools and lack of access among many poor blacks to adequate health care. Black leaders were also concerned about the high level of incarceration of African American men, another long-standing problem that Obama had not addressed as president. Some Democratic strategists with close ties to Obama told me of their worry that the black legislators might openly rebel against their president, which could conceivably diminish his high job-approval ratings in the black electorate.

This began to happen in late autumn. Members of the Congressional Black Caucus boycotted a key House committee vote on financial regulations, arguing that Congress and the White House hadn't done enough to help African Americans while the establishment in Washington was rushing to help Wall Street. Obama responded the next day by saying, "The most important thing I can do for the African American community is the same thing I can do for the American community, period, and that is get the economy going again and get people hiring again."[31] He added that he sympathized with the goals of the black caucus, such as making sure that black-owned small businesses had access to credit, but added, "It's a mistake to start thinking in terms of particular ethnic segments of the United States rather than to think that we are all in this together and we are all going to get out of this together."

NAACP President Benjamin T. Jealous said, "This president is literally the embodiment of the hopes and dreams of millions of people. But he has come to a crossroads of his first year in office."[32] Speaking of health care and Obama's goal of winning congressional approval for a bill even if it didn't contain the "public option" of government-provided care, Jealous, who favored that option, added that Obama was "headed toward a moment that the White House would consider a victory but that his base considers a loss."

* * *

THE VAST MAJORITY of Americans seemed to be evaluating Obama based not on his race but on his policies. That was his objective. In a very basic sense, the problems facing the country, ranging from the near-collapse of the financial system that started under his predecessor George W. Bush to a painful recession and the wars in Iraq and Afghanistan, were crowding out most racial concerns. Obama portrayed himself as a calm, collected decision maker in the tradition of Franklin D. Roosevelt and John F. Kennedy, not a special pleader for African Americans.

In an Oval Office interview in September 2009, Obama told me about his approach to problem solving and how it applied to race. "The things that, for me, work day to day become that much more important in a crisis: being able to pull together the best people and have them work as a team, insisting on analytical rigor in evaluating the nature of the problem, making sure that dissenting voices are heard and that a range of options are explored, being willing to make a decision after having looked at all the options, and then insisting on good execution as well as timely feedback, so that [if] you have to correct the decision that you make, that you are able to do so in time, being able to stay calm and steady when the stakes are high. You know, all those things are, I think, principles I try to apply in any circumstance. I find them particularly useful when the decisions are tough and the consequences of action are most weighty."[33]

I was struck by how there seemed to be nothing at all racial about Obama's approach to the presidency. He was describing generic attributes of leadership that transcended race and focused instead on inspiring and mobilizing others and finding the right answers to complex problems under adverse conditions. Few people have those traits, regardless of their race, and Obama appeared to understand this—but to put himself in that special transcendent category. I asked him what had prepared him to be an effective leader, since he had virtually no executive experience prior to taking office. He laughed in amusement and said, "I don't know—in the sense that I don't think anything prepares you for the presidency."[34] This same thought could have been expressed by every one of his predecessors, from George Washington to George W. Bush, and had no racial undertones whatsoever.

Obama's confidants at this point argued that the race issue was fading. When I asked senior White House adviser David Axelrod, who had been his chief campaign strategist, whether people saw Obama as "a black president" or simply as "the president," Axelrod said race wasn't uppermost on their minds. "I think we largely overcame that in the campaign," he noted. "I think it was a noteworthy historic fact when he took office because a barrier had fallen, but I don't think people judge him in that way at all. I think there's a level of familiarity with him that allows folks to judge him as a person and not on the basis of race or any other externality."[35]

Of course it would have been counterproductive for Obama or his aides to say anything else. White Americans were always on the lookout for signs that Obama might give preferential treatment to blacks, and it would have been political suicide for him to act in any way like a black president who was giving other blacks an edge.

Axelrod also said that John F. Kennedy had endured a large degree of public opposition and suspicion in the 1960 campaign because he was Roman Catholic, but it didn't seem to be much of an issue after he took office. "I think that's the natural way," Axelrod said. "I think that frequent exposure, watching someone do the job, helps dispel a lot of the negative thoughts, to the extent they're worrying. Whether they support him or not, I think most people have embraced him as president."

But race was still hovering in the background. In mid-October of 2009, as Obama was completing his first nine months in office, a Gallup poll found that hope seemed to be fading that racial conflict could be ended once and for all.[36] Fifty-six percent of Americans thought that a solution could be worked out to America's racial problems, down from 67 percent in a survey conducted the day after Obama's victory on November 4, 2008. Only 42 percent of blacks felt that a solution would eventually be worked out, compared with 50 percent the previous June and July after it became clear that Obama would win the Democratic presidential nomination.

In November, polls found a growing racial disparity in how Americans were evaluating him. Only 39 percent of white Americans approved of Obama's job performance, compared with more than 60 percent when he was inaugurated in January, according to the Gallup Poll. Black voters, meanwhile, remained loyal to him, with 90 percent saying he was doing a good job even though in many black communities, especially in the big cities, the economy was much worse than in white areas, and unemployment for African American men was much higher than the national rate of 10.2 percent, according to a survey by Hart Research Associates/Public Opinion Strategies in October–November 2009.[37]

In that same survey 69 percent of whites agreed with the statement that "Race relations are still a problem in the USA, but we have come a long way," while only 46 percent of African Americans agreed with that statement. Forty-seven percent of African Americans agreed with the statement that "race relations are still a problem in the USA, and we still have a long way to go," compared with 27 percent of whites. Eighty-seven percent of African Americans said President Obama was "doing more to unite the country," while only 47 percent of whites felt that way. Forty-one percent of whites were more hopeful and optimistic about the next ten years, compared with 76 percent of African Americans.

When polled on one race-related issue, both blacks and whites expressed similar views. Sixty percent of blacks and 59 percent of whites told pollsters that Obama's race had little or no effect "on the way he handles his job as president." Obama aides told me that they believed his effort to bill himself as a "race-neutral" president appeared to be taking hold. According to Cornell Belcher, one of the few black leaders in survey research, Obama had become a unique figure, an individual and not someone who appealed only to blacks. "Because of who he is, he was inoculated from the stereotypes [during the campaign], the idea that somehow African Americans don't share your values or are more morally loose or less intelligent," Belcher said.[38] "What were the X factors? Does a biracial family heritage figure? His Ivy League education? The image of a strong family man speaking out about personal responsibility?" To Obama advisers, all of those factors played a part in making him a popular figure as an individual, even if people opposed his policies.

Yet many political strategists felt that racial animosity and suspicion were still serious challenges even though they were camouflaged because voters didn't want to talk about these feelings to pollsters. "There are some people for whom that [race] is another reason to hate Barack Obama," said Will Marshall, president of the Progressive Policy Institute, a centrist think tank for Democrats.[39]

"He doesn't run away from it [race]," Marshall said. He regards his election as "vindication of the promise of color-blindness." Marshall added that the world saw Obama's election as the first African American president as a very positive development. He noted that the Nobel Peace Prize was awarded to Obama in 2009 after he had been in office only a few weeks because the Nobel award committee felt that Obama's ascension redeemed in part America's promise of inclusion and pluralism, and was an effort to encourage Obama to be a peacemaker.

Michael Steele, the chairman of the Republican National Committee and the first African American to hold that post, told me in the fall of 2009: "I would say that people always saw him as a black president and they still do. But not in the context in which people have traditionally approached that with respect to a candidate—'Oh, he's the black candidate.' It is as matter-of-fact as anything else about the president that we know. And so that's a good place for America to be. You don't want your leadership hung up on issues like, 'Gee, if I do something, will people think I'm doing it because I'm black?' That's just not helping people of the country and it's certainly not helping for the leadership."[40]

Steele said there were still racial issues that needed to be worked out, such as affirmative action and the desire of blacks and whites to live separately in some places—issues that he said were "intrinsic to communities and individuals, and only those communities and those individuals over time will work those things through." But Steele added that, "The president being an African American helps us move further down that road. I think that my being the chairman of this party helps us move further down that road. When you step back and look at it you see two blacks sitting atop the political structures of this country. And who'd have thought that four years ago, let alone forty years ago? So it speaks to the advancement that we as individuals and as communities can make without even thinking about it. And I think that's a wonderful part of the story."

* * *

ANOTHER ASPECT of Obama's racial policies that got little media attention was his appointment of blacks to key positions. He followed the pattern of several of his predecessors in naming blacks to a few cabinet-level positions, notably Eric Holder as attorney general. But it was in filling lower-level but still highly important jobs with blacks that he made a real mark. Among these appointments were Valerie Jarrett as senior adviser, Melody Barnes as his domestic policy adviser, Rob Nabors as deputy director of the Office of Management and Budget, Patrick Gaspard as political director, Desiree Rogers as White House social secretary, and retired Admiral Stephen Rochon, who was retained as director of the executive residence and chief usher, in charge of all household staff and operations at the White House. Except for Rogers, they weren't on TV or in the newspapers very much, but their jobs were consequential and they were at the center of power.

As noted in Chapter One, Obama named more blacks to federal jobs than any of his predecessors: 15 percent. This compared with 10 percent under George W. Bush and 13 percent under Bill Clinton.

But he didn't want to call attention to any of this. Black voters would naturally realize it when they saw all the black people working in the administration. And white voters, Obama theorized, would see the black officials as simply policymakers, with race an interesting but minor factor as long as they did their jobs well and the country was on a positive course. Obama's goal, his aides told me, was to show that blacks in government really shouldn't be seen as any different than whites. It was part of his objective of making his administration race-neutral.

*   *   *

EVEN THOUGH he was trying to maintain this race neutrality in public, Obama felt a special bond with the African American household staff. Many on the household staff had been hoping for an African American president all their lives. Over the years, some of them had endured low wages, long hours, and difficult bosses in order to serve the institution of the presidency and witness history at close quarters. With Obama, all their hopes and dreams of equality and progress had, in a sense, come to fruition and they were proud of him in a very personal way. Sam Sutton Jr., a longtime presidential valet, who is black, even refused a scheduled retirement from government service and the offer of an appealing new job outside the White House in order to serve the first African American president, which he considered the honor of a lifetime.

Obama returned the affection. In our interview, President Obama not only praised Sutton for his dedication but talked about the black household staffers as if they were family. "I think, not just me, but Michelle and the girls and my mother-in-law are especially touched by our relationship with the staff, because I think they care about the office and they care about all the other presidents and their families who have come before us—I don't think it's a stretch to say that when they see Michelle and they think to themselves, boy, she reminds me of my daughter, or when they see Malia and Sasha, and they say, boy, those two look just like my granddaughters, that it's important to them. And they've been just incredibly gracious and they feel like family. I think that they had great affection for previous families and those bonds were special, as well, but there's no doubt that they have a special pride, I think, in being part of serving the first African American family in the White House."[41]

During the first weeks of his presidency, on April 9, 2009, he and first lady Michelle Obama held an emotional memorial service in the White House for Smile "Smiley" Saint-Aubin, a household staff mainstay who died only a few weeks after Obama took office. Obama said he didn't know Smiley long, but he and his family came to have deep admiration for him.

The president said in his eulogy that Smiley "made this house our home." He informally taught some French to the president's two daughters, Obama said, "treating every phrase they uttered as the most brilliant and eloquent statement ever made in that language." Smiley also would patiently answer the girls' questions about what was for dinner and happily tell them how the White House operates day to day. When Smiley got sick, Sasha and Malia made cards to send him in the hospital. Malia wrote, "We miss you so much. It isn't nearly as much fun at the White House without you." Sasha wrote, "You have done so much great things for us."

The bond between the Obamas and the residence staff is strong. "There is a sense of family and informality," said a confidant of the president. "They treat him with complete deference and respect. But you'll also see a familiar banter back and forth. They tease him. He teases them."

A New Prototype for the First Lady

Meanwhile, Michelle Obama was becoming a big hit as first lady.

A fascinating part of her personal narrative was that it was Michelle, not Barack, whose ancestors were slaves. Barack's mother was a white woman, Ann Dunham, from Kansas, and his father was a black man,

Barack Obama Sr., from Kenya, and he was not descended from any anyone who had been in bondage. But Michelle's great-great-great grandparents were an unknown white man and Melvinia Shields, a slave who was born in South Carolina and moved as a child to Georgia.[42] So she had much more of a personal connection to America's bitter racial history than her husband did.

But, like her husband, First Lady Michelle Obama didn't want to dwell on race. She and her staff remained acutely aware of the negative reputation she developed among some white voters in the 2008 campaign when she said that, for the first time in her adult life, she was finally proud to be an American, ostensibly because her husband was doing well in the Democratic campaign. Her critics felt this revealed her as an angry black woman who had a grudge against white people, and she quickly distanced herself from the remark. Amid a firestorm of attacks, her aides said she was merely talking about the political system, not the country as a whole, but her comment prompted criticism that she was not sufficiently patriotic.

After that episode, she was careful to seem upbeat and positive. As first lady, Michelle declined to involve herself in controversy and she avoided getting involved in policy-making, as Hillary Rodham Clinton had done amid withering criticism when she served as first lady during the 1990s. Instead, Mrs. Obama tried to show that she had the same values and concerns as other middle-class Americans, regardless of race—ranging from emphasizing her role as a loving mother to stressing the importance of education, raising public alarms about childhood obesity and poor nutrition, and committing herself to helping military families trying to cope with the stress of wartime. She also fascinated many people with her elegance and her poise. Democratic pollster Geoff Garin said that within two months of becoming first lady in 2009, she was a "superstar."

Michelle showed a glamorous sense of style, which heightened media interest in her, as it had heightened media interest in Jacqueline Kennedy, the wife of President John F. Kennedy, in the early 1960s. Michelle gradually attained a very high level of popularity, with nearly 80 percent of Americans approving of how she was handling her role as first lady. This was much higher than her husband's approval rating, which was hovering at about 50 percent at the start of 2010. "On a very basic level, they relate to her as a great mom, someone who is strong and smart and very caring," Garin told me.[43]

As first lady, she has rarely referred to herself as the first African American to hold that title, and her staff and friends say she sees her role as more traditional than some had expected, especially feminists.

Although she is a lawyer who enjoyed a highly successful career in the past, she said her first priority is to be the best mother to Malia and Sasha, and being the wife and helpmate to the man she continued to call "Barack." Her goal, she says, is to provide as normal a family life in the White House as she can. This is what first ladies have said from the start of the Republic.

During her first year, she cleverly allowed and encouraged extensive media coverage of this aspect of her life. The overwhelmingly positive stories that emerged included the "date nights" she and her husband arranged to get away from the White House for dinner at local restaurants and, in one much-publicized case, dinner and a show in New York City. She and her husband were also shown in endearing family moments with their children as they took them out for ice cream, attended the girls' athletic events and parent-teacher conferences at their school in Washington, and included them on official trips to Ghana, the Vatican, and Russia.

Beyond the strong commitments to her family, Michelle selected a handful of noncontroversial projects to work on, as most of her recent predecessors had done. In Michelle's case, that meant being an advocate for federal assistance to military families, encouraging public service, and, with increasing emphasis, advocating what she called "healthy eating and healthy families." In 2009, her first year, she got considerable media attention for a White House garden she created and she called attention to the importance of vegetables and fruit as requirements for good nutrition. Over time, this evolved into a special emphasis on fighting childhood obesity, which happened to be a particular scourge of African American women, according to various studies. So in her own way, Michelle Obama was involving herself in an issue of special importance to the black community, without seeming to be overly racial.

She was helped by images of her digging in the dirt behind the White House and harvesting sweet potatoes and lettuce, some of which ended up on the president's table and some of which were consumed by guests at the East Wing. Still more was sent to feed the homeless around Washington. Those images also helped Mrs. Obama shed the "angry black woman" image.

The Earth Mother persona also provided a counterpoint to her reputation as a fashionista. This glitzy image was intensified by the media and the fashion industry, Michelle's supporters said, but it was also encouraged when she allowed herself to be photographed in glamorous poses by slick magazines.

There were other areas in which Mrs. Obama managed to inject an element of racial sensitivity into the White House. One was in her choice of entertainers for official functions, which included more blacks as headliners and guests than ever before. This approach reached a crescendo in early February 2010 when the Obamas marked the start of Black History Month by hosting what they called "A Celebration of Music from the Civil Rights Movement" at the White House. The concert featured African American icons of the music industry including Natalie Cole, Jennifer Hudson, John Legend, Smokey Robinson, and Seal, and the Howard University Choir (along with a handful of white performers including Bob Dylan and John Mellencamp). Morgan Freeman and Queen Latifah were the emcees. The concert was televised the following night on public broadcasting stations across the country, and National Public Radio carried portions of it throughout the month. "The whole point is exposure and bringing people together who wouldn't ordinarily come together," said senior White House adviser Valerie Jarrett.[44]

Mrs. Obama made the rounds of majority-black schools in the majority-black capital city. At Anacostia High School in one of Washington's poorest sections, she told the students her life story. "We didn't have a lot of money," she said. "I lived in the same house my mother lives in now.... I went to public schools. The fact is I had somebody around me who helped me understand hard work. I had parents who told me, 'Don't worry about what other people say about you.' I worked really hard. I did focus on school. I wanted an A. I wanted to be smart. Kids would say, 'You talk funny; you talk like a white girl.' I didn't know what that meant."[45]

This theme became part of Michelle's mission. She told friends that she wanted to serve as a role model to young African Americans, especially girls, so they would realize that they could grow up to be an achiever like the first lady and live in a wonderful place like the White House.

Early on, the first lady held a dinner for 100 girls in the eleventh and twelfth grades from Washington and nearby public schools. A large percentage of those girls were African American, and few had ever expected to be invited to the White House under any circumstances. Mrs. Obama also included high-achieving women to inspire and motivate the girls. "Part of that goal is to open up their eyes to the possibilities and to provide them with direct exposure to role models with whom they could relate, and inspire them to be the best that they can be," Jarrett told me later.

Meanwhile, few public figures criticized the White House on racial grounds. "This is a time-out in a sense," said Frank Donatelli, chairman of the conservative GOPAC political action committee and former White House political adviser to Ronald Reagan.[46] "Maybe we can finally get past seeing everything through a racial prism." He said that, with some exceptions, there was less emphasis on whether political issues had a racial dimension. "Now that we have a black president, that barrier has fallen, and that is a good thing," Donatelli said.

CHAPTER THIRTEEN
CHARISMA AND REALITY

As he began his second year in office, Obama's presidency was not going well. His legislation to overhaul the health-care system was still bogged down in Congress. The unemployment rate, which polls showed was the top concern of most Americans, remained stubbornly high at about 10 percent, and much worse in many African American communities. Obama's job-approval ratings had dropped markedly from the astronomical levels of his first few months to below 50 percent.

Adding to his woes, in January 2010 the race issue erupted again in an unusual and unexpected way. Democratic Senator Harry Reid of Nevada, the Senate majority leader and an Obama ally, was embarrassed because of some racially insensitive comments he had made to John Heilemann and Mark Halperin, the authors of a new book, *Game Change,* about the Obama campaign. It turned out that Reid had predicted in 2008 that Obama could succeed as an African American presidential candidate partly because he was "light-skinned" and because he didn't speak with a "Negro dialect."

Reid quickly apologized, and many black leaders, including the president and Attorney General Eric Holder, defended him as a decent man who was not a racist.[1] But Republicans tried to score political points, with party chairman Michael Steele and Senator John Cornyn of Texas, chairman of the National Republican Senatorial Committee, calling on Reid to resign as majority leader. He refused, but the furor showed how race remained just below the surface of American life. Racial polarization was again on the rise. In January 2010, 96 percent of African Americans approved Obama's job performance, virtually unchanged from his 100-day mark in April 2009. But whites were losing faith in him, with only 44 percent approving his job performance, compared with 62 percent the previous April, according to a *Washington Post*/ABC News poll in January 2010.[2]

Republican pollster Bill McInturff said, "I don't think you can find a guy who's done more to try to put this issue [of race] off the table." But McInturff added, "I don't think the press really understands how difficult this guy's position is" because his support among whites was so "precarious."[3] This was largely because the economy was in such distress, and most whites except perhaps for young people didn't have a close bond with Obama to begin with.

African Americans' views on achieving racial equality also were growing more negative, even though black voters remained in strong support of Obama. According to McInturff, only 11 percent of blacks said that African Americans had reached racial equality, down by 9 percentage points in year, and 32 percent said equality would not be attained in their lifetimes, up by 9 points. Four in ten whites said African Americans already had reached racial equality while 31 percent said it would happen soon.

Obama addressed this pessimism among blacks in an address at the Vermont Avenue Baptist Church in Washington on January 18, 2010, to mark the holiday devoted to Reverend Martin Luther King Jr. Calling for patience and pragmatism, the president said, "Sometimes I get a little frustrated when folks just don't want to see that even if we don't get everything, we're getting something.... King understood that the desegregation of the armed forces didn't end the civil rights movement, because black and white soldiers still couldn't sit together at the same lunch counter when they came home. But he still insisted on the rightness of desegregating the armed forces. 'Let's take a victory,' he said, 'and then keep on marching.' Forward steps, large and small, were recognized for what they were—which was progress."[4]

He continued, "There was a hope shared by many that life would be better from the moment that I swore that oath." But he said, "Let us hold fast to that faith, as Joshua held fast to the faith of his fathers, and together, we shall overcome the challenges of a new age. Together, we shall seize the promise of this moment. Together, we shall make a way through winter and we're going to welcome the spring. Through God all things are possible."[5]

On February 10, 2010, Obama and top aide Valerie Jarrett met in the Oval Office with civil rights leaders who were concerned that he wasn't paying enough attention to fighting unemployment among African Americans. It was his first meeting exclusively with civil rights leaders since he took office. The government had just issued a monthly report that the overall unemployment rates in January had dropped from 10 percent to 9.7 percent, but joblessness among blacks had increased to 16.5 percent.

But the black activists didn't directly pressure Obama to take a race-based approach. Instead, they urged him to address the problems of the poor, regardless of race—which paralleled the approach Obama already had adopted. The effect was to give Obama more latitude to deal with the economy as he saw fit, without black leaders stepping up the pressure on him.

Those who attended included Reverend Al Sharpton, founder of the National Action Network, who told reporters afterward, "We're not looking for race-based programs, but, like the president, we want to make sure that everyone is included. We need to make sure that those efforts to spur job creation are equally and fairly distributed so that, when the rubber meets the road, we're all in the car."[6]

NAACP President Benjamin T. Jealous, who also attended, said the meeting focused less on race than on the geography of the economic downturn and how it was particularly severe in some urban areas such as Detroit and rural areas such as those in North and South Carolina. "The reality is that poverty has been greatly democratized by this recession," Jealous said. "What all Americans have in common is that they are hurting and struggling and want to see the pace of progress quicken."[7]

*   *   *

ON MARCH 12, 2010, President Obama welcomed me into the Oval Office for an interview for this book. Dressed in an elegant dark-blue business suit and tie with an American flag pin in his left lapel, he was serene and confident. He sat in a comfortable chair in front of the fireplace and I sat close by at the end of a sofa—the same setting where he and his predecessors customarily welcomed heads of state, congressional leaders, and other dignitaries for photo opportunities and policy talks. Behind him was the portrait of George Washington that has hung in the Oval Office for many years. Flanking that portrait were two busts added by Obama reflecting his own values and heroes—behind him on his right was a likeness of Martin Luther King Jr. and on his left was one of Abraham Lincoln.

It was a particularly interesting moment at which to talk with Obama about race. Earlier that week was the forty-fifth anniversary of Bloody Sunday, when Alabama state troopers and local police attacked peaceful demonstrators marching for civil rights from Selma to Montgomery, Alabama, on March 7, 1965. Our interview also came the day after Obama had met with disgruntled members of the Congressional Black Caucus, who weren't pleased with his level of attention to their demands for more federal assistance targeted to the African American community, which was bearing the brunt of the recession that was then hurting millions across the country.

Obama was in a reflective mood. He began the interview by saying he had been "fully briefed" on my topic and was ready for me to "dive in." He proceeded to methodically defend his effort to build a race-neutral administration. "Americans since the victories of the civil rights movement I think have broadly come to accept the notion that everybody has to be treated equally, everybody has to be treated fairly," the president told me. "And I think that the whole debate about how do you make up for past history creates a complicated wrinkle in that principle of equality."

Calmly, candidly, and with typical intellectual precision, Obama gave one of his most extensive analyses of the country's racial situation and his goals for improving it. He made clear that he was president of all Americans, not just of African Americans, and didn't want to be thought of only as a black president, even though he acknowledged that the country had been extremely proud in November 2008 when a majority of voters made history by electing him. He said he wasn't sure how many Americans still saw him "through the lens of race," although he acknowledged that, within the black community, "there is a great pride that's undeniable" and many African American children "may feel a special affinity to me as a role model." He compared all this with Irish Catholic Americans who felt enormous pride in John F. Kennedy's election as the first Irish Catholic president in 1960.

I asked him if he was very conscious of his own race as he conducted the business of the presidency, and his answer was insightful. "You just don't think about it; you really don't," he replied. "You've got too many other things to worry about."

Then I asked Obama to describe his main goal in dealing with race issues, and he said, "I'll tell you a couple things. My main goal is to be the best possible president and help to put the country on the best possible track going forward. If I do that, then a couple of things will have happened. It means our education system is going to be fixed and so more kids are going to be having opportunities to excel and compete in the twenty-first-century economy, and that means there are going to be a whole bunch of black and brown kids who are doing well who otherwise wouldn't be.

"If I succeed, then it means that we'll have a health-care system that provides basic health care for every American, and a whole bunch of folks who don't have it, including a whole bunch of blacks and Hispanics, will then have it.

"If I succeed, the economy will have been growing, and our history indicates that when the economy is growing and people feel good about their prospects, that social tensions diminish.

"I've always been of the view that if you are able to close the gap in the economic status of African Americans relative to the general population, that that would do more than any race commission or explicit race-based strategy to reduce tensions. And so my—the legacy I hope to leave is a more prosperous, more secure, more confident America. And if that happens, then I think you're also going to see continued improvement in race relations in this country."

I asked him how much he felt an obligation or responsibility as the first African American president to advance racial justice and make up for some of the past disparities between blacks and whites. He replied, "Well, I think that every president should feel an obligation to deal with not only issues of discrimination but also the legacy of slavery and segregation that has been such a profound part of our history. You know, obviously it's hard for me to engage in a mind experiment and say, well, if I weren't African American would I feel less strongly about it or more strongly about it—and I know I feel strongly about it. I do come to this issue with personal experiences that are unlike any previous presidents'.

"But I also think that anybody in this office who cares deeply about the future of the country would be looking and saying to themselves the population is changing; the future workforce is going to have a lot more African American and Latino and Asian workers. And if those populations don't feel fully assimilated into the culture, aren't performing at high levels educationally, are caught in cycles of poverty—that that's not good for America's future. And that's certainly how I feel—and I would like to think that any president would feel that way."

Obama added: "I think for most Americans equality means that you treat everybody the same. There's a notion, I think shared by a lot of African Americans, that would say that having been denied opportunities in the past some special steps need to be taken. You know, that's the argument around affirmative action obviously and a number of other controversies over the last several decades.

"The reason I don't feel torn in two directions on this debate is because I actually believe that right now the same things that would most help African Americans are the same things that would help the society at large."

He was talking about programs to improve education, which had cleared Congress; his ambitious health insurance initiative, which finally passed after a year-long struggle; and ongoing programs to create jobs.

*   *   *

BUT THE CRITICISM of Obama from some black activists was increasing. Author Sophia A. Nelson wrote in the *Washington Post* on March 20 that "a quiet storm has been brewing among African American leaders for months over the devastating effects that U.S. economic woes are having on blacks across the nation."[8] African American commentator Tavis Smiley, for example, questioned whether black leaders such as Jealous and Sharpton were too reluctant to hold Obama accountable. Smiley urged Obama to develop an agenda specifically addressing the needs of African Americans.

Nelson went on to cite research suggesting that "blacks have been disproportionately and devastatingly affected by the recession, foreclosure crisis, and loss of wealth in the U.S. economy since 2007."

"A 2008 study suggested that the typical African American family had only a dime for every dollar of wealth possessed by the typical white family," Nelson wrote. "Only 18 percent of blacks and Latinos had retirement accounts, compared with 43.4 percent of whites." And Nelson argued that blacks needed disproportionately greater help in weathering the recession than whites.

"Race remains America's deepest and most enduring dividing line," Nelson said. "That is not something the president alone, not even a black one, can fix. This is a challenge that black Americans must address within our communities, and it is one that President Obama must be bold enough to take up as a unique challenge of his administration."

In July, the drumbeat for Obama to adopt a "black agenda" grew louder. Smiley and scholar Michael Eric Dyson accused the president of not doing enough to create jobs in black communities and urged him to talk more openly about racial prejudice.[9]

But for most Americans, Obama's politics still seemed to be race-neutral, and they liked it that way. "He's not a racial figure," said Republican analyst Matthew Dowd, the former pollster and strategist for President George W. Bush, in May 2010.[10] Many commentators agreed that adopting a racial agenda would alienate too many whites.

And no less a respected leader than Colin Powell agreed with Obama's refusal to let race define his presidency. Powell told me that his own experience was instructive in this larger context. Throughout his years as a career soldier and then as White House national security advisor and secretary of state, he had tried to live his life based on performance, and insisted that people judge him by his performance and not the color of his skin.[11]

Powell conceded that "we still have a race issue in this country. We haven't reached a nirvana" because the nation now has a black president, and "we haven't entered a post-racial era. We haven't entered the world we all hoped for yet."

But Powell counseled black young people not to become preoccupied with racial issues, and not to be overly sensitive to possible prejudice. These young people need to "get on with it," Powell said, and focus on being the best they can be. "If you don't perform," Powell added, "you won't go anywhere anyway."

*   *   *

YET AS HIS PRESIDENCY advanced, and while his policies were largely race-neutral, Obama gradually associated himself more openly with his and his wife's African American roots. When he filled out his Census form in early 2010, he identified himself as "black" rather than biracial, which would have been more accurate. Obama's advisers said he filled out the form according to the way he felt about himself and how others regarded him for most of his life.

He also had a framed copy of the Emancipation Proclamation hung in the Oval Office. Events at the White House featured more African American entertainers and sports figures, as well as increasing numbers of African American children who were invited there to be inspired about what was possible in their lives. White House Press Secretary Robert Gibbs told me that Obama was deeply moved by "the notion that all the African American kids in school can now turn on the television and see that being anything that you want to be includes being president of the United States, and the psychological difference that that has, almost immediately, and specifically for African American kids."[12]

Gibbs added that the historic change struck him with special force one morning as he was eating breakfast with his six-year-old son. On the table was a placemat bearing images of all the presidents, "going from white wigs to Barack Obama," Gibbs recalled. It was all very ordinary to his son. "He's only known two presidents in his life, and one of them was an African American. He'll never grow up at a time in which people will ever wonder whether it's possible, and I think that's a pretty amazing thing."

Obama also made a special appeal to the graduating class of Hampton University, at the historically black school's 2010 commencement in Hampton, Virginia. Obama said that "all of us have a responsibility, as Americans, to change" the relatively low academic achievement levels of African Americans. He called on the black graduates to be "role models for your brothers and sisters." And he urged them to resist the temptation to use technological advances such as iPods, iPads, and Xboxes that make information "a distraction, a diversion, a form of entertainment, rather than a tool of empowerment, rather than the means of emancipation." Obama said the graduates shouldn't accept limitations set by others, and used the example of groundbreaking civil rights activist Dorothy Height, whom he had praised at her funeral in Washington the previous month. "That refusal to accept a lesser fate," he said, "that insistence on a better life, that, ultimately, is the secret not only of African American survival and success, it has been the secret of America's survival and success."[13]

Michelle Obama's anti–childhood obesity campaign was clearly chosen to have a strong appeal to whites but also because it resonated so strongly with blacks (and Latinos), who have a higher risk for obesity. "African American parents know how important this is," and the Obamas don't need to make an overly racial appeal to make the point, says Republican pollster Bill McInturff.[14]

* * *

THERE WERE MANY effects stemming from Obama's presidency, both those that were expected and those that were not. One was a surprising surge in the number of black Republican candidates in the mid-term elections of November 2010.[15] At least thirty-two African Americans were running for Congress as Republicans as of May, the largest number since Reconstruction, according to *The New York Times*. The last time there was a black Republican serving in the House was 2003, when J. C. Watts of Oklahoma left office after eight years. *The New York Times* found that "many of the candidates suggest that they felt empowered by Mr. Obama's election, that it made them realize that what had once seemed impossible—for a black candidate to win election with substantial white support—was not." The states where these candidates were running included Arkansas, Arizona, and Florida.

Valerie Jarrett told me, "I think at the time of his victory there was an enormous amount of historical significance to this country being able to elect a person who was African American as president. I think that there are probably people who still see him as an African American president favorably and unfavorably. But the vast majority of people, I think, see him as *their* president. I think that because he inherited such a crisis on all fronts—two wars, an economic meltdown, a fiscal meltdown, the largest deficit in our nation's history, and a health crisis, energy crisis, education crisis, confidence crisis around the world—because of this extraordinary moment in history when he stepped in, I don't think there has been a lot of time to focus on his race. People just want to know, 'Are you going to be able to improve the quality of my life?'"

But Obama, in his most candid moments, acknowledged that race was still a problem. In May 2010, he told guests at a private White House dinner that race was probably a key component in the rising opposition to his presidency from conservatives, especially right-wing activists in the anti-incumbent "tea party" movement that was then surging across the country. Many middle-class and working-class whites felt aggrieved and resentful that the federal government was helping other groups, including bankers, automakers, irresponsible people who had defaulted on their mortgages, and the poor, but wasn't helping them nearly enough, he said.

A guest suggested that when tea party activists said they wanted to "take back" their country, their real motivation was to stir up anger and anxiety at having a black president, and Obama didn't dispute the idea. He agreed that there was a "subterranean agenda" in the anti-Obama movement—a racially biased one—that was unfortunate. But he sadly conceded that there was little he could do about it.

His goal, he said, was to be as effective and empathetic a president as possible for all Americans. If he could accomplish that, it would advance racial progress for blacks more than anything else he could do.

Obama's concerns about the tea party and the mood of the country were reinforced by the midterm elections of November 2, 2010. Prompted at least in part by anger at his policies, voters gave Republicans control of the House of Representatives and moved several Senate seats to the GOP.

In effect, Americans used the elections to send two messages to Obama: put the brakes on his costly, activist approach to government, and focus much more intently on creating jobs amid an unemployment rate that had remained over 9 percent for many months. Four in ten Americans told pollsters that they were worse off financially than they were two years earlier, and half said Obama's policies were hurting the country, according to polling by Edison Research.[16]

There was another problem. It turned out that most white voters had turned against Obama and his fellow Democrats while support from African Americans remained strong. It seemed to be a return to the racial polarization of the past. White Americans told pollsters that they weren't opposed to Obama simply because he was black; it was more complicated than that. White middle-class and working-class people didn't think Obama understood them and their problems, and his policies weren't doing them much good.

But as he prepared for his reelection campaign in 2012, Barack Obama retained the belief that Americans, in the end, would evaluate him on the basis of his ideas, his character, and his abilities, not the ancient stereotypes of skin color and race. His presidency would remain what it was from the start—a test of American reality versus American ideals, reflecting a conflict as old as the Republic.

NOTES

Chapter One

1. Huppke, Rex and Stacy St. Clair. 2008. "The Grant Park Rally." www.chicagotribune .com (November 5), p. 10.

2. Author's interview with President Obama, March 12, 2010.

3. Author's interview with Valerie Jarrett, January 25, 2010.

4. Walton, Hanes Jr. and Robert C. Smith. 2008. *American Politics and the African American Quest for Universal Freedom*. New York: Pearson Longman, pp. 209–210.

5. *Journal of Blacks in Higher Education*. 2008. "Blacks and the White House: from slave builders to the master of the house." (Winter), p. 26.

6. Ibid.

7. White House Historical Association/Exhibits. 2009. "The Working White House," www.whitehousehistory.org (December 30). See also Wills, Garry. 2003. *"Negro President": Jefferson and the Slave Power*. New York: Houghton Mifflin Company, p. 236.

8. Felzenberg, Alvin Stephen. 2008. *The Leaders We Deserved (And a Few We Didn't): Rethinking the Presidential Rating Game*. New York: Basic Books, p. 264.

9. Brooks, Noah. 1906. *Abraham Lincoln and the Downfall of American Slavery*. New York: G.P. Putnam's Sons, p. 303.

10. Walton and Smith. *American Politics and the African American Quest for Universal Freedom*, p. 242.

11. Kamen, Al. 2010. "No record-breaking year for presidential appointments." *The Washington Post* (January 20), p. A3.

12. Kurin, Richard and Marjorie Hunt. 1996. "In the service of the presidency: workers' culture at the White House." *Prologue: Quarterly of the National Archives and Records Administration* 28, no. 4 (Winter 1996), p. 273.

13. Ibid., p. 276.

14. Ibid.

15. Author's interview with Valerie Jarrett, January 25, 2010.

16. Author's interview with Gary Walters, retired chief usher at the White House, January 25, 2010. See also Isserman, Maurice and Michael Kazin. 2004. *America Divided: The Civil War of the 1960s*. New York: Oxford University Press, p. 25.

17. E-mail response to the author, April 22, 2010.

18. Holland, Jesse J. 2007. *Black Men Built the Capitol: Discovering African-American History in and Around Washington, DC.* Guilford, CT: The Globe Pequot Press, p. 57.

19. Ibid., pp. 57–58.

20. Bordewich, Fergus M. 2008. *Washington: The Making of the American Capital.* New York: Amistad, p. 193.

21. Kurin and Hunt. "In the service of the presidency," p. 274.

22. Ibid.

23. Ibid.

24. *Journal of Blacks in Higher Education.* 2008. "Blacks and the White House: from slave builders to the master of the house" (Winter), p. 26.

25. *Life.* 1969 (May 9), p. 67.

26. Author's interview with White House historian William Seale, July 31, 2009.

27. *Baltimore Afro-American.* 1927. "Valet handled Harding love notes." November 19, p. 1.

28. Harper, Lucius C. 1939. "Harding had colored kin, records show." In "Dustin' off the News." *The Chicago Defender* (November 25).

29. Bruce, Preston, with Katharine Johnson, Patricia Hass, and Susan Hainey. 1984. *From the Door of the White House.* New York: Lothrop, Lee and Shepard Books, pp. 170–171.

30. Kitchen Sisters. 2008. "Hercules and Hemings: presidents' slave chefs." www.npr.org (February 19).

31. White House Historical Association/Exhibits. 2009. "The Working White House," www.whitehousehistory.org (December 30).

32. Parks, Lillian Rogers, with Frances Spatz Leighton. 1961. *My Thirty Years Backstairs at the White House.* New York: Fleet Publishing Corporation, p. 121.

33. Ibid., p. 122.

34. Ibid., p. 123.

35. Ibid., pp. 154–155.

36. Kitchen Sisters. "Hercules and Hemings."

37. Author's interview with Chris Emery, February 17, 2010.

38. Author's interview with Colin Powell, May 28, 2010.

39. Parks with Leighton. *My Thirty Years Backstairs at the White House,* p. 43.

40. Ibid.

41. Ibid., pp. 43–44.

42. Ibid., p. 44.

43. Ibid.

44. Taylor, Kristin Clark. 1993. *The First to Speak: A Woman of Color Inside the White House.* New York: Doubleday, pp. 97–99.

45. Branch, Taylor. 2009. *The Clinton Tapes: Wrestling History with the President.* New York: Simon and Schuster, p. 535.

46. Taylor. *The First to Speak,* p. 183.

47. Powell, Colin L., with Joseph E. Persico. 1995. *My American Journey.* New York: Random House, p. 401.

48. Ibid., p. 399.

Chapter 2

1. Wood, Gordon S. 2003. "Slaves in the family." *The New York Times Book Review* (December 14), p. 10. See also Wilkins, Roger. 2001. *Jefferson's Pillow: The Founding Fathers and the Dilemma of Black Patriotism.* Boston: Beacon Press, p. 9.

2. Mazyck, Walter H. 1932. *George Washington and the Negro.* Washington, DC: The Associated Publishers, Inc., p. 7.

3. Anthony, Carl Sferrazza. 1992. "Skirting the issue." *American Visions 7*, no. 5 (Oct/Nov), p. 28.

4. Anthony, Carl Sferrazza. 1990. *First Ladies: The Saga of the Presidents' Wives and Their Power 1789–1961*. New York: William Morrow and Company, Inc., p. 58.

5. Wood, Gordon S. 2003. "Slaves in the family." *The New York Times Book Review* (December 14), p. 10.

6. Mazyck. *George Washington and the Negro*, p. 13.

7. Latrobe, Benjamin Henry. 1977. *The Papers of Benjamin Henry Latrobe*, Yale University, p. 170.

8. Holland, Jesse J. 2007. *Black Men Built the Capitol: Discovering African-American History in and Around Washington, DC*. Guilford, CT: The Globe Pequot Press, p. 54.

9. Wiencek, Henry. 2003. *An Imperfect God: George Washington, His Slaves and the Creation of America*. New York: Farrar, Straus and Giroux, p. 13.

10. Ferling, John. 2009. *The Ascent of George Washington: The Hidden Political Genius of an American Icon*. New York: Bloomsbury Press, pp. 284–285.

11. Ibid., p. 285.

12. Ibid.

13. Wills, Garry. 2003. *"Negro President": Jefferson and the Slave Power*. New York: Houghton Mifflin Company, p. 210. See also Wiencek. *An Imperfect God*, pp. 314–316.

14. Bordewich, Fergus M. 2008. *Washington: The Making of the American Capital*. New York: Amistad, p. 233.

15. Wiencek. *An Imperfect God*, p. 319.

16. Wills. *"Negro President,"* p. 209.

17. Wiencek. *An Imperfect God*, p. 320.

18. Ibid., pp. 311–314.

19. Holland. *Black Men Built the Capitol*, p. 56.

20. Wiencek. *An Imperfect God*, pp. 321–334.

21. Bordewich. *Washington*, pp. 233–234.

22. Ibid., p. 234.

23. LaBan, Craig. 2010. "A birthday shock from Washington's chef." www.philly.com (February 22).

24. Holland. *Black Men Built the Capitol*, p. 55.

25. Kitchen Sisters. 2008. "Hercules and Hemings: presidents' slave chefs." www.npr.org (February 19), p. 2.

26. Holland. *Black Men Built the Capitol*, p. 55.

27. Wiencek. *An Imperfect God*, p. 308. See also Walsh, Kenneth T. 2005. *From Mount Vernon to Crawford: A History of the Presidents and Their Retreats*. New York: Hyperion, p. 22.

28. Mazyck, Walter H. 1932. *George Washington and the Negro*. Washington, DC: The Associated Publishers, Inc., p. 128.

29. Ibid.

30. Burns, James MacGregor and Susan Dunn. 2004. *George Washington*. New York: Times Books, p. 154.

31. Walsh. *From Mount Vernon to Crawford*, p. 20.

32. Anthony. *First Ladies*, p. 71.

33. Anthony. "Skirting the issue," p. 28. See also Anthony. *First Ladies*, p. 70.

34. Wiencek. *An Imperfect God*, pp. 219–220.

35. Gates, Henry Louis Jr. 2009. *Lincoln on Race and Slavery*. Princeton, NJ: Princeton University Press, p. xxiii.

36. Jackson, Donald. 1989. *A Year at Monticello, 1795*. Golden, CO: Fulcrum, Inc., pp. 29–30.

37. Gordon-Reed, Annette. 1997. *Thomas Jefferson and Sally Hemings: An American Controversy*. Charlottesville: University Press of Virginia, p. 172.

38. Author's interview with Monticello historical guide Sharon Lugar, February 17, 2004.

39. Bear, James. A. Jr., ed. 1967. *Jefferson at Monticello: Recollections of a Monticello Slave and of a Monticello Overseer*. Charlottesville: University Press of Virginia, p. 23.

40. Jackson. *A Year at Monticello*, p. 32.

41. Bear. *Jefferson at Monticello*, pp. 15–16.

42. Wills. *"Negro President,"* p. 210.

43. Kitchen Sisters. "Hercules and Hemings," p. 3.

44. Bear. *Jefferson at Monticello*, p. 105.

45. Ibid.

46. Halliday, E. M. 2001. *Understanding Thomas Jefferson*. New York: HarperCollins Publishers, pp. 233–234.

47. Milkis, Sidney M. and Michael Nelson. 1999. *The American Presidency: Origins and Development, 1776–1998*. Washington, DC: Congressional Quarterly (CQ) Press, p. 105. See also Lorant, Stefan. 1968. *The Glorious Burden: The American Presidency*. New York: Harper and Row Publishers, p. 97.

48. Jennings, Paul. 1865. *A Colored Man's Reminiscences of James Madison*. Brooklyn: George C. Beadle (available from the Montpelier Foundation), p. 14.

49. Ibid., pp. 7–8.

50. Kurin, Richard and Marjorie Hunt. 1996. "In the service of the presidency: workers' culture at the White House." *Prologue: Quarterly of the National Archives and Records Administration* 28, no. 4 (Winter 1996), pp. 272–273.

51. Jennings. *A Colored Man's Reminiscences*, pp. 9–10.

52. Ibid., p. 13.

53. Anthony. "Skirting the issue," p. 28.

54. Jennings. *A Colored Man's Reminiscences*, p. 15.

55. Montpelier.org. 2009. "Historic Montpelier celebrates 195th anniversary of George Washington portrait rescue from the White House." Press release, available on www .montpelier.org/press (August 24).

56. Walton, Hanes Jr. and Robert C. Smith. 2008. *American Politics and the African American Quest for Universal Freedom*. New York: Pearson Longman, p. 199.

57. White House Historical Association/Exhibits. 2009. The Census of 1830. www .whitehousehistory.org (December 30).

58. Felzenberg, Alvin Stephen. 2008. *The Leaders We Deserved (And a Few We Didn't): Rethinking the Presidential Rating Game*. New York: Basic Books, p. 264.

59. Eisenhower, John S. D. 2008. *Zachary Taylor*. New York: Times Books, p. 99.

Chapter 3

1. Gates, Henry Louis Jr. 2009. *Lincoln on Race and Slavery*. Princeton, NJ: Princeton University Press, p. xxxii.

2. Ibid., pp. xxi–xxii.

3. McPherson, James M. 2008. *Tried by War: Abraham Lincoln as Commander in Chief*. New York: The Penguin Press, p. 267.

4. Kendrick, Paul and Stephen Kendrick. 2008. *Douglass and Lincoln: How a Revolutionary Black Leader and a Reluctant Liberator Struggled to End Slavery and Save the Union*. New York: Walker and Company, p. 9.

5. Brooks, Noah. 1906. *Abraham Lincoln and the Downfall of American Slavery*. New York: G.P. Putnam's Sons, p. 300.

6. Kendrick and Kendrick. *Douglass and Lincoln*, p. 111.

7. Washington, John E. 1942. *They Knew Lincoln*. New York: E.P. Dutton, p. 101. See also Pinsker, Matthew. 2003. *Lincoln's Sanctuary: Abraham Lincoln and the Soldiers' Home*. New York: Oxford University Press, p. 68.

8. Washington. *They Knew Lincoln*, p. 101.

9. Pinsker. *Lincoln's Sanctuary*, p. 11.

10. Donald, David Herbert. 1999. *Lincoln at Home: Two Glimpses of Abraham Lincoln's Family Life*. New York: Simon and Schuster, p. 48.

11. Beschloss, Michael. 2007. *Presidential Courage: Brave Leaders and How They Changed America 1789–1989*. New York: Simon and Schuster, p. 109. See also Felzenberg, Alvin Stephen. 2008. *The Leaders We Deserved (And a Few We Didn't): Rethinking the Presidential Rating Game*. New York: Basic Books, pp. 19–27, 90–91, 124–125.

12. Quarles, Benjamin. 1962. *Lincoln and the Negro*. New York: Oxford University Press, p. 186.

13. Gates. *Lincoln on Race and Slavery*, pp. xxxiii–xxxiv.

14. Ibid., pp. xxxiv–xxxv.

15. Beschloss. *Presidential Courage*, p. 110.

16. Gates. *Lincoln on Race and Slavery*, pp. lii–liii. See also Quarles. *Lincoln and the Negro*, pp. 191–194.

17. McPherson. *Tried by War*, pp. 201–202.

18. Ibid., pp. 202–203.

19. Kendrick and Kendrick. *Douglass and Lincoln*, p. 5.

20. Washington. *They Knew Lincoln*. Cited in "Lincoln as his servants knew him." *Baltimore Afro-American* (Feb. 11, 1956), p. 19G.

21. Kendrick and Kendrick. *Douglass and Lincoln*, p. 8.

22. McPherson. *Tried by War*, p. 203.

23. Holland, Jesse J. 2007. *Black Men Built the Capitol: Discovering African-American History in and Around Washington, DC*. Guilford, CT: The Globe Pequot Press, p. 66.

24. Keckley, Elizabeth. 1988. *Behind the Scenes, or Thirty Years a Slave, and Four Years in the White House*. New York: Oxford University Press, p. 83.

25. Quarles. *Lincoln and the Negro*, pp. 200–202.

26. Anthony, Carl Sferrazza. 1992. "Skirting the issue." *American Visions* 7, no. 5 (Oct/Nov), p. 29.

27. Keckley. *Behind the Scenes*, pp. 86–89.

28. Ibid., pp. 102–103.

29. Ibid., pp. 104–105.

30. Quarles. *Lincoln and the Negro*, p. 203.

31. Ibid., pp. 200–202.

32. Ibid., p. 203.

33. Keckley. *Behind the Scenes*, pp. 127–131.

34. Ibid., pp. 132–133.

35. Ibid., pp. 130–131.

36. Beschloss. *Presidential Courage*, p. 98.

37. Ibid.

38. Ibid., pp. 189–192.

39. Hadley, Clara Boyton. 1932. "Freed slaves: a true story of Lincoln and Douglass." *Atlanta Daily World* (February 19), p. 6.

40. Quarles. *Lincoln and the Negro*, p. 194.

41. Ibid., pp. 194–195.

42. Ibid., p. 195.

43. MacGregor, Morris J. 1999. *The Emergence of a Black Catholic Community: St. Augustine's in Washington*. Washington, DC: The Catholic University of America Press, pp. 4–5.

44. Quarles. *Lincoln and the Negro*, p. 196.

45. Report by John E. Washington in *They Knew Lincoln*, cited in *Baltimore Afro-American*. 1956. "Lincoln as his servants knew him." February 11, p. 19G.

46. Ibid.

47. Harper, Lucius C. 1947. "Negro heard Lincoln's Gettysburg speech before anyone." In "Dustin' off the News." *The Chicago Defender* (November 15), p. 1.

48. Slade, William. "Mr. Lincoln's White House." At www.mrlincolnswhitehouse.org.

49. Ibid.

50. Anthony. "Skirting the issue," p. 28.

51. Ibid., p. 29

52. Ibid., p. 30.

53. Ibid.

Chapter 4

1. Sinkler, George. 1972. *The Racial Attitudes of American Presidents from Abraham Lincoln to Theodore Roosevelt.* Garden City, NY: Anchor Books, p. 96.

2. Ibid., p. 97.

3. Ibid., pp. 97–98.

4. Felzenberg, Alvin Stephen. 2008. *The Leaders We Deserved (And a Few We Didn't): Rethinking the Presidential Rating Game.* New York: Basic Books, p. 273.

5. Trefousse, Hans L. 1989. *Andrew Johnson: A Biography.* New York: W.W. Norton and Company, p. 196.

6. Sinkler. *The Racial Attitudes of American Presidents from Abraham Lincoln to Theodore Roosevelt,* p. 107.

7. Ibid. p. 129.

8. Ibid., p. 98.

9. Ibid., p. 107.

10. Walton, Hanes Jr. and Robert C. Smith. 2008. *American Politics and the African American Quest for Universal Freedom.* New York: Pearson Longman, p. 199. See also Isserman, Maurice and Michael Kazin. 2004. *America Divided: The Civil War of the 1960s.* New York: Oxford University Press, p. 24.

11. Felzenberg. *The Leaders We Deserved (And a Few We Didn't),* pp. 274–275.

12. Ibid., p. 275.

13. Ibid., p. 277.

14. Whitney, David C. 1967. *The American Presidents.* Garden City, NY: Doubleday and Company, Inc., p. 154.

15. Ibid., p. 155.

16. Ibid.

17. Anthony, Carl Sferrazza. 1990. *First Ladies: The Saga of the Presidents' Wives and Their Power 1789–1961.* New York: William Morrow and Company, Inc., p. 205.

18. Bowen, David Warren. 1989. *Andrew Johnson and the Negro.* Knoxville: The University of Tennessee Press, p. 131.

19. Ibid., p. 51.

20. Whitney. *The American Presidents,* p. 45.

21. Bowen. *Andrew Johnson and the Negro,* p. 52.

22. Trefousse. *Andrew Johnson,* p. 45.

23. Bowen. *Andrew Johnson and the Negro,* p. 130.

24. Ibid., p. 137.

25. Ibid., pp. 1–2.

26. Ibid., p. 3.

27. Ibid.

28. Ibid., pp. 4–5.

29. Ibid., p. 6.

30. *Chicago Defender.* 1938. "Ex-president's slave on 'We the People' radio program." January 8, p. 10.

Chapter 5

1. Meyer, Howard N. 1966. *Let Us Have Peace: The Story of Ulysses S. Grant.* New York: The MacMillan Company, p. 32.

2. McFeely, William S. 1982. *Grant: A Biography.* New York: W.W. Norton and Company, pp. 71–72.

3. Ibid., p. 62. See also Sinkler, George. 1972. *The Racial Attitudes of American Presidents from Abraham Lincoln to Theodore Roosevelt.* Garden City, NY: Anchor Books, p. 146.

4. Sinkler. *The Racial Attitudes of American Presidents from Abraham Lincoln to Theodore Roosevelt,* p. 147.

5. Ibid., p. 156.

6. Walton, Hanes Jr. and Robert C. Smith. 2008. *American Politics and the African American Quest for Universal Freedom.* New York: Pearson Longman, p. 199.

7. Wilentz, Sean. 2010. "Who's buried in the history books?" *The New York Times Week in Review* (March 14), p. 9.

8. Felzenberg, Alvin Stephen. 2008. *The Leaders We Deserved (And a Few We Didn't): Rethinking the Presidential Rating Game.* New York: Basic Books, pp. 282–284.

9. Ibid., p. 285.

10. Ibid., p. 282.

11. Ibid., pp. 283–284.

12. *Baltimore Afro-American.* 1922. "First colored man given a federal job." August 11, p. 7.

13. *Atlanta Daily World.* 1935. "Orderly, 102, dead." January 22, p. 1.

14. Felzenberg. *The Leaders We Deserved (And a Few We Didn't),* pp. 285–286.

15. Ibid., p. 286.

16. Ibid., pp. 286–288. See also Milkis, Sidney M. and Michael Nelson. 1999. *The American Presidency: Origins and Development, 1776–1998.* Washington, DC: Congressional Quarterly (CQ) Press.

17. Felzenberg. *The Leaders We Deserved (And a Few We Didn't),* p. 288.

18. Walton and Smith. *American Politics and the African American Quest for Universal Freedom,* p. 199.

19. Sinkler. *The Racial Attitudes of American Presidents from Abraham Lincoln to Theodore Roosevelt,* p. 381.

20. Ibid., pp. 381–382.

21. Ibid., p. 408.

22. Ibid., p. 387.

23. Ibid., p. 388.

24. Ibid., p. 400.

25. Gould, Lewis L. 1991. *The Presidency of Theodore Roosevelt.* Lawrence: University Press of Kansas, p. 23.

26. Sinkler. *The Racial Attitudes of American Presidents from Abraham Lincoln to Theodore Roosevelt,* p. 418.

27. Ibid., p. 428.

28. Ibid., p. 418.

29. Felzenberg. *The Leaders We Deserved (And a Few We Didn't),* p. 290.

30. Morris, Edmund. 2001. *Theodore Rex.* New York: Random House, p. 58.

31. Quoted in Morris, *Theodore Rex,* pp. 261–262.

32. Sinkler. *The Racial Attitudes of American Presidents from Abraham Lincoln to Theodore Roosevelt,* p. 423.

33. Ibid., p. 424.

34. Ibid., p. 419.

35. *Pittsburgh Courier.* 1927. "Intimate impressions of Rooseveltian personality recorded by former secretary." (April 23), p. A2.

36. Morris. *Theodore Rex*, pp. 52–53.
37. Ibid., p. 55. See also Felzenberg. *The Leaders We Deserved (And a Few We Didn't)*, p. 291.
38. Morris. *Theodore Rex*, pp. 54–55.
39. Quoted in Morris, *Theodore Rex*, pp. 54–55.
40. Morris. *Theodore Rex*, p. 58.
41. Seale, William. 1986. *The President's House: A History*. Washington, DC: The White House Historical Association in cooperation with the National Geographic Society, p. 653.
42. Morris. *Theodore Rex*, p. 453.
43. Ibid.
44. Ibid., p. 454.
45. Ibid., pp. 454–455.
46. Ibid., p. 455.
47. Ibid., pp. 465, 467.
48. Felzenberg. *The Leaders We Deserved (And a Few We Didn't)*, pp. 294–295.
49. Ibid., p. 294.
50. Cooper, John Milton Jr. 2009. *Woodrow Wilson, A Biography*. New York: Alfred A. Knopf, pp. 170–171.
51. Ibid.
52. *Norfolk Journal and Guide*. 1931. "Native Virginian, ex-slave, was mentioned for presidential nomination, married 50 years." (October 10), p. A11.
53. Cooper. *Woodrow Wilson*, p. 205.
54. Lightman, David. 2009. "Racial barriers fell slowly in capital." McClatchy News Service (January 16).
55. Cooper. *Woodrow Wilson*, p. 25.
56. Patler, Nicholas. 2004. *Jim Crow and the Wilson Administration: Protesting Federal Segregation in the Early Twentieth Century*. Boulder: The University Press of Colorado, p. 137.
57. Ibid.
58. Cooper. *Woodrow Wilson*, pp. 205–206.
59. Ibid., pp. 270–271.
60. Patler. *Jim Crow and the Wilson Administration*, p. 177.
61. Ibid., p. 178.
62. Cooper. *Woodrow Wilson*, p. 205.
63. Patler. *Jim Crow and the Wilson Administration*, p. 206.
64. Cooper. *Woodrow Wilson*, p. 273.
65. Ibid., p. 407.
66. Ibid., pp. 407–408.
67. Ibid., pp. 409–410.
68. Felzenberg. *The Leaders We Deserved (And a Few We Didn't)*, p. 298.
69. Parks, Lillian Rogers, with Frances Spatz Leighton. 1961. *My Thirty Years Backstairs at the White House*. New York: Fleet Publishing Corporation, pp. 154–155.
70. Ibid.
71. Ibid., p. 155.
72. Office of History and Preservation, Office of the Clerk, U.S. House of Representatives. 2008. *Black Americans in Congress 1870–2007*. Washington, DC: U.S. Government Printing Office, p. 280.
73. Anthony, Carl Sferrazza. 1992. "Skirting the issue." *American Visions 7*, no. 5 (Oct/Nov), p. 30.
74. Hoover, Herbert. 1952. *The Memoirs of Herbert Hoover: The Cabinet and the Presidency 1920–1933*. New York: The MacMillan Company, p. 323.
75. Parks with Leighton. *My Thirty Years Backstairs at the White House*, p. 219.
76. Ibid., p. 226.

77. Ibid.

78. Ibid., pp. 228–229.

79. *Norfolk Journal and Guide*. 1932. "They went to Hoover's photo party." (October 29), p. 2.

80. *Baltimore Afro-American*. 1932. "The Hoover photograph: I told you so." October 8, editorial.

81. Midnight, J. O. 1930. "Hoover photos are as scarce as his race appointments." *Baltimore Afro-American* (January 18), p. A1.

Chapter 6

1. Brands, H. W. 2008. *Traitor to His Class*. New York: Doubleday, p. 515. See also Walton, Hanes Jr. and Robert C. Smith. 2008. *American Politics and the African American Quest for Universal Freedom*. New York: Pearson Longman, pp. 199–200.

2. O'Reilly, Kenneth. 1995. *Nixon's Piano: Presidents and Racial Politics from Washington to Clinton*. New York: The Free Press, p. 116.

3. Anthony, Carl Sferrazza. 1992. "Skirting the issue." *American Visions* 7, no. 5 (Oct/Nov), pp. 30–31.

4. Calvin, Dolores. 1942. "Louis Armstrong band plays president ball." *Philadelphia Times*, January 24, p. 15.

5. *Pittsburgh Courier*. 1934. "No color line at White House." (August. 11), p. A1.

6. Keiler, Allan. 2000. *Marian Anderson: A Singer's Journey*. New York: Scribner, p. 130.

7. West, J. B., with Mary Lynn Kotz. 1973. *Upstairs at the White House: My Life with the First Ladies*. New York: Coward, McCann and Geoghegan, Inc., pp. 31–32.

8. Anthony. "Skirting the issue," p. 28.

9. West with Kotz. *Upstairs at the White House*, pp. 31–32.

10. Parks, Lillian Rogers, with Frances Spatz Leighton. 1981. *The Roosevelts: A Family in Turmoil*. Englewood Cliffs, NJ: Prentice-Hall, Inc., p. 71.

11. Ibid., pp. 71–72.

12. Brands. *Traitor to His Class*, p. 515. See also Walton and Smith. *American Politics and the African American Quest for Universal Freedom*, p. 516.

13. Ibid.

14. Ibid.

15. Ibid.

16. Author's interview with Robert Dallek, October 6, 2009.

17. West with Kotz. *Upstairs at the White House*, pp. 30–31.

18. Goodwin, Doris Kearns. 1994. *No Ordinary Time: Franklin and Eleanor Roosevelt: The Home Front in World War II*. New York: Simon and Schuster, p. 627.

19. Patler, Nicholas. 2004. *Jim Crow and the Wilson Administration: Protesting Federal Segregation in the Early Twentieth Century*. Boulder: The University Press of Colorado, p. 208.

20. Walton and Smith. *American Politics and the African American Quest for Universal Freedom*, p. 200.

21. Cohen, Adam. 2009. *Nothing to Fear: FDR's Inner Circle and the Hundred Days that Created Modern America*. New York: Penguin Press, p. 226.

22. Goodwin. *No Ordinary Time*, pp. 445–446.

23. Ibid., p. 446.

24. Ibid.

25. Ibid., p. 447.

26. Fields, Alonzo. 1960/1961. *My 21 Years in the White House*. New York: Coward-McCann, Inc., pp. 41–42.

27. Parks with Leighton. *The Roosevelts*, p. 32.

28. Ibid., p. 192.

29. Ibid., pp. 192, 194–195.

30. Ibid., p. 33.

31. Fields. *My 21 Years in the White House,* pp. 42–43.

32. Kurin, Richard and Marjorie Hunt. 1996. "In the service of the presidency: workers' culture at the White House." *Prologue: Quarterly of the National Archives and Records Administration* 28, no. 4 (Winter 1996), p. 276.

33. *Baltimore Afro-American.* 1940. "Reporter visits FDR's Ga. Home." Staff correspondence, September 14, p. 1.

34. McKay, Cliff. 1941. "Roosevelt hails new hospital." *Atlanta Daily World* (January 16), p. 1.

35. *Atlanta Daily World.* 1945. "ANP 'Says Warm Springs treats Negro polio victims now.'" September 8, p. 1.

36. Marton, Kati. 2001. *Hidden Power: Presidential Marriages that Shaped Our Recent History.* New York: Pantheon, p. 74.

37. United Press. 1936. "Negro runner says F.D.R. snubbed him." *El Paso Herald-Post* (October 16), p. 8.

38. *New York Times.* 1976. "Owens proud of latest medal." In People in Sports (August 26).

39. Parks with Leighton. *The Roosevelts,* p. 18.

40. Ibid., p. 21.

41. Parks, Lillian Rogers, with Frances Spatz Leighton. 1961. *My Thirty Years Backstairs at the White House.* New York: Fleet Publishing Corporation, p. 258.

42. Ibid.

43. Ibid., pp. 258–259.

44. Ibid., p. 58.

45. Ibid., pp. 236–237.

46. Ibid., p. 237.

47. Parks with Leighton. *The Roosevelts,* p. 21.

48. Ibid., p. 22. See also *Pittsburgh Courier.* 1933. "President-elect Roosevelt to use Georgian as valet." (January 7), p. 3.

49. Weaver, Frederick S. 1936. "President Roosevelt's valet says attitude of Nation's executive is friendly; also says that he reads colored papers." *Atlanta Daily World* (March 18), p. 1.

50. Parks with Leighton. *My Thirty Years Backstairs at the White House,* p. 241.

51. Parks with Leighton. *The Roosevelts,* p. 22.

52. Ibid., p. 46.

Chapter 7

1. O'Reilly, Kenneth. 1995. *Nixon's Piano: Presidents and Racial Politics from Washington to Clinton.* New York: The Free Press, p. 145.

2. Ibid., p. 146.

3. Truman, Margaret. 1973. *Harry S. Truman.* New York: William Morrow and Company, Inc., p. 392.

4. Felzenberg, Alvin Stephen. 2008. *The Leaders We Deserved (And a Few We Didn't): Rethinking the Presidential Rating Game.* New York: Basic Books, p. 316.

5. Ibid., pp. 316–317.

6. Geselbracht, Raymond H. 2007. *The Civil Rights Legacy of Harry S. Truman.* Kirksville, MO.: Truman State University Press, p. 141.

7. Felzenberg. *The Leaders We Deserved (And a Few We Didn't),* pp. 317–318.

8. Dallek, Robert. 2008. *Harry S. Truman.* New York: Times Books, pp. 65–66.

9. Ibid., p. 66.

10. Ibid.

11. Felzenberg. *The Leaders We Deserved (And a Few We Didn't)*, p. 316.

12. Dallek. *Harry S. Truman*, p. 71. See also Truman. *Harry S. Truman*, p. 553.

13. O'Reilly. *Nixon's Piano*, pp. 153–154.

14. Ibid., p. 154.

15. Dallek. *Harry S. Truman*, p. 71.

16. Davis, Michael D. and Hunter R. Clark. 1992. *Thurgood Marshall: Warrior at the Bar, Rebel on the Bench*. New York: Birch Lane Press, p. 123.

17. Kurin, Richard and Marjorie Hunt. 1996. "In the service of the presidency: workers' culture at the White House." *Prologue: Quarterly of the National Archives and Records Administration* 28, no. 4 (Winter 1996), p. 277.

18. Parks, Lillian Rogers, with Frances Spatz Leighton. 1961. *My Thirty Years Backstairs at the White House*. New York: Fleet Publishing Corporation, p. 57.

19. Ibid., p. 58.

20. Hamilton, Charles V. 1991. *Adam Clayton Powell Jr.: The Political Biography of an American Dilemma*. New York: Collier Books, p. 165.

21. West, J. B., with Mary Lynn Kotz. 1973. *Upstairs at the White House: My Life with the First Ladies*. New York: Coward, McCann and Geoghegan, Inc., pp. 94–95.

22. *Cleveland Call and Post*. 1946. "Truman irked when Robeson claims U.S. lynchings same as Axis crimes." September 28.

23. Fields, Alonzo. 1960/1961. *My 21 Years in the White House*. New York: Coward-McCann, Inc., pp. 119–122, 126–128.

24. Parks with Leighton. *My Thirty Years Backstairs at the White House*, p. 302.

25. Fields. *My 21 Years in the White House*, p. 135.

26. Ibid., pp. 136–137.

27. Ibid., pp. 184–185.

28. Parks with Leighton. *My Thirty Years Backstairs at the White House*, p. 284.

29. Ibid., p. 282.

30. Ibid.

31. Ibid., p. 289.

32. Holland, Jesse J. 2007. *Black Men Built the Capitol: Discovering African-American History in and Around Washington, DC*. Guilford, CT: The Globe Pequot Press, p. 65.

33. Felzenberg. *The Leaders We Deserved (And a Few We Didn't)*, pp. 318–319.

34. Ibid., p. 319.

35. Ibid., p. 320.

36. *Pittsburgh Courier*. 1957. "Ike, Nixon apologize to Negro over Delaware racial snub!" (October 19), p. 13.

37. Parks with Leighton. *My Thirty Years Backstairs at the White House*, p. 319.

38. Ibid.

39. Ibid., pp. 311–312.

40. Anthony, Carl Sferrazza. 1992. "Skirting the issue." *American Visions* 7, no. 5 (Oct/Nov), pp. 28–30.

41. Anthony, Carl Sferrazza. 1990. *First Ladies: The Saga of the Presidents' Wives and Their Power 1789–1961*. New York: William Morrow and Company, Inc., pp. 581–582.

42. *Atlanta Daily World*. 1956. "Eisenhower greets 22 Negro beauty queens." August 20, p. 1.

43. Parks with Leighton. *My Thirty Years Backstairs at the White House*, p. 320.

44. *New York Times*. 1957. "President greets friends of valet." Special to *The New York Times* (June 13), p. 22.

45. Parks with Leighton. *My Thirty Years Backstairs at the White House*, p. 321.

46. Ibid.

47. Morrow, E. Frederic. 1963. *Black Man in the White House*. New York: Macfadden Books, pp. 215, 216.

48. Ibid., pp. 11, 16.

49. Ibid., p. 198.

50. Haygood, Wil. 1993. *King of the Cats: The Life and Times of Adam Clayton Powell Jr.* New York: Amistad, p. 183.

Chapter 8

1. Felzenberg, Alvin Stephen. 2008. *The Leaders We Deserved (And a Few We Didn't): Rethinking the Presidential Rating Game.* New York: Basic Books, p. 321.

2. O'Brien, Michael. 2005. *John F. Kennedy: A Biography.* New York: Thomas Dunne Books, p. 364.

3. Beschloss, Michael. 2007. *Presidential Courage: Brave Leaders and How They Changed America 1789–1989.* New York: Simon and Schuster, p. 237.

4. Robinson, Jackie, with Alfred Duckett. 1995. *I Never Had It Made.* New York: HarperCollins, pp. 137–138.

5. Ibid., p. 138.

6. O'Brien, Michael. 2005. *John F. Kennedy: A Biography.* New York: Thomas Dunne Books, p. 595.

7. Ibid., 594.

8. Walton, Hanes Jr. and Robert C. Smith. 2008. *American Politics and the African American Quest for Universal Freedom.* New York: Pearson Longman, p. 201.

9. Bryant, Nick. 2006. *The Bystander: John F. Kennedy and the Struggle for Black Equality.* New York: Basic Books, pp. 211–212.

10. Ibid., p. 210.

11. Walton, *American Politics and the African American Quest for Universal Freedom,* p. 201.

12. Felzenberg. *The Leaders We Deserved (And a Few We Didn't),* p. 322.

13. Anthony, Carl Sferrazza. 1990. *First Ladies: The Saga of the Presidents' Wives and Their Power 1789–1961.* New York: William Morrow and Company, Inc., p. 31.

14. Bryant. *The Bystander,* p. 219.

15. Beschloss. *Presidential Courage,* p. 236.

16. O'Brien. *John F. Kennedy: A Biography,* p. 741.

17. Beschloss. *Presidential Courage,* pp. 236–237.

18. O'Brien. *John F. Kennedy: A Biography,* pp. 742–743. See also Marton, Kati. 2001. *Hidden Power: Presidential Marriages that Shaped Our Recent History.* New York: Pantheon, p. 124.

19. Dallek, Robert. 1998. *Flawed Giant: Lyndon Johnson and His Times 1961–1973.* New York: Oxford University Press, pp. 30–31.

20. Ibid., p. 31. See also O'Brien. *John F. Kennedy: A Biography,* ch. 29.

21. Beschloss. *Presidential Courage,* p. 259.

22. Ibid. See also O'Brien. *John F. Kennedy: A Biography,* p. 833.

23. Bennett, Lerone Jr. 1980. "Sammy Davis Jr. on Sammy Davis Jr. . . . sex, suicide, success, Richard Nixon, Frank Sinatra, black and white women, blacks and Jews." *Ebony* (March), p. 130.

24. Ibid.

25. Kotz, Nick. 2005. *Judgment Days: Lyndon Baines Johnson, Martin Luther King Jr., and the Laws that Changed America.* New York: Houghton Mifflin Company, pp. 42–43.

26. Dallek. *Flawed Giant,* p. 32.

27. Felzenberg. *The Leaders We Deserved (And a Few We Didn't),* p. 322.

28. Ibid., p. 323.

29. Bruce, Preston, with Katharine Johnson, Patricia Hass, and Susan Hainey. 1984. *From the Door of the White House.* New York: Lothrop, Lee and Shepard Books, p. 95.

30. Ibid., pp. 95–96.

31. Ibid., p. 96.
32. Ibid., p. 97.
33. Ibid., p. 78.
34. Ibid., pp. 79–80.
35. Ibid., p. 88.
36. Beschloss. *Presidential Courage,* p. 261.
37. Ibid.
38. *Chicago Daily Defender.* 1961. "White House photogs told to accept Negro by May 19." April 25, p. 3.
39. BNET. 1998. "Pioneer *Jet* photographer Maurice Sorrell dies at age 84 in Washington D.C." www.bnet.com, July 13.
40. Quoted in *Los Angeles Sentinel.* 1964. "Jackie breaks social bars at White House." February 13, p. C6.
41. Bryant. *The Bystander,* p. 473.
42. Ibid., pp. 11, 12, 465, 473.

Chapter 9

1. Dallek, Robert. 1998. *Flawed Giant: Lyndon Johnson and His Times 1961–1973.* New York: Oxford University Press, pp. 23–24.
2. Ibid., p. 24.
3. Ibid., p. 30.
4. Kotz, Nick. 2005. *Judgment Days: Lyndon Baines Johnson, Martin Luther King Jr., and the Laws that Changed America.* New York: Houghton Mifflin Company, p. 178.
5. Ibid., pp. 252–253.
6. Ibid., pp. 251–252.
7. Dallek. *Flawed Giant,* p. 113.
8. Kotz. *Judgment Days,* p. 32 (footnote).
9. Dallek. *Flawed Giant,* pp. 111–112. See also Kotz. 2005. *Judgment Days,* p. 94.
10. Ibid., p. 441.
11. Ibid., pp. 111–112.
12. Ibid., p. 112.
13. Walton, Hanes Jr. and Robert C. Smith. 2008. *American Politics and the African American Quest for Universal Freedom.* New York: Pearson Longman, p. 202.
14. Kotz. *Judgment Days,* pp. 65–66.
15. Ibid., p. 87.
16. McNamara, Robert S., with Brian Van DeMark. 1995. *In Retrospect: The Tragedy and Lessons of Vietnam.* New York: Times Books, pp. 282–283.
17. Kotz. *Judgment Days,* p. 88.
18. Ibid.
19. Davis, Michael D. and Hunter R. Clark. 1992. *Thurgood Marshall: Warrior at the Bar, Rebel on the Bench.* New York: Birch Lane Press, p. 248.
20. Dallek. *Flawed Giant,* p. 20.
21. Robinson, Jackie, with Alfred Duckett. 1995. *I Never Had It Made.* New York: HarperCollins, p. 200.
22. Anthony, Carl Sferrazza. 1992. "Skirting the issue." *American Visions* 7, no. 5 (Oct/Nov), p. 32.
23. Ibid.
24. Ibid.
25. Rich, Frank. 2010. "Fourth of July 1776, 1964, 2010." *New York Times,* Sunday opinion (July 4), p. 8.
26. Graham, Hugh Davis. 1992. *Civil Rights and the Presidency: Race and Gender in American Politics 1960–1972.* New York: Oxford University Press, p. 99.

27. Ibid.

28. Bruce, Preston, with Katharine Johnson, Patricia Hass, and Susan Hainey. 1984. *From the Door of the White House*. New York: Lothrop, Lee and Shepard Books, p. 120.

29. Ibid., pp. 120–121.

30. Graham. *Civil Rights and the Presidency*, p. 100.

31. Marton, Kati. 2001. *Hidden Power: Presidential Marriages that Shaped Our Recent History*. New York: Pantheon, pp. 165–166.

32. Ibid., p. 166.

33. Bruce. *From the Door of the White House*, pp. 107–108.

34. West, J. B., with Mary Lynn Kotz. 1973. *Upstairs at the White House: My Life with the First Ladies*. New York: Coward, McCann and Geoghegan, Inc., p. 325.

35. Ibid., pp. 324–326.

36. Ibid., pp. 326–327.

37. Marton. *Hidden Power*, p. 151.

38. Bruce. *From the Door of the White House*, pp. 129–130.

39. Ibid., p. 130.

Chapter 10

1. Author's interview with Bill Galston, September 22, 2009.

2. Walton, Hanes Jr. 1997. *African American Power and Politics: The Political Context Variable*. New York: Columbia University Press, p. 20. See also O'Reilly, Kenneth. 1995. *Nixon's Piano: Presidents and Racial Politics from Washington to Clinton*. New York: The Free Press, pp. 278–279.

3. Black, Conrad. 2007. *Richard Nixon: A Life in Full*. New York: Public Affairs, p. 643.

4. Felzenberg, Alvin Stephen. 2008. *The Leaders We Deserved (And a Few We Didn't): Rethinking the Presidential Rating Game*. New York: Basic Books, p. 324.

5. Ibid., pp. 324–325.

6. Walton, Hanes Jr. and Robert C. Smith. 2008. *American Politics and the African American Quest for Universal Freedom*, New York: Pearson Longman, p. 202.

7. Traub, James. 1990. "Daniel Patrick Moynihan, liberal? Conservative? Or just Pat?" nytimes.com (September 16).

8. Walters, Del. 2008. "Out damned spot: under the 'stain' lies a truth about race in America." www.ebonyjet.com (April 9).

9. Savage, Charlie. 2009. "On Nixon tapes, ambivalence on abortion, not Watergate." www.nytimes.com (January 23).

10. *Journal of Blacks in Higher Education*. 2008. "Blacks and the White House: from slave builders to the master of the house." (Winter), p. 26.

11. Bennett, Lerone Jr. 1980. "Sammy Davis Jr. on Sammy Davis Jr. . . . sex, suicide, success, Richard Nixon, Frank Sinatra, black and white women, blacks and Jews." *Ebony* (March), p. 130.

12. Ambrose, Stephen E. 1991. *Nixon, Volume Three: Ruin and Recovery 1973–1990*. New York: Simon and Schuster, pp. 66, 149–152.

13. Schoenebaum, Eleanora W., ed. 1979. *Political Profiles: The Nixon/Ford Years*. New York: Facts on File, pp. 75–76.

14. Bruce, Preston, with Katharine Johnson, Patricia Hass, and Susan Hainey. 1984. *From the Door of the White House*. New York: Lothrop, Lee and Shepard Books, p. 160.

15. O'Reilly. *Nixon's Piano*, p. 332.

16. Ibid., pp. 332–334.

17. Brinkley, Douglas. 2007. *Gerald R. Ford*. New York: Times Books, p. 67.

18. O'Reilly. *Nixon's Piano*, p. 332.

19. Goldstein, Richard. 2008. "Earl Butz, secretary felled by racial remark, is dead at 98." *The New York Times* (February 4).

20. Noah, Timothy. 2008. "Earl Butz, history's victim: how the gears of racial progress tore up Nixon's agriculture secretary." www.slate.com, February 4.

21. Weidenfeld, Sheila Rabb. 1979. *First Lady's Lady: With the Fords at the White House.* New York: G.P. Putnam's Sons, p. 38.

22. Anthony, Carl Sferrazza. 1991. *First Ladies: The Saga of the Presidents' Wives and Their Power 1961–1990.* New York: William Morrow and Company, Inc., p. 242.

23. Ford, Gerald R. 1979. *A Time to Heal: The Autobiography of Gerald R. Ford.* New York: Harper and Row.

24. Hutchison, Earl Ofari. 2010. "Gerald Ford: the conflicted president on civil rights." www.blacknews.com (May 14).

25. Walsh, Kenneth T. 1997. *Ronald Reagan: Biography.* New York: Park Lane Press, pp. 16–17. See also Cannon, Lou. 2003. *Governor Reagan: His Rise to Power.* New York: Public Affairs, pp. 30–31.

26. Cannon. *Governor Reagan,* p. 456.

27. Weber, Ralph E. and Ralph A. Weber, eds. 2003. *Dear Americans: Letters from the Desk of President Ronald Reagan.* New York: Doubleday, pp. 88–89.

28. Skinner, Kiron K., Annelise Anderson, and Martin Anderson. 2003. *Reagan: A Life in Letters.* New York: Free Press, p. 13.

29. Author's interview with Frank Donatelli, March 4, 2010.

30. Cannon. *Governor Reagan,* p. 458.

31. Walton and Smith. *American Politics and the African American Quest for Universal Freedom,* p. 202.

32. Felzenberg. *The Leaders We Deserved (And a Few We Didn't),* p. 327.

33. Walton. 1997. *African American Power and Politics,* p. 312.

34. Felzenberg. *The Leaders We Deserved (And a Few We Didn't),* pp. 328–329. See also Wilentz, Sean. 2008. *The Age of Reagan: A History, 1974–2008.* New York: HarperCollins, p. 182.

35. *Journal of Blacks in Higher Education.* 2008. "Blacks and the White House: from slave builders to the master of the house." (Winter), p. 26.

36. Author's e-mail interview with George H. W. Bush, April 22, 2010.

37. Ibid.

38. Randolph, Laura B. 1989. "Barbara Bush speaks out." *Ebony* (September), p. 58.

39. Ibid.

40. Ibid.

41. Ibid., p. 56.

42. Ibid.

43. Ibid., p. 58.

44. Author's e-mail interview with George H. W. Bush, April 22, 2010.

45. Randolph. "Barbara Bush speaks out," p. 58.

46. Ibid., p. 60.

47. Walton and Smith. *American Politics and the African American Quest for Universal Freedom,* pp. 202–203.

48. Wilentz. *The Age of Reagan,* pp. 311–312.

49. O'Reilly. *Nixon's Piano,* p. 402.

50. Author's interview with Colin Powell, May 28, 2010.

51. Powell, Colin L., with Joseph E. Persico. 1995. *My American Journey.* New York: Random House, p. 568.

Chapter 11

1. Morris, Kenneth E. 1996. *Jimmy Carter: American Moralist*. Athens: The University of Georgia Press, p. 151.

2. O'Reilly, Kenneth. 1995. *Nixon's Piano: Presidents and Racial Politics from Washington to Clinton*. New York: The Free Press, p. 336.

3. Ibid., p. 337.

4. Carter, Jimmy. 1975. *Why Not the Best? The First Fifty Years*. Nashville, TN: Broadman Press, pp. 36–37.

5. Ibid.

6. O'Reilly. *Nixon's Piano*, p. 338.

7. Carter. *Why Not the Best?*, pp. 36–37.

8. O'Reilly. *Nixon's Piano*, p. 339.

9. Ibid.

10. Morris. *Jimmy Carter*, p. 155.

11. Wilentz, Sean. 2008. *The Age of Reagan: A History, 1974–2008*. New York: HarperCollins, pp. 76–77. See also O'Reilly. *Nixon's Piano*, pp. 341–345.

12. O'Reilly. *Nixon's Piano*, p. 343.

13. Ibid., pp. 344–345.

14. Morris. *Jimmy Carter*, pp. 263–265.

15. Ibid., p. 264.

16. Walton, Hanes Jr. and Robert C. Smith. 2008. *American Politics and the African American Quest for Universal Freedom*. New York: Pearson Longman, p. 202.

17. Anthony, Carl Sferrazza. 1992. "Skirting the issue." *American Visions* 7, no. 5 (Oct/Nov), p. 31.

18. Carter, Jimmy. 1995. *Keeping Faith: Memoirs of a President*. Fayetteville: University of Arkansas Press, p. 26.

19. Ibid., pp. 32–33.

20. Davis, Michael D. and Hunter R. Clark. 1992. *Thurgood Marshall: Warrior at the Bar, Rebel on the Bench*. New York: Birch Lane Press, p. 363.

21. Clinton, Bill. 2004. *My Life*. New York: Alfred A. Knopf, p. 37.

22. Branch, Taylor. 2009. *The Clinton Tapes: Wrestling History with the President*. New York: Simon and Schuster, pp. 474–475.

23. Clinton. *My Life*, p. 13.

24. Ibid., p. 39.

25. Ibid., pp. 11–12.

26. Walton and Smith. *American Politics and the African American Quest for Universal Freedom*, p. 203.

27. Author's interview with Thurgood Marshall Jr., June 16, 2010.

28. Smith, Sally Bedell. 2007. *For Love of Politics: Bill and Hillary Clinton: The White House Years*. New York: Random House, p. 119.

29. Clinton. *My Life*, p. 296.

30. Ibid., p. 779.

31. Merida, Kevin. 1998. "Caught between loyalty and principle." *The Washington Post* (October 4), p. 1.

32. Quoted in Parker, Kathleen. 2010. "Our first female president." *The Washington Post* (June 30), p. A17.

33. Author's interview with Bill Galston, June 16, 2010.

34. Walton and Smith. *American Politics and the African American Quest for Universal Freedom*, p. 203.

35. Ibid.

36. Branch. *The Clinton Tapes*, p. 273.

37. Walton and Smith. *American Politics and the African American Quest for Universal Freedom,* p. 206.

38. Harris, John F. 2006. *The Survivor: Bill Clinton in the White House.* New York: Random House, p. 189.

39. Ibid., pp. 189–190.

40. Walton and Smith. *American Politics and the African American Quest for Universal Freedom,* p. 206.

41. Ibid., pp. 206–207.

42. Branch. *The Clinton Tapes,* p. 440.

43. Ibid., pp. 452–453.

44. Ibid., p 534.

45. Ibid., pp. 534–535.

46. Ibid., p. 535.

47. Harris. *The Survivor,* p. 188.

48. Smith. *For Love of Politics,* p. 287.

49. Fletcher, Michael A. 1998. "Clinton gets race report, rejects criticism." *The Washington Post* (September 19), p. A8.

50. Harris. *The Survivor,* p. 264–265.

51. Ibid., p. 265.

52. Ibid., pp. 317–318.

53. Author's interview with Chris Emery, February 17, 2010.

54. Bush, Laura. 2010. *Spoken from the Heart.* New York: Scribner, p. 72.

55. Walton and Smith. *American Politics and the African American Quest for Universal Freedom,* p. 207.

56. E-mail correspondence with George W. Bush, July 15, 2010.

57. Ibid.

58. Walton and Smith. *American Politics and the African American Quest for Universal Freedom,* pp. 207–208.

59. Ibid., p. 208.

60. Ibid.

61. Ibid.

62. E-mail correspondence with George W. Bush, July 15, 2010.

63. Powell, Colin L., with Joseph E. Persico. 1995. *My American Journey,* New York: Random House, p. 400.

64. Ibid., pp. 400, 568.

65. Ibid., p. 401.

66. Walton and Smith. *American Politics and the African American Quest for Universal Freedom,* pp. 282–283.

67. E-mail correspondence with George W. Bush, July 15, 2010.

68. Lusane, Clarence. 2006. *Colin Powell and Condoleezza Rice: Foreign Policy, Race, and the New American Century.* Westport, CT: Praeger, p. 2.

69. Ibid.

70. Ibid., p. 3.

71. Ibid., p. 79.

Chapter 12

1. Heilemann, John and Mark Halperin. 2010. *Game Change: Obama and the Clintons, McCain and Palin, and the Race of a Lifetime.* New York: HarperCollins, p. 72.

2. Balz, Dan and Haynes Johnson. 2009a. "A political odyssey: how Obama's team forged

a path that surprised everyone, including the candidate." *The Washington Post* (August 2), p. A11.

3. Obama, Barack. 2006. *The Audacity of Hope: Thoughts on Reclaiming the American Dream*. New York: Crown Publishers, p. 231.

4. Ibid., p. 249.

5. Ibid., pp. 255–256.

6. King, Colbert I. 2010. "Mr. OMB gets a parental pass." *The Washington Post* (January 16), p. A17.

7. Cobb, William Jelani. 2010. *The Substance of Hope: Barack Obama and the Paradox of Progress*. New York: Walker and Company, p. 7.

8. Balz, Dan and Haynes Johnson. 2009b. *The Battle for America 2008*. New York: Viking Penguin, p. 200.

9. Balz and Johnson. "A political odyssey," p. A11.

10. Balz and Johnson. *The Battle for America 2008*, pp. 203–204.

11. Ibid., p. 211.

12. Balz and Johnson. "A political odyssey," p. A11.

13. E-mail correspondence with George H. W. Bush, April 22, 2010.

14. Simon, Roger. 2009. "What happened to post-racial America?" www.politico.com (August 7).

15. Author's interview with Cornell Belcher, October 13, 2009.

16. BBC News. 2009. "Key excerpts; Obama's Ghana speech. www.bbc.co.uk/News/ (July 11).

17. Saul, Michael. 2009. "President Obama honors civil rights pioneers with speech at NAACP centennial convention." www.nydailynews.com (July 16).

18. Ibid.

19. Robinson, Eugene. 2009. "Black America's new reality." *The Washington Post* (July 19), p. A21.

20. Author interviews with Kellyanne Conway on September 16, 2009, and Stan Greenberg on September 15, 2009.

21. Murray, Mark. 2009. "Carter: race plays role in Obama dislike." www.msnbc.msn.com (September 15).

22. Ibid.

23. Dowd, Maureen. 2009. "Boy, oh, boy." *The New York Times Week in Review* (September 13), p. 17.

24. Ehrenreich, Barbara and Dedrick Muhammad. 2009. "The recession's racial divide." *The New York Times Week in Review* (September 13), p. 17.

25. Author's interview with Valerie Jarrett, January 25, 2010.

26. Author's interview with David Axelrod, September 14, 2009.

27. Author's interview with Geoff Garin, October 19, 2009.

28. Author's interview with Barack Obama, March 12, 2010.

29. Fletcher, Michael A. 2009. "For Obama, warm regards." *The Washington Post* (September 27), p. A7.

30. Author's interview with Democratic pollster Cornell Belcher, November 24, 2009.

31. Hyde, Justin and Richard Wolf. 2009. "President Obama says he won't put focus on blacks' troubles." www.usatoday.com (December 3).

32. Fletcher. "For Obama, warm regards," p. A7.

33. Author's interview with Barack Obama, September 29, 2009.

34. Ibid.

35. Author's interview with David Axelrod, November 3, 2009.

36. Agence France-Press. 2009. www.afp.com/afpcom/en/ (October 30).

37. Data from Hart Research/Public Opinion Strategies, USA Networks Survey, taken October 30–November 4, 2009.

38. Remnick, David. 2010. *The Bridge: The Life and Rise of Barack Obama*. New York: Alfred A. Knopf, p. 508.

39. Author's interview with Will Marshall, October 22, 2009.

40. Author's interview with Michael Steele, October 28, 2009.

41. Author's interview with Barack Obama, March 12, 2010.

42. Swarns, Rachel L. and Jodi Kantor. 2009. "In first lady's roots, a complex path from slavery." *The New York Times,* www.nytimes.com (October 8).

43. Author's interview with Geoff Garin, March 12, 2009.

44. Author's interview with Valerie Jarrett, January 25, 2010.

45. Givhan, Robin. 2010. "First lady reaps what she sowed." *The Washington Post* (January 17), p. E6.

46. Author's interview with Frank Donatelli, May 3, 2010.

Chapter 13

1. CNN. 2010. "McCain complains of 'double standard' for Reid." www.cnn.com, January 12.

2. Cohen, Jon and Jennifer Agiesta. 2010. "Poll shows growing disappointment, polarization over Obama's performance." *The Washington Post* (January 17), p. A8.

3. Author's interview with Bill McInturff, June 28, 2010.

4. Shear, Michael D. and Hamil R. Harris. 2010. "In speech honoring King, Obama calls for patience from allies." *The Washington Post* (January 18), p. A2.

5. Ibid.

6. Parsons, Christi and Janet Hook. 2010. "Obama meets black leaders on job disparities." *The Baltimore Sun,* www.baltimoresun.com (February 10).

7. Fletcher, Michael A. 2010. "President Obama and civil rights leaders discuss economy and black Americans." *The Washington Post* (February 11), p. A3.

8. Nelson, Sophia A. 2010. "Unequal in the age of Obama." *The Washington Post (*March 20), p. A15.

9. Henderson, Nia-Malika and Perry Bacon Jr. 2010. "Loyalty, but with limits." *The Washington Post* (July 11), p. A3.

10. Author's interview with Matthew Dowd, May 20, 2010.

11. Author's interview with Colin Powell, May 28, 2010.

12. Author's interview with Robert Gibbs, May 5, 2010.

13. *The Washington Post.* 2010. "Education vital to U.S. success, Obama says." (May 10), p. A3.

14. Author's interview with Bill McInturff, June 28, 2010.

15. Steinhauer, Jennifer. 2010. "Black hopefuls pick this year in G.O.P. races." *The New York Times,* www.nytimes.com (May 5).

16. Associated Press. 2010. "Exit poll: 'Economy dominates voters' worries,'" (associatedpress.com (November 2).

BIBLIOGRAPHY

Abbott, Lawrence F., ed. 1924. *The Letters of Archie Butt, Personal Aide to President Roosevelt.* Garden City, NY: Doubleday.

Agence France-Press. 2009. www.afp.com/afpcom/en/ (October 30).

Ambrose, Stephen E. 1991. *Nixon, Volume Three: Ruin and Recovery 1973–1990.* New York: Simon and Schuster.

Anthony, Carl Sferrazza. 1990. *First Ladies: The Saga of the Presidents' Wives and Their Power 1789–1961.* New York: William Morrow and Company, Inc.

Anthony, Carl Sferrazza. 1991. *First Ladies: The Saga of the Presidents' Wives and Their Power 1961–1990.* New York: William Morrow and Company, Inc.

Anthony, Carl Sferrazza. 1992. "Skirting the issue." *American Visions* 7, no. 5 (Oct/Nov), p. 28.

Atlanta Daily World. 1935. "Orderly, 102, dead." January 22, p. 1.

Atlanta Daily World. 1945. "ANP 'Says Warm Springs treats Negro polio victims now.'" September 8, p. 1.

Atlanta Daily World. 1956. "Eisenhower greets 22 Negro beauty queens." August 20, p. 1.

Baltimore Afro-American. 1922. "First colored man given a federal job." August 11, p. 7.

Baltimore Afro-American. 1927. "Valet handled Harding love notes." November 19, p. 1.

Baltimore Afro-American. 1932. "The Hoover photograph: I told you so." October 8, editorial.

Baltimore Afro-American. 1940. "Reporter visits FDR's Ga. Home." Staff correspondence, September 14, p. 1.

Balz, Dan and Haynes Johnson. 2009a. "A political odyssey: how Obama's team forged a path that surprised everyone, including the candidate." *The Washington Post* (August 2), p. A11.

Balz, Dan and Haynes Johnson. 2009b. *The Battle for America 2008*. New York: Viking Penguin.

Bauer, Stephen M., with Frances Spatz Leighton. 1991. *At Ease in the White House: The Uninhibited Memoirs of a Presidential Social Aide*. Secaucus, NJ: Birch Lane Press.

BBC News. 2009. "Key excerpts; Obama's Ghana speech. www.bbc.co.uk/news/ (July 11).

Bear, James. A. Jr., ed. 1967. *Jefferson at Monticello: Recollections of a Monticello Slave and of a Monticello Overseer*. Charlottesville: University Press of Virginia.

Bennett, Lerone Jr. 1980. "Sammy Davis Jr. on Sammy Davis Jr. . . . sex, suicide, success, Richard Nixon, Frank Sinatra, black and white women, blacks and Jews." *Ebony* (March), p. 130.

Beschloss, Michael. 2007. *Presidential Courage: Brave Leaders and How They Changed America 1789–1989*. New York: Simon and Schuster.

Beschloss, Michael R. 1997. *Taking Charge: The Johnson White House Tapes, 1963–1964*. New York: Simon and Schuster.

Black, Conrad. 2007. *Richard Nixon: A Life in Full*. New York: Public Affairs.

BNET. 1998. "Pioneer *Jet* photographer Maurice Sorrell dies at age 84 in Washington D.C." www.bnet.com, July 13.

Bordewich, Fergus M. 2008. *Washington: The Making of the American Capital*. New York: Amistad.

Bowen, David Warren. 1989. *Andrew Johnson and the Negro*. Knoxville: The University of Tennessee Press.

Branch, Taylor. 1998. *Pillar of Fire: America in the King Years 1963–65*. New York: Simon and Schuster.

Branch, Taylor. 2009. *The Clinton Tapes: Wrestling History with the President*. New York: Simon and Schuster.

Brands, H.W. 2008. *Traitor to His Class*. New York: Doubleday.

Brinkley, Douglas. 2007. *Gerald R. Ford*. New York: Times Books.

Brooks, Noah. 1906. *Abraham Lincoln and the Downfall of American Slavery*. New York: G.P. Putnam's Sons.

Bruce, Preston, with Katharine Johnson, Patricia Hass, and Susan Hainey. 1984. *From the Door of the White House*. New York: Lothrop, Lee and Shepard Books.

Bryant, Nick. 2006. *The Bystander: John F. Kennedy and the Struggle for Black Equality*. New York: Basic Books.

Burlingame, Michael and John R. Turner Ettlinger, eds. 1997. *Inside Lincoln's*

White House: The Complete Civil War Diary of John Hay. Carbondale: Southern Illinois University Press.

Burns, James MacGregor and Susan Dunn. 2004. *George Washington.* New York: Times Books.

Bush, Laura. 2010. *Spoken from the Heart.* New York: Scribner.

Calvin, Dolores. 1942. "Louis Armstrong band plays president ball." *Philadelphia Times,* January 24, p. 15.

Cannon, Lou. 1991. *President Reagan: The Role of a Lifetime.* New York: Public Affairs.

Cannon, Lou. 2003. *Governor Reagan: His Rise to Power.* New York: Public Affairs.

Carter, Jimmy. 1975. *Why Not the Best? The First Fifty Years.* Nashville, TN: Broadman Press.

Carter, Jimmy. 1995. *Keeping Faith: Memoirs of a President.* Fayetteville: University of Arkansas Press.

Chicago Defender. 1938. "Ex-president's slave on 'We the People' radio program." January 8, p. 10.

Chicago Daily Defender. 1961. "White House photogs told to accept Negro by May 19." April 25, p. 3.

Cleveland Call and Post. 1946. "Truman irked when Robeson claims U.S. lynchings same as Axis crimes." September 28.

Clinton, Bill. 2004. *My Life.* New York: Alfred A. Knopf.

CNN. 2010. "McCain complains of 'double standard' for Reid." www.cnn.com, January 12.

Cobb, William Jelani. 2010. *The Substance of Hope: Barack Obama and the Paradox of Progress.* New York: Walker and Company.

Cohen, Adam. 2009. *Nothing to Fear: FDR's Inner Circle and the Hundred Days that Created Modern America.* New York: Penguin Press.

Cohen, Jon and Jennifer Agiesta. 2010. "Poll shows growing disappointment, polarization over Obama's performance." *The Washington Post* (January 17), p. A8.

Cooper, John Milton Jr. 2009. *Woodrow Wilson, A Biography.* New York: Alfred A. Knopf.

Dallek, Robert. 1998. *Flawed Giant: Lyndon Johnson and His Times 1961–1973.* New York: Oxford University Press.

Dallek, Robert. 2008. *Harry S. Truman.* New York: Times Books.

Davis, Michael D. and Hunter R. Clark. 1992. *Thurgood Marshall: Warrior at the Bar, Rebel on the Bench.* New York: Birch Lane Press.

Donald, David Herbert. 1999. *Lincoln at Home: Two Glimpses of Abraham Lincoln's Family Life.* New York: Simon and Schuster.

Donald, Henderson H. 1971. *The Negro Freedman: Life Conditions of the American Negro in the Early Years After Emancipation*. New York: Cooper Square Publishers.

Dowd, Maureen. 2009. "Boy, oh, boy." *The New York Times Week in Review* (September 13), p. 17.

Ehrenreich, Barbara and Dedrick Muhammad. 2009. "The recession's racial divide." *The New York Times Week in Review* (September 13), p. 17.

Eisenhower, John S. D. 2008. *Zachary Taylor*. New York: Times Books, 2008.

Felzenberg, Alvin Stephen. 2008. *The Leaders We Deserved (And a Few We Didn't): Rethinking the Presidential Rating Game*. New York: Basic Books.

Ferling, John. 2009. *The Ascent of George Washington: The Hidden Political Genius of an American Icon*. New York: Bloomsbury Press.

Fields, Alonzo. 1960/1961. *My 21 Years in the White House*. New York: Coward-McCann, Inc.

Fletcher, Michael A. 1998. "Clinton gets race report, rejects criticism." *The Washington Post* (September 19), p. A8.

Fletcher, Michael A. 2009. "For Obama, warm regards." *The Washington Post* (September 27), p. A7.

Fletcher, Michael A. 2010. "President Obama and civil rights leaders discuss economy and black Americans." *The Washington Post* (February 11), p. A3.

Ford, Gerald R. 1979. *A Time to Heal: The Autobiography of Gerald R. Ford*. New York: Harper and Row.

Gallagher, Mary Barelli. 1970. *My Life with Jacqueline Kennedy*. New York: Paperback Library, Coronet Communications, Inc.

Garrett, Romeo B. 1982. *The Presidents and the Negro*. Peoria, IL: Bradley University.

Gates, Henry Louis Jr. 2009. *Lincoln on Race and Slavery*. Princeton, NJ: Princeton University Press.

Gerald R. Ford Library. Ford papers: accession numbers 80-13, 91-NLF-002, 92-NLF-020, 92-NLF-026, 94-NLF-007. Ann Arbor, MI.

Geselbracht, Raymond H. 2007. *The Civil Rights Legacy of Harry S. Truman*. Kirksville, MO: Truman State University Press.

Givhan, Robin. 2010. "First lady reaps what she sowed." *The Washington Post* (January 17), p. E6.

Golden, Harry. 1964. *Mr. Kennedy and the Negroes*. Greenwich, CT: Crest Books.

Goldstein, Richard. 2008. "Earl Butz, secretary felled by racial remark, is dead at 98." *The New York Times* (February 4).

Goodwin, Doris Kearns. 1994. *No Ordinary Time: Franklin and Eleanor Roosevelt: The Home Front in World War II*. New York: Simon and Schuster.

Gordon-Reed, Annette. 1997. *Thomas Jefferson and Sally Hemings: An American Controversy.* Charlottesville: University Press of Virginia.

Gould, Lewis L. 1991. *The Presidency of Theodore Roosevelt.* Lawrence: University Press of Kansas.

Graham, Hugh Davis. 1992. *Civil Rights and the Presidency: Race and Gender in American Politics 1960–1972.* New York: Oxford University Press.

Hadley, Clara Boyton. 1932. "Freed slaves: a true story of Lincoln and Douglass." *Atlanta Daily World* (February 19), p. 6.

Halliday, E. M. 2001. *Understanding Thomas Jefferson.* New York: HarperCollins Publishers.

Hamby, Alonzo L. 1995. *Man of the People: A Life of Harry S. Truman.* New York: Oxford University Press.

Hamilton, Charles V. 1991. *Adam Clayton Powell Jr.: The Political Biography of an American Dilemma.* New York: Collier Books.

Harper, Lucius C. 1939. "Harding had colored kin, records show." In "Dustin' off the News." *The Chicago Defender* (November 25).

Harper, Lucius C. 1947. "Negro heard Lincoln's Gettysburg speech before anyone." In "Dustin' off the News." *The Chicago Defender* (November 15).

Harris, John F. 2006. *The Survivor: Bill Clinton in the White House.* New York: Random House.

Haygood, Wil. 1993. *King of the Cats: The Life and Times of Adam Clayton Powell Jr.* New York: Amistad.

Heilemann, John and Mark Halperin. 2010. *Game Change: Obama and the Clintons, McCain and Palin, and the Race of a Lifetime.* New York: HarperCollins.

Henderson, Nia-Malika and Perry Bacon Jr. 2010. "Loyalty, but with limits." *The Washington Post* (July 11), p. A3.

Holland, Jesse J. 2007. *Black Men Built the Capitol: Discovering African-American History in and Around Washington, DC.* Guilford, CT: The Globe Pequot Press.

Hoover, Herbert. 1952. *The Memoirs of Herbert Hoover: The Cabinet and the Presidency 1920–1933.* New York: The MacMillan Company.

Huppke, Rex and Stacy St. Clair. 2008. "The Grant Park Rally." www .chicagotribune.com (November 5), p. 10

Hutchison, Earl Ofari. 2010. "Gerald Ford: the conflicted president on civil rights." www.blacknews.com (May 14).

Hyde, Justin and Richard Wolf. 2009. "President Obama says he won't put focus on blacks' troubles." www.usatoday.com (December 3).

Isserman, Maurice and Michael Kazin. 2004. *America Divided: The Civil War of the 1960s.* New York: Oxford University Press.

Jackson, Donald. 1989. *A Year at Monticello, 1795*. Golden, CO: Fulcrum, Inc.

Jet. 1998. "Pioneer *Jet* photographer Maurice Sorrell dies at age 84 in Washington, DC." 94, no. 7 (July 13).

Jeffries, Ona Griffin. 1960. *In and Out of the White House... From Washington to the Eisenhowers*. New York: Wilfred Funk, Inc.

Jennings, Paul. 1865. *A Colored Man's Reminiscences of James Madison*. Brooklyn: George C. Beadle (available from the Montpelier Foundation).

Johnson, Haynes. 1975. *The Working White House*. New York: Praeger Publishers.

Journal of Blacks in Higher Education. 2008. "Blacks and the White House: from slave builders to the master of the house" (Winter), p. 26.

Kamen, Al. 2010. "No record-breaking year for presidential appointments." *The Washington Post* (January 20), p. A3.

Keckley, Elizabeth. 1988. *Behind the Scenes, or Thirty Years a Slave, and Four Years in the White House*. New York: Oxford University Press.

Keiler, Allan. 2000. *Marian Anderson: A Singer's Journey*. New York: Scribner.

Kendrick, Paul and Stephen Kendrick. 2008. *Douglass and Lincoln: How a Revolutionary Black Leader and a Reluctant Liberator Struggled to End Slavery and Save the Union*. New York: Walker and Company.

King, Colbert I. 2010. "Mr. OMB gets a parental pass." *The Washington Post* (January 16), p. A17.

Kitchen Sisters. 2008. "Hercules and Hemings: presidents' slave chefs." www.npr.org (February 19).

Kotz, Nick. 2005. *Judgment Days: Lyndon Baines Johnson, Martin Luther King Jr., and the Laws that Changed America*. New York: Houghton Mifflin Company.

Kurin, Richard and Marjorie Hunt. 1996. "In the service of the presidency: workers' culture at the White House." *Prologue: Quarterly of the National Archives and Records Administration* 28, no. 4 (Winter 1996), p. 273.

LaBan, Craig. 2010. "A birthday shock from Washington's chef." www.philly.com (February 22).

Latrobe, Benjamin Henry. 1977. *The Papers of Benjamin Henry Latrobe*, Yale University.

Life. 1969. May 9, p. 67.

Lightman, David. 2009. "Racial barriers fell slowly in capital." McClatchy News Service (January 16).

Logan, Rayford W. 1954. *The Negro in American Life and Thought: The Nadir 1877–1901*. New York: Dial Press.

Logan, Rayford W. and Michael R. Winston. 1971. *The Negro in the United*

States, Volume II: The Ordeal of Democracy. New York: Van Nostrand Rein-hold Company.

Lorant, Stefan. 1968. *The Glorious Burden: The American Presidency.* New York: Harper and Row Publishers.

Los Angeles Sentinel. 1964. Quoted in "Jackie breaks social bars at White House." February 13, p. C6.

Lusane, Clarence. 2006. *Colin Powell and Condoleezza Rice: Foreign Policy, Race, and the New American Century.* Westport, CT: Praeger.

MacGregor, Morris J. 1999. *The Emergence of a Black Catholic Community: St. Augustine's in Washington.* Washington, DC: The Catholic University of America Press.

Marton, Kati. 2001. *Hidden Power: Presidential Marriages that Shaped Our Recent History.* New York: Pantheon.

Mazyck, Walter H. 1932. *George Washington and the Negro.* Washington, DC: The Associated Publishers, Inc.

McFeely, William S. 1982. *Grant: A Biography.* New York: W.W. Norton and Company.

McJimsey, George. 2000. *The Presidency of Franklin Delano Roosevelt.* Lawrence: University Press of Kansas.

McKay, Cliff. 1941. "Roosevelt hails new hospital." *Atlanta Daily World* (January 16), p. 1.

McNamara, Robert S., with Brian Van DeMark. 1995. *In Retrospect: The Tragedy and Lessons of Vietnam.* New York: Times Books.

McPherson, James M. 2008. *Tried by War: Abraham Lincoln as Commander in Chief.* New York: The Penguin Press.

Meacham, Jon. 2004. *Franklin and Winston: An Intimate Portrait of an Epic Friendship.* New York: Random House.

Mendell, David. 2007. *Obama: From Promise to Power.* New York: Amistad.

Merida, Kevin. 1998. "Caught between loyalty and principle." *The Washington Post* (October 4), p. 1.

Meyer, Howard N. 1966. *Let Us Have Peace: The Story of Ulysses S. Grant.* New York: The MacMillan Company.

Midnight, J. O. 1930. "Hoover photos are as scarce as his race appointments." *Baltimore Afro-American* (January 18), p. A1.

Milkis, Sidney M. and Michael Nelson. 1999. *The American Presidency: Origins and Development, 1776–1998.* Washington, DC: Congressional Quarterly (CQ) Press.

Montpelier.org. 2009. "Historic Montpelier celebrates 195th anniversary of George Washington portrait rescue from the White House." Press release, available on www.montpelier.org/press (August 24).

Morris, Edmund. 2001. *Theodore Rex.* New York: Random House.

Morris, Kenneth E. 1996. *Jimmy Carter: American Moralist.* Athens: The University of Georgia Press.

Morrow, E. Frederic. 1963. *Black Man in the White House.* New York: Macfadden Books.

Murray, Mark. 2009. "Carter: race plays role in Obama dislike." www.msnbc.msn.com (September 15).

Nelson, Sophia A. 2010. "Unequal in the age of Obama." *The Washington Post* (March 20), p. A15.

New York Times. 1957. "President greets friends of valet." Special to *The New York Times* (June 13), p. 22.

New York Times. 1976. "Owens proud of latest medal." In People in Sports (August 26).

Noah, Timothy. 2008. "Earl Butz, history's victim: how the gears of racial progress tore up Nixon's agriculture secretary." www.slate.com, February 4.

Norfolk Journal and Guide. 1931. "Native Virginian, ex-slave, was mentioned for presidential nomination, married 50 years." (October 10), p. A11.

Norfolk Journal and Guide. 1932. "They went to Hoover's photo party." (October 29), p. 2.

Obama, Barack. 2006. *The Audacity of Hope: Thoughts on Reclaiming the American Dream.* New York: Crown Publishers.

O'Brien, Michael. 2005. *John F. Kennedy: A Biography.* New York: Thomas Dunne Books.

Office of History and Preservation, Office of the Clerk, U.S. House of Representatives. 2008. *Black Americans in Congress 1870–2007.* Washington, DC: U.S. Government Printing Office.

O'Reilly, Kenneth. 1995. *Nixon's Piano: Presidents and Racial Politics from Washington to Clinton.* New York: The Free Press.

Pach, Chester J. Jr. and Elmo Richardson. 1991. *The Presidency of Dwight D. Eisenhower.* Lawrence: University Press of Kansas.

Paludan, Phillip Shaw. 1994. *The Presidency of Abraham Lincoln.* Lawrence: University Press of Kansas.

Parker, Kathleen. 2010. "Our first female president." *The Washington Post* (June 30), p. A17.

Parks, Lillian Rogers, with Frances Spatz Leighton. 1961. *My Thirty Years Backstairs at the White House.* New York: Fleet Publishing Corporation.

Parks, Lillian Rogers, with Frances Spatz Leighton. 1981. *The Roosevelts: A Family in Turmoil.* Englewood Cliffs, NJ: Prentice-Hall, Inc.

Parsons, Christi and Janet Hook. 2010. "Obama meets black leaders on job disparities." *The Baltimore Sun,* www.baltimoresun.com (February 10).

Patler, Nicholas. 2004. *Jim Crow and the Wilson Administration: Protesting*

Federal Segregation in the Early Twentieth Century. Boulder: The University Press of Colorado.

Petro, Joseph. 2005. *Standing Next to History: An Agent's Life Inside the Secret Service.* New York: Thomas Dunne Books.

Pinsker, Matthew. 2003. *Lincoln's Sanctuary: Abraham Lincoln and the Soldiers' Home.* New York: Oxford University Press.

Pittsburgh Courier. 1927. "Intimate impressions of Rooseveltian personality recorded by former secretary." (April 23), p. A2.

Pittsburgh Courier. 1933. "President-elect Roosevelt to use Georgian as valet." (January 7), p. 3.

Pittsburgh Courier. 1934. "No color line at White House." (August 11), p. A1.

Pittsburgh Courier. 1957. "Ike, Nixon apologize to Negro over Delaware racial snub!" (October 19), p. 13.

Popadiuk, Roman. 2009. *The Leadership of George Bush: An Insider's View of the Forty-First President.* College Station: Texas A&M University Press.

Powell, Adam Clayton Jr. 1994. *Adam by Adam: The Autobiography of Adam Clayton Powell Jr.* New York: Citadel Press.

Powell, Colin L., with Joseph E. Persico. 1995. *My American Journey.* New York: Random House.

Quarles, Benjamin. 1962. *Lincoln and the Negro.* New York: Oxford University Press.

Quarles, Benjamin. 1969. *The Negro in the Making of America.* New York: Collier Books.

Randolph, Laura B. 1989. "Barbara Bush speaks out." *Ebony* (September), p. 58.

Remnick, David. 2010. *The Bridge: The Life and Rise of Barack Obama.* New York: Alfred A. Knopf.

Rich, Frank. 2010. "Fourth of July 1776, 1964, 2010." *New York Times,* Sunday opinion (July 4), p. 8.

Robinson, Eugene. 2009. "Black America's new reality." *The Washington Post* (July 19), p. A21.

Robinson, Jackie, with Alfred Duckett. 1995. *I Never Had It Made.* New York: HarperCollins.

Saul, Michael. 2009. "President Obama honors civil rights pioneers with speech at NAACP centennial convention." www.nydailynews.com (July 16).

Savage, Charlie. 2009. "On Nixon tapes, ambivalence on abortion, not Watergate." www.nytimes.com (January 23).

Schoenebaum, Eleanora W., ed. 1979. *Political Profiles: The Nixon/Ford Years.* New York: Facts on File.

Seale, William. 1986. *The President's House: A History.* Washington, DC: The

White House Historical Association in cooperation with the National Geographic Society.

Shear, Michael D. and Hamil R. Harris. 2010. "In speech honoring King, Obama calls for patience from allies." *The Washington Post* (January 18), p. A2.

Simon, Roger. 2009. "What happened to post-racial America?" www.politico.com (August 7).

Sinkler, George. 1972. *The Racial Attitudes of American Presidents from Abraham Lincoln to Theodore Roosevelt.* Garden City, NY: Anchor Books.

Skinner, Kiron K., Annelise Anderson, and Martin Anderson. 2003. *Reagan: A Life in Letters.* New York: Free Press.

Slade, William. "Mr. Lincoln's White House." At www.mrlincolnswhitehouse.org.

Smith, Sally Bedell. 2007. *For Love of Politics: Bill and Hillary Clinton: The White House Years.* New York: Random House.

Steinhauer, Jennifer. 2010. "Black hopefuls pick this year in G.O.P. races." *The New York Times,* www.nytimes.com (May 5).

Swarns, Rachel L. and Jodi Kantor. 2009. "In first lady's roots, a complex path from slavery." *The New York Times,* www.nytimes.com (October 8).

Taylor, Kristin Clark. 1993. *The First to Speak: A Woman of Color Inside the White House.* New York: Doubleday.

Trefousse, Hans L. 1989. *Andrew Johnson: A Biography.* New York: W.W. Norton and Company.

Truman, Margaret. 1973. *Harry S. Truman.* New York: William Morrow and Company, Inc.

United Press. 1936. "Negro runner says F.R. snubbed him." *El Paso Herald-Post* (October 16), p. 8.

Updegrove, Mark K. 2008. *Baptism by Fire: Eight Presidents Inaugurated in a Time of Crisis.* New York: Thomas Dunne Books.

Walsh, Kenneth T. 2005. *From Mount Vernon to Crawford: A History of the Presidents and Their Retreats.* New York: Hyperion.

Walsh, Kenneth T. 1997. *Ronald Reagan: Biography.* New York: Park Lane Press.

Walters, Del. 2008. "Out damned spot: under the 'stain' lies a truth about race in America." www.ebonyjet.com (April 9).

Walton, Hanes Jr. 1997. *African American Power and Politics: The Political Context Variable.* New York: Columbia University Press.

Walton, Hanes Jr. and Robert C. Smith. 2008. *American Politics and the African American Quest for Universal Freedom.* New York: Pearson Longman.

Washington, John E. 1942. *They Knew Lincoln.* New York: E.P. Dutton.

Washington, John E. 1956. *They Knew Lincoln.* Cited in "Lincoln as his servants knew him." *Baltimore Afro-American* (Feb. 11, 1956), p. 19G.

The Washington Post. 2010. "Education vital to U.S. success, Obama says." (May 10), p. A3.

Weaver, Frederick S. 1936. "President Roosevelt's valet says attitude of nation's executive is friendly; also says that he reads colored papers." *Atlanta Daily World* (March 18), p. 1.

Weber, Ralph E. and Ralph A. Weber, eds. 2003. *Dear Americans: Letters from the Desk of President Ronald Reagan.* New York: Doubleday.

Weidenfeld, Sheila Rabb. 1979. *First Lady's Lady: With the Fords at the White House.* New York: G.P. Putnam's Sons.

West, Cornel. 2008. "President-elect Barack Obama: opening a new era and ending the age of Reagan, Obama must now act, Cornel West writes." www .usnews.com (November 5).

West, J. B., with Mary Lynn Kotz. 1973. *Upstairs at the White House: My Life with the First Ladies.* New York: Coward, McCann and Geoghegan, Inc.

White House Historical Association/Exhibits. 2009. "The Working White House," www.whitehousehistory.org (December 30).

Whitney, David C. 1967. *The American Presidents.* Garden City, NY: Doubleday and Company, Inc.

Wiencek, Henry. 2003. *An Imperfect God: George Washington, His Slaves and the Creation of America.* New York: Farrar, Straus and Giroux.

Wilentz, Sean. 2008. *The Age of Reagan: A History, 1974–2008.* New York: HarperCollins.

Wilentz, Sean. 2010. "Who's buried in the history books?" *The New York Times Week in Review* (March 14), p. 9.

Wilkins, Roger. 2001. *Jefferson's Pillow: The Founding Fathers and the Dilemma of Black Patriotism.* Boston: Beacon Press.

Wills, Garry. 2003. *"Negro President": Jefferson and the Slave Power.* New York: Houghton Mifflin Company.

Wolk, Allan. 1971. *The Presidency and Black Civil Rights: Eisenhower to Nixon.* Rutherford, NJ: Fairleigh Dickinson University Press.

Wood, Gordon S. 2003. "Slaves in the family." *The New York Times Book Review* (December 14), p. 10.

INDEX